MEMOIRS OF A CAPE CODDER

A Cape Cod Country Boy's Trip To Boston and Back

By

Stephen A. Hopkins

This book is a work of non-fiction. Names and places have been changed to protect the privacy of all individuals. The events and situations are true.

ISBN: 1-4107-8861-X (e-book)
ISBN: 1-4107-8860-1 (Paperback)

This book is printed on acid free paper.

1stBooks - rev. 08/18/04

Oct 2010

For Synthia

Hope you enjoy

Stev Hopkins

All stories in this narrative are true. The thoughts, observations, and opinions I include as part of many of the stories are mine alone, presented as honestly and openly as possible. Some who read this book, to be sure, may disagree with some of the conclusions I have expressed, and that is fine and to be expected. When a person in a story, particularly those in the chapter "A Trial Practice," is presented in a flattering, constructive way, I have usually used his or her real name. The names of the innocent or those whose roles in the stories could be perceived as less than flattering are either omitted or changed as designated.

Although some names have been changed, the characters, conversations and testimony are as accurate as the author can recall.

PROLOGUE

When I arranged for the publication in 2001 of my first book, "Three Dollars Just Same", containing stories I had written about growing up on Cape Cod and my activities thereafter, I thought that that would be the end of my story telling. But I soon found myself thinking of other people, places, and events that affected my life, both in growing up on Cape Cod and thereafter, and I was unable to resist the urge to convert these additional memories into descriptive stories.

My initial motivation, when I began writing in early 1998 was to give my children and grandchildren some idea of how Cape Cod had influenced my life. But then, as I continued writing, I found myself going beyond that limited goal to talk about the various other influences on my life after my childhood on the Cape.

Once I started along that path, I could not stop. Even after the first book was going through the printing process, I would think of new ideas for other stories. Friends would remind me of a particular person or event, suggesting I should write about it, and after mulling it over in my mind, I would find myself typing a story on the particular subject.

Maybe this is simply a characteristic, which befalls some people when they have retired in what we now quaintly call "those senior years". When my earlier stories first began appearing in 1998 in The Cape Codder, a local weekly newspaper, Sam Sherman, a long-time childhood friend, sent a letter to The Cape Codder containing wry comments about my story-telling (then, of course, going on to tell a story of his own, which he is prone to do).

Sam's letter began with reference to my stories as follows: "You can always tell when a fellow has reached retirement age. He has little to do, so he lies (in more ways than one) around thinking of the good old days and the hilarious things that happened to him, imagining that people are interested in such drivel, so he decides to put pen to paper."

Well, Sam's observations, as usual, were presented in a needling, mischievous way, which might have the effect of discouraging most people from saying anything about their life experiences. But Sam knows me well enough to understand that his jibes would not discourage me in the least from pursuing my goals.

Behind Sam's teasing, however, there was a grain of truth in what he had to say. Some people, in their later years, do think of the "good old days" and do feel the urge to write about those earlier times. And I suspect, and surely hope, that others will be interested either in recapturing those times or learning what it was like growing up on the Cape in those yesteryears and then dealing with events and challenges of life thereafter.

Clarence Darrow, the great trial attorney, wrote a number of books during his career, but after he retired, at the age of 75, he wrote a book entitled "The Story of My Life", which was published in 1932, the year I was born. In the preface on pages five and six, Clarence Darrow discussed with insight, depth and sensitivity the urges which prompt a person in his last years to write about his life:

"The young man's reflections of unfolding life concern the future, the great broad tempestuous sea on whose hither shore he stands eagerly waiting to learn of other lands and climes. The reactions and recollections of the old concern the storming journey drawing to a close. No longer does the aging transient yearn for new adventures or unexplored highways. His ambition is to find some snug harbor where he can doze and dream the fleeting days away. So elderly men who speak or write turn to autobiography. This is all they have to tell and they cannot sit idly in silence and wait for the night to come."

Clarence Darrow put into words far better than I could do, what motivates an older person, such as myself, to reflect upon the persons, places and events he encountered in the journey through life, and seek to put those reflections into written form to be read, and hopefully, enjoyed and appreciated by others. Moreover, the goal, at least for me, in these endeavors, has not been an effort to glorify myself but rather to describe how a person, place or event, for whatever it was worth, influenced my journey through life.

As I have attempted to show by my stories, the biggest influence upon me, without doubt, were my years growing up as a boy on Cape Cod. In reading Clarence Darrow's book, I did not come away with the impression that he felt a particular closeness to Kinsman, the town he grew up in as a boy in Ohio, and yet, this is what he said about his hometown:

"My mind goes back to Kinsman because I lived there in my childhood, and to me it was once the centre of the world, and however far I have roamed since then it has never fully lost that place in the storehouse of miscellaneous memories gathered along the path of life." Orleans does have a special significance to me for many reasons, and if Mr. Darrow's hometown created special memories for him, then surely, the lower Cape, for me, created even greater memories.

As I attempted to do in the stories carried in my first book, my stories here, which do include some stories from that first book, focus upon and describe for the reader, the persons, places, and events which affected my life and the direction my journey has taken, particularly how Cape Cod, and all it offered, had such a positive influence upon the direction of that journey.

In some respects, a person's trip through life is like walking along the edge of the water toward the distant inlet and the sea beyond. When you have completed this journey, your footprints will disappear with the action of the wind and tide, and eventually there is little left as evidence of your trip. Perhaps this is another way of expressing what Clarence Darrow meant in the comments he included in the Introduction to his book, explaining a person's desire to record his memoirs, thereby creating a written chronicle of your journey and those who influenced you during your trip.

TABLE OF CONTENTS

CHAPTER I. GROWING UP ON CAPE COD

Most of the children in the Orleans-Eastham area, who were born in the Thirties, were delivered at the house of Nettie Knowles, who served as a midwife during those times. Ironically, the house was located beside the Cove Burying Ground, the oldest cemetery in Eastham, located on what is now Route 6 in the southern part of the Town.

I was one of the babies delivered in that house. This momentous event occurred on April 25 1932 in a room located adjacent to the large gravestone marker for Giles Hopkins who, after coming across the ocean as a teenager on the Mayflower with his family, eventually settled in the 1640's in the Tonset area of Orleans, near the Town Cove, where he lived until his death in 1690.

Giles was the oldest son of Stephen Hopkins who became a prominent leader in the Plymouth Colony. Direct descendents of Stephen Hopkins have lived in the Tonset area of East Orleans continuously since the time Giles moved there back in the 1640's.

My father was Reuben S. B. Hopkins who, after a stint in the Coast Guard, had established himself as one of the first electricians in Orleans. His father was Josiah Hopkins, a farmer and carpenter who lived on Tonset Road. Dad had seven brothers and three sisters. My mother was Lucy Flora Knowles who grew up in Eastham. Her father was Abbott Knowles, a piano tuner who also raised turnips and asparagus. Mother was the oldest of seven siblings, three girls and four rambunctious boys.

Stephen A. Hopkins

Life on Cape Cod in the Thirties was far different than it is now. First of all, there were few houses in those years and they were widely scattered. On the entire length of Hopkins Lane, where we lived, there were only six houses and one side street off Hopkins Lane, known then as Dry Swamp Road (now Pine Needle Way). At last count, there are approximately 27 houses and two housing projects on Hopkins Lane alone, as well as seven roads off Hopkins Lane upon which there are about 80 additional houses.

But the differences between then and now are not limited to changes in housing density. Today, Orleans, and the Cape in general, is wrapped in the lush greenery of trees and bushes, so thick that in some instances, in the summer months, you cannot see your neighbor's house. Back in the Thirties, however, the entire area consisted primarily of pastureland and open fields. From the second floor of our house on Hopkins Lane, I could see Nauset Beach perhaps two miles away and the ocean beyond. This view is now completely obstructed with trees.

Trees were used for fuel in those times, which in part accounted for open fields. In addition, families had more grazing farm animals in those years, maintained for their own consumption, and this resulted in large areas being used for pasture or for the raising of hay.

Some families owned wood lots, consisting of hard wood trees, and in those early years, these lots were considered far more valuable than property located along the shore, which because of its exposure to the weather, was not viewed as having much value. Cape Cod was primarily a rural area in those years, and young lads growing up in those times were really "country boys" in every respect.

There was no television in those times, and apart from an occasional movie at the theater up-town, the only outside entertainment for children were the 15 minute radio shows each evening, such as The Green Hornet, The Shadow ("who knows what evil lurks in the heart of man?...the Shadow knows!"), and The Lone Ranger. My mother religiously listened to the afternoon soap operas of Helen Trent and Ma Perkins.

But children in the Thirties and Forties were able to devise all kinds of games and diversions, among themselves, to keep busy and amused. Homes were widely scattered, but we willingly traveled a half-mile to participate in whatever game was being developed. When girls were involved, the typical game was kick-the-can which we often played until it became too dark to see. Pickup baseball games were regularly played on nearby fields.

After the commencement of World War II, we boys got together at my house regularly on Saturdays to play "War Games", with two teams opposing each other, using toy guns, out in the woods adjoining my house. All of these activities were interwoven with swimming, boating, and fishing activities on the nearby shores, so typical of Cape Cod life.

In addition to play activities, however, most boys 10 years of age and older (sometimes even earlier) were expected to handle specific chores within the family and assume part-time jobs outside the family, such as mowing lawns or delivering newspapers, in order to earn extra money.

Local children in those times carried on their activities in what was truly a classless society. None of us, to my knowledge, ever gave a thought to whether our families would be considered upper, lower or middle class. Perhaps some of our parents were conscious of these distinctions, but as far as I could see, they did not express any of these thoughts to me or my contemporaries.

The first time I began to discern class distinctions was while I was going to college at the University of Massachusetts. During my summer vacations, I began to participate socially with the children of some of the more affluent summer residents, many of whom had attended prestigious prep schools and were attending Ivy League colleges.

On the whole, I found these new friends bright, friendly, and fun, and in many instances, with the urging of their parents, they, like the local boys, also held jobs during the summer months. I could not help but feel, however, that some of them had a condescending attitude toward me, a local boy from a modest background. There was, for me, for the first time, a subliminal sense of class distinctions.

While I was in the midst of my boyhood activities, however, I gave little thought to the quality of what I was doing, the sense of equality which existed among us, and what kind of a foundation my boyhood on Cape Cod was creating for future years. Later, when I was an adult, with my own family, I realized, looking back, what a wonderful childhood I had had and how fortunate I had been to have grown up on Cape Cod as a "country boy" in those years.

Stephen A. Hopkins

TENDING THE FARM

In the early 1940's, in the aftermath of the Great Depression and during the war years when food products, gasoline and other necessities were scarce, children in most of the families on Cape Cod assumed work responsibilities within the home and also part-time outside jobs to earn money for personal and family use. Involved in this, I am sure, was the basic concept of self-sufficiency, so highly valued by people on the Cape. Everybody was expected to pitch in to help support the family.

Back in the early 1940's, we had a garden near the house which provided vegetables, and a farm which comprised of chickens, ducks, pigs, and a cow. Other families had similar farms of differing compositions. Now I know some people, from areas such as Pennsylvania, could scoff at the idea that this constituted a farm, but for us on Cape Cod it indeed was a farm...what else could you call it? Anyway, although I was required from time to time to weed the garden, a job I did not relish, my Dad was primarily responsible for the garden operation. I, on the other hand, as a young lad, was responsible for the "the farm."

The Hopkins farm usually consisted of a dozen hens, three or four roosters, flocks of Pekin and Muscovy ducks, and a dozen mallard ducks. The ducks stayed on or near the small pond near our house, while the chickens were housed in a small shed, with a wire cage attached. The white Pekin ducks and the multicolored Muscovy ducks, growing to be big and plump, were a source of food, but the mallards, always cheerful and energetic birds, were kept as pets rather than as a source of food. We had a small pond near the barnyard, and the mallards swam around happily in the pond in search of water bugs, worms and other similar tidbits. They built nests on the edge of the pond and regularly produced little ducklings that followed their mother duck closely around the water edge and, like a little convoy, through the waters of the pond as well.

The main feature of the farm, however, was Daisy the cow. We first acquired her in 1941 when I was nine years old. She furnished milk, of course, for us, and in addition, produced a heifer from time to time. The milk was placed in a large pan, kept in a cool place, and the cream was allowed to rise to the top where it congealed in a thick covering about one inch deep. One of my favorite taste treats was to scoop off cream with a spoon, apply it to a piece of bread, salt the cream, and eat the resulting concoction.

Daisy was an unusual looking cow. First of all, one side of her belly was plump and bulgy, while the other side was gaunt, with ribs visible. She had horns which curved into her forehead, and it was necessary to saw off the tips of the horns periodically with a hack saw to avoid the horns from going into the forehead. One of her hoofs on her right rear leg did not grow straight in a normal way, but actually grew in a twisted manner, like the horn of a unicorn.

Many stories could be told about Daisy's escapades. Basically, she was rather moody...docile and cooperative one moment, and obstinate and difficult the next. I, of course, had to feed and care for her each morning and evening, as I did all of the other farm creatures, and, since I also milked Daisy each morning and evening, I came to know her mood swings well. For example, if during liking she was in a bad mood, she became jumpy with her back legs, and if I did not pull the pail quickly out of the way during one of her outbursts, she could, and sometimes did, stick her unicorn hoof into the bucket.

Although I always, always had to milk the cow twice a day, without fail, I never really minded it. Apart from the occasional jumpings, it normally was a quiet, peaceful time to sit and reflect, as I flexed my fingers, pulling up and down, to obtain the milk.

The author, age nine, with his ducks

When I was in the eighth grade, for example, I was chosen from my class to compete in the school's declamation contest, assigned to recite Longfellow's "Paul Revere's Ride." I spent the quiet isolation of milking time to memorize and practice this lengthy poem. Also, I had convinced myself that my milking, helped build strength into my fingers, hands, and wrists which would later help me in my athletic endeavors. Dad probably instilled that idea in my mind.

Once in a while, I had an audience while I milked. Cousins and friends would show up to watch from the doorway to the stable. I had developed the ability to turn Daisy's teat as I milked and send a stream of milk horizontally. As my visitor stood watching, I would unexpectantly and surreptitiously squeeze out a stream of milk into his face, with startling results...my version of water pistol.

Yes, I did have a long, close relationship with Daisy, the cow. Sometime shortly after World War II had ended and I entered high school and had less time for chores, Daisy was shipped out, and except for the mallard ducks, which were kept as pets, the farm operation ceased. But even in later years, there was something compelling to me about raising and caring for farm creatures, and when I was living with my growing family in the Old Town area of Marblehead, I raised mallards, those happy carefree ducks, in our backyard for no other reason than to have them around as family pets.

MY CAREER AS A HUNTER

In my earlier years as a boy on the Cape, I soon learned that hunting was an integral part of my family's activities. Among the 10 uncles I had, six on my Dad's side and four on my mother's side, six of them were heavily involved in hunting, mostly for ducks, but occasionally for rabbits and pheasants as well.

During the Depression years of the 1930's, part of the motivation to hunt was to put food on the table, but in addition, in looking back, I realize that the drive to hunt was a cultural thing engendered by family traditions.

From time to time one of my "hunting uncles" would drop by the house to leave four or five ducks they had shot. When this occurred, I had mixed feelings: on the one hand, I always ended up with the task of plucking feathers off the ducks, but on the other hand, I was caught up in what, for me then at least, was the challenge and mystique of hunting. Having in mind that hunting was a tradition on both sides of my family, I felt compelled to hunt, even though my Dad did not.

As I got older, around nine years of age, I took over the responsibilities of tending our little farm. The chickens, ducks and cow required grain, and with stores of grain in our shed, we were soon faced with the problem of families of rats. To limit the rat population, I was allowed to use the 22-caliber rifle my Dad had obtained to control the woodchucks, which were vandalizing his vegetable garden, to shoot the rats.

As rats came out from under the shed to eat grain left on the ground, from my vantage location at the kitchen window, I attempted to pick them off. My hunting instincts were activated and I began thinking of other ways I could hunt with the 22 rifle in keeping with the family tradition.

I was too young to go duck hunting and did not, in any event, have a shotgun, which was necessary to use in shooting at highflying ducks. There were, however, numerous gray squirrels in the tall pine trees across the street. I had read stories about how the frontiersmen, such as Daniel Boone,

7

regularly shot and ate squirrels as part of their diet. Equipped with this knowledge, I decided I ought to provide my family with a food supply, like my "hunting uncles", by hunting those squirrels for food. Thus began my hunting career.

Having received permission from my parents, I stalked the gray squirrels as they scampered high in the trees, and when they stopped to rest or eat a pinecone, I aimed and shot. Although several of the shots missed, I was able in a relatively short time, bag three plump squirrels. I did feel certain pangs upon seeing the lifeless creatures, but I was a hunter, and had to put down those feelings.

Naturally, part of the hunting process requires that these squirrels be cleaned and skinned, something I had never done before. I used my common sense, however, as to what to do, and eventually succeeded in preparing my bounty for my mother to bake in the oven. Mind you, we had never eaten squirrel before. As the baking process proceeded, I looked forward to having what I thought would be a succulent meal from nature.

When the squirrels were taken out of the oven and placed on a platter, they were curled up and shriveled, not at all what I had expected. The meat, we soon discovered, was tough and gamy. Maybe, if you were in the wilderness and had nothing to eat but squirrel, perhaps it would have been an acceptable food source, but I began to wonder whether for all the work of shooting and preparing the squirrels for cooking, particularly with other better things to eat, a meal of squirrels was worth the effort.

But I was a hunter, and so back into the woods I went several weeks later with my trusty rifle. Soon I spotted a squirrel on a tree limb, chirping happily away. I took my deadly aim and hit him squarely. Down he came from the tree, and I went over to retrieve him. As I picked him up, I began dwelling upon how happy he seemed with his life in the trees a moment before, all ended by my shot. I carried him gently home, got a shovel from the garage, and returned to the tree where he had been, where I buried him.

After that, I thought of families of ducks flying together freely and happily. I visualized deer walking gently and gracefully through the woods. And after the squirrel, I could no longer imagine myself shooting those wild creatures. My career as a hunter was forever ended.

CHAMP, THE ROOSTER

The chickens we raised as part of our little farm usually consisted of approximately fifteen hens and three roosters. This flock would be reduced over time by our taking an occasional chicken for a meal, or by illness or old age. We would replenish the flock, however, by letting a hen nest to hatch chicks, usually five to eight in a brood.

Most people have heard about how chickens have a well-defined pecking order system. Picking up on that, perhaps, it seems clear that we humans have also developed a type of pecking order. Being an observant lad, I noticed that the pecking order among chickens begins even when they are little chicks, and these relationships continue as the chick develops into either a hen or a rooster. Seldom is the downtrodden chick, low in the pecking order, able to become an impressive and dominant adult. But there is always, of course, the exception to the rule. This is a story of one such exception.

One of the hens in our flock had a typical brood of six chicks. As is normal, the larger, more aggressive chicks clamored on top of and over the smaller chicks to reach the food offered to them, and thus, they could grow larger and stronger, while the smaller chicks, left behind, did not mature as rapidly. As the chicks grew larger and developed small pinfeathers and combs, they began showing characteristics of being either a pullet (small hen) or a rooster.

In the particular brood my story relates to, I saw that we had two roosters, one larger, with black feathers, the other smaller, with the typical markings of a Rhode Island Red. Blackie became the dominant rooster, somewhat the big bully of the barnyard, and he seemed to take pleasure in picking on the smaller red rooster. It got so bad that I finally decided to take the little rooster out of the hen-yard and keep him separate in the shed where we stored out feed and hay. Soon I was giving the little red rooster special attention, feeding him extra corn and holding him in my arms as he ate from my hand or rested quietly and contentedly. When I entered the shed, the red would run to greet me, much like a dog would do.

Over time, the little rooster grew larger and was becoming a handsome bird. He had beautiful coloring and a large comb and impressive wattles. Large spurs were growing on his legs, and he now strutted around with a sense of pride. I decided to name my pet rooster "Champ."

Blackie, however, was still very much the controlling force in the hen-yard. He did not have an impressive comb; indeed, he did not have an attractive head. But, he was a big, muscular bird.

Champ had finally reached a point when he was drawn to return to the hen-yard, even if it meant confronting Blackie. Indeed, as soon as Champ was placed back in the yard, Blackie attacked him. After a fierce struggle, involving flapping leaps at each other, Blackie was able to prevail, and I took Champ back to the protection of the shed. Champ and I continued our close relationship, but I could see that he wanted very much to be a part of the flock.

Months passed, and one day I returned home from school to find Champ, his head covered with blood, walking with pride and dignity among the hens in the yard. Blackie was not present, and I began searching for him in the area near the hen-yard. Finally, I found Blackie lying behind a bush, in a beaten and exhausted condition. Somehow, Champ had gotten out of the shed and into the hen-yard where the two roosters had had a "fight to the finish" to decide who would be where in the pecking order, and the downtrodden runt of the brood finally overcame the big aggressive bully. Blackie did recover, but he never was the same rooster and did not challenge Champ's new position as "head of the flock."

Champ remained the head rooster for a number of years. I was proud of this beautiful bird for what he was able to accomplish. One year I entered him in the competition at the Barnstable County Four-H Fair. When I carried him in his cage into the building where the roosters were being judged, he seemed to understand immediately what his role was. Surrounded by many other roosters, he preened and strutted in his cage, glaring at these usurpers, while occasionally asserting his presence with a loud "cocker-doodle-do." The judges had no choice but to give him the first-place blue ribbon. Defying the pecking order system, my pet rooster had indeed become "the Champ."

DAISY AND THE PEACH TREE

As noted in the earlier story, "Tending The Farm," I was responsible for the care and maintenance of the family cow, Daisy, feeding and milking her and seeing that her stall and stable were clean and comfortable.

The pasture in which Daisy roamed was surrounded by a one-wire electric fence, which gave a sharp jolt to anybody who touched it. Usually, it was very effective in keeping Daisy confined. Sometimes, however, I was never sure how she did it, Daisy was able to get through the wire and out of the pasture area. The reasons for these escapes were varied.

The first time, I recall, had to do with her maternal instincts. Daisy regularly produced calves, and when she approached full term, we attempted to keep her confined to her stable. This one morning, however, I went to the stable and found the stable door open and Daisy gone. I searched the pasture area, but could not locate her. Somehow, she had gotten through the electric fence and out of the pasture. There were dense woods on three sides of the pasture, and searching for Daisy in those woods would have been difficult.

In addition to Daisy, we also raised chickens, ducks and pigs on the Hopkins family farm. One of the pigs, a large white female I called Whitey (pretty original, eh?), was particularly friendly with Daisy, and when Whitey was allowed out of her pen, she would follow Daisy around the pasture, staying close.

I got the bright idea to let Whitey out of her pen to see whether she could locate Daisy in the woods. Whitey trotted quickly along through the pasture and into the woods in a straight northerly direction, with me puffing along in hot pursuit.

The pig finally came up to a clump of small trees and stopped on the outside. Sure enough, standing inside the clump was Daisy, with a newly born calf at her feet. After a spell, I was able to coax Daisy back to the pasture, with the calf at her side, and into her stable, as Whitey trailed respectfully behind.

The second incident of Daisy escaping the confines of the enclosed pasture did not, however, have such a happy ending. My Dad for a number of years had nurtured a small peach tree in the side-yard. This little tree was subject to a lot of careless abuse. For example, my neighborhood buddies and I often played baseball (using a tennis ball) in the yard, and it was not unusual for one of us to run into the little tree while sprinting for a grounder or fly ball.

Still, my Dad patiently brought the tree along to the point that one summer, after bountiful blossoms, it developed a lovely crop of peaches, 72 to be exact. As the summer progressed, my friends and I were very careful to protect the peach tree, expecting later to enjoy the fruits of our efforts. The branches of the little tree bent down under the weight of these large peaches, and Dad propped them up with wooden braces.

As the peaches grew ever bigger, they took on beautiful colors as they ripened. They were big. They were luscious. We all pressed Dad to pick the peaches, but Dad wanted to wait until they were at the height of ripeness. Finally, he figured they would be fully ripe in two days, and planned to take photographs of them just before they were picked.

Daisy's stable was next to this sideyard, and the tree, with its peaches, was easily visible to Daisy. And alas, she, too, we were to discover, found the peaches tempting. The next afternoon, when nobody was at the house, Daisy somehow got through the electric fence and quickly consumed all of the peaches, pits and all, as well as a good portion of the leaves and branches of the little tree. Dad arrived home that night to find his tree decimated. Although I was furious at what had happened, amazingly, Dad was calm and philosophical about it.

After her feast, Daisy had wandered off, belching and uncomfortable. The next morning, I found her staggering around in the pasture much like a drunk on four legs. We theorized that the peaches, moving from one stomach to another, along with her daily portion of grain, had created a type of peach brandy, resulting in her tipsy condition. I did not, however, have any sympathy for her.

The little tree never did recover from the abuse Daisy administered that day, and it never again developed the fruit it carried that summer. Dad, moreover, lost the enthusiasm he had had in prior years in tending the tree, and it stood in the yard after that in a forlorn state. The peach tree survived the constant carelessness of overzealous ball players for many years, but was undone in a span of few moments by Daisy the Cow.

Daisy the cow, with calf, circa 1945

LEARNING TO SWIM

As described in my story, Summer Jobs, I spent two summers as the Red Cross Water Safety Director for the Lower Cape, teaching life saving and swimming classes in the individual towns. And as noted in my later story about underwater swimming, contests between members of my family have been a tradition for almost 60 years. Now, in my retirement years, I try to swim laps on a daily basis, either off the beach or in our pool.

But how did this all this swimming initially begin? Back when I was a young boy, the Town did not sponsor swimming lessons as it does today. Indeed, some parents in those earlier years did not even encourage their children to learn to swim. It was not unusual, moreover, to discover that many old Cape Cod types could not swim, even those who routinely were at sea (see the story "Captain Dan, the Jackknife Man".)

In my family, however, although swimming lessons were not available, my parents encouraged me, indeed expected me, to learn to swim. Although my Dad helped me in the fundamentals when he had time, I was, nevertheless, pretty much left to my own devises in terms of learning how to swim. And at the age of eight, or thereabouts, I made a concerted effort to learn this skill.

Stanley Snow, who had been a classmate of mine since the first grade, spent his summers at the family cottage on the Town Cove. They had a long dock with spans supporting the walkway, embedded in the mud, each span about eight feet apart. The dock went out to a float a distance of approximately 60 feet. Along with Stan and a number of other boys the same age living nearby, we discovered that the dock, with its supporting spans, was a perfect setup for learning to swim.

We would wade out to the first span, and with frantic dog-paddle strokes, we would swim to the next span, grasping it with our arms. Moving around this span, we would work up our courage, and push off the beam to swim as fast as we could go to the next span. As we moved out toward the float, we realized, of course, that the water was getting deeper and deeper, far over our heads. But this added to our efforts to cross the distance to the next span.

Once we reached the float, we hoisted ourselves onto the surface and sat briefly congratulating ourselves for accomplishing the mission. Once we had had a chance to rest, we ran back to the shore to repeat the process.

After days of doing this, we found that we could swim out in the open water, off the float, diving from and swimming in a half circle back to the float. Nobody suggested this to us, and like with many things when we were growing up, we developed this method of learning to swim entirely on our own. And I've been swimming ever since, although with a far better technique than the frantic dog paddle I employed in those earlier years.

HUNTING FOR SHELLFISH

My Dad, Reuben Hopkins, never became involved in hunting, a popular pastime of my uncles, but he was avid in the pursuit of clams, quahogs, and later, mussels, and he enlisted me at an early age in his excursions for shellfish.

Soft-shelled clams, fried or steamed, are delicious, and I always relished a dinner of steamers. First, you stripped the covering off the neck, cleaned the clam in a cup of hot broth to get off the grit, and then dipped it in melted butter. A joy to the palate!

Digging clams, however, is hard, backbreaking work. Located six inches down in often a firm combination of sand and mud, the steamer is difficult to reach. A short-handled, long-pronged rack is used to excavate and reach the clam, but the digging must be performed carefully so as to avoid crushing the soft-shell of the clam which was embedded below. If clams are plentiful on a particular clam flat, and the digger is reasonably efficient, a bucket-full of steamers, through laborious efforts, can be obtained in 20 to 30 minutes.

There is, however, a technique to digging clams. A novice, who has no instructions, will have a very difficult time locating them. For example, Gonzaque Denis, a Frenchman married to my cousin Carol, both of whom live in Paris and come to Cape Cod each summer, was looking for something to do and decided he would dig for clams. So one day he went across in his little boat to the flats opposite Pricilla's Landing, to get some steamers. He took along a rake and bucket.

Gonzague watched what the commercial diggers were doing and attempted to copy them. He did not know, however, how deep the clams were and since the rake he had had shorter tongs then what was usually used for steamers, he never did dig deep enough to reach the clams nestled below. After about 40 minutes of fruitless digging, as he watched the other diggers quickly filling their buckets, he finally gave up in frustration and headed home.

Gonzague told me about his futile attempt to dig clams, and so several days later I went over to the flats with him, taking along several rakes with longer tongs. I showed him where the best holes were, how far down to dig, how to feel for the top of the clam below, and the technique of removing them without breaking their delicate shells.

After a few tries, and much to his delight, he soon was able to locate and extract clams, one after another. Our bucket was filled quickly and he proudly returned home to display his success. As with most things, digging clams can be successful if you know what you're doing. But it is tough work and never easy.

What stands out most vividly in my memory of my early clamming activities were the trips Dad and I took to the marshes off Snow Shore to harvest quahogs which were then abundant in the slough holes on the marshes. These holes were scattered across the marsh, some small and circular, about 10 feet across, while others were irregular in shape and as long as seventy feet.

The water in the holes was usually about 15 to 18 inches in depth and the bottom of the holes consisted of soft mud, some five inches thick. Hiding in the mud, just below the surface of the mud, were quahogs of varying sizes: little necks, two inches across; cherrystones, three inches across, and quahogs, or "chowders", four inches or more across.

During the late Thirties and into the early Fifties, quahogs were very plentiful in the slough holes on the marshes. Unfortunately, those marshes were, and still are areas, where greenheads reproduce and live when they are not chasing after somebody to bite. During the greenhead season, usually the month of July, those who entered the marsh areas looking for a bucket-full of cherrystones had to contend with sharp, painful bites from the pesky greenheads.

Various digging techniques were used to locate quahogs in the slough holes. The more fastidious clammer, standing along the edge of the hole, would use a long handled rack to probe the bottom trying to locate a quahog. With this technique, however, they could not reach the center of the hole and could not cover all areas of the hole. Moreover, during greenhead season, they were wholly exposed to the bites of those unrelenting insects.

My Dad and I used an entirely different method, which Dad had earlier devised. Wearing just bathing suits and floppy hats, we climbed into the hole, crouched low in the water on our hands and knees, and slowly moved across the hole, side by side, searching back and forth with our hands for the feel of a quahog.

There were few rocks in these holes, and if you felt something solid, it inevitably was a quahog. We would toss the quahog, be it a little neck, cherrystone or chowder, onto the nearby bank, and keep moving slowly forward through the mud. After travelling throughout the entire hole, we would climb out, collect what we had harvested in our bucket, and move on to the next hole. In those earlier years, we could easily fill our bucket in 15 or 20 minutes, with little effort.

Apart from the fact that this was the most efficient method of getting quahogs, it also provided us with a certain amount of protection from greenheads during the weeks they dominated the marsh areas. By crouching down in the water of the hole, with brimmed hats on our heads, we could escape the swarming flies while we moved across the slough hole. When we moved from one hole to the water of another, however, we ran as fast as we could to outdistance the greenheads in our wake.

Another great spot to get quahogs in those early years was the Salt Pond in Eastham. During my visits to my grandparents, and later my cousins, who lived on Locust Road, a short distance from the Salt Pond, we would often head down to the Salt Pond at low tide in the warmer months, wade out into the water up to our waists, and feel out the quahogs with our feet. Once we felt what we thought was a quahog, we would dive down to retrieve it. Sometimes, of course, we discovered what we felt was actually a rock. The fun of looking for quahogs this way was that it combined clamming with swimming.

Later, when the slough holes had become barren, I discovered, during our annual summer visits to the family cottage on the Mill Pond on Nauset Heights, that there were quahogs close to the shore, right below the bluff in front of the cottage. For a number of years, quahogs could be found in large quantities in the muddy bottom at low tide in about 18 inches of water. I effectively used the same "hands and knees" technique as my Dad and I had used successfully for years in the slough holes.

During the years I was growing up on the Cape, there were large mussel beds scattered throughout the tidal waters on the Cape. Near our cottage on Nauset Heights, in Roberts Cove, which was on the channel side, connected to the Mill Pond, there was a large thick bed of mussels, which filled most of the Cove. The Cove was a perfect place for mussels to hitch together with their "beards" to create a giant community.

17

Mussels were eaten regularly in Europe in those early years, but Cape Codders, for whatever reason, did not eat them. Some people even thought they were inedible. It was only later, in the Sixties, that harvesting of mussels began here, especially by commercial fishermen, like Russell Chase, who were shipping them off to New York City.

Since mussels laid together on the surface of the bottom, in shallow water, they could be picked up with no effort. With them so plentiful near our cottage, we first began eating them after my service in the Army in Europe. We steamed them in water, similar to steaming the soft-shelled clam, dipping them in melted butter when they were cooked.

Although they often had a yellow, sometimes orange coloring (maybe the reason some Cape Codders avoided them), I liked them immediately. For one thing, they were not gritty like steamers often are. Also, unlike steamers which require the removal of the covering of the neck before eating, the mussel has no neck. All you have to do is dip it in you melted butter and eat it. Since our early experimentation, mussels became a regular part of our diet.

Over time, other folks have also discovered how delicious mussels really are. As time went on and demand for them has increased, the supply of mussels in our coves has dwindled in recent years.

Moreover, although I have tried those slough holes and my other favorite spots looking for quahogs, they, too, have become scarce. Clams still exist on certain flats, but hey, although I love them, digging for clams can be backbreaking work, not nearly as easy as getting those quahogs and mussels.

GOING FISHING, THEN AND NOW

In several of my stories, I have talked about digging for shellfish along the shores and in the marshes. But I have not discussed fishing or taking shellfish by boat. One of my earliest experiences with fishing had to do with the fish weirs which were located on the sand flats near Skaket Beach, now one of Orleans' most popular bathing areas.

These weirs were composed of a ring of netting, approximately six to eight feet high, attached to a circle of poles, the circle being about 150 feet in diameter. These weirs, used in the Thirties, would be in a foot of water at low tide and totally submerged at high tide. All manner of fish would be caught in the weir as the tide went out, stranding them within the netting of the weir. Fishermen then went into the weir, either on foot or in a boat, to net the edible fish caught inside. I have a distinct memory of watching as a very young lad how those fish were captured from the weir.

There were a wide variety of fish inside the weir when the tide went out, including a few sand sharks. But the one creature that I most remember being in the weir was the very ugly goosefish, now called the "monk" fish. These fish have enormous heads and small narrow tails. One wonders how they are able to propel themselves with those small tails, which incidentally, are now considered a delicacy.

The goosefish lies on the bottom with its jaw wide open, displaying a set of sharp pointed teeth. Hanging over its open mouth is a thin appendage with a little lure dangling on the end. If an unsuspecting fish is attracted to the lure, the jaws of the goosefish snap shut upon the hapless victim.

The goosefish blends in perfectly with the bottom and is difficult to see. Apparently, a goose, walking along looking for something to eat, may step into the open jaw of the predator and sometimes became one of its victims, hence the derivation of the name. If the goose is swimming along in shallow waters, the goosefish will leap up and grab its leg.

Other early experiences I recall involving fishing on the water were also trips into Cape Cod Bay, but much farther out then those fish weirs. My parents were friendly with Everett and Doris Pond, who lived on Rock Harbor Road, near the harbor itself. They had two daughters, Pricilla and Betsy, who were about the ages of my sister and me, and we often visited with them at their home and played games in the large backyard, which had numerous fruit trees.

Everett Pond's occupation was that of a plumber, but he did have a dragger which he ran out of Rock Harbor into Cape Cod Bay from time to time, where he would drag for quahogs and sea clams. When I was probably seven years old, my Dad took me along on several trips with Everett Pond

19

on his boat. These were my first experiences with going out on the "high seas" in an open boat. I recall those trips now with mixed feelings.

When you're on shore, looking out on the waters at a distance, the sea appears calm and quiet, but when you are out some distance from land, as I soon discovered, the waves and swells can mount up significantly, causing the boat to rock up and down or roll from side to side.

On my first trip, the swaying of the boat soon resulted in me becoming sea sick, and as is so typical the reaction, all I wanted to do was go below deck and lie in the bunk. My Dad tried to explain that "going below" was the last thing you should do when seasick because the confinement of the space and the fumes of the engine would only make you feel worse. And he was, of course, correct.

Everett Pond, in the meantime had to complete his dragging operations, and he chugged around, from place to place, putting out the boom of his drag, and dragging it along the bottom here and there for quahogs and sea clams. Lying below, moaning in misery, I hardly paid any attention to what was happening up on deck. Eventually, we headed back to port, and as we got into the calm waters near the shore and the rocking and rolling subsided, I began to feel better.

The second time we were invited to accompany Everett, I resisted, but with Dad's encouragement, I bravely agreed to go. This time, however, I heeded my Dad's advice, and when I began to feel queasy, I stayed up on deck, in the fresh air, where I could look at the horizon. This time, I observed the dragging operations and focussed my attention on what the drag was bringing up, rather then how my stomach felt.

Although the trip was as bouncy as the first trip, I did not get seasick and enjoyed what was going on. This was surely a learning experience. (When I was travelling across the north Atlantic on a troop ship in March 1955, instead of staying below deck in my bunk as many of my friends did, I endured the cold and stayed up on deck as long as I could, thus avoiding being seasick. My friends who stayed below were sick the entire trip.)

Later, when I was maybe age ten, my Dad began taking me regularly in the small boat he owned into the middle of the Town Cove or the Mill Pond where we would bait handlines with pieces of quahog for sea worms and fish for flounder. Flounder, and sometimes fluke, were very plentiful in the Forties and we could easily catch a bucketful of these tasty fish in less than an hour's time. We would take them home, clean them, and my mother would coat them with flour and fry them in a pan. Always delicious.

Unfortunately, as the years passed, flounder became more and more scarce. Some of my children always wanted me to take them fishing, and I would take them out in our boat into the Mill Pond in front of our family cottage, to areas where we previously could catch a dozen flounder in an hour, but now were lucky to catch two flounder. And as time went on, we couldn't catch any.

I am convinced that the ever-increasing numbers of comarants, which dive underwater to catch small fish to eat, have killed off all the baby flounder to the extent that there are no more. When I used to snorkel in the shallow areas of these waters, I would always see baby flounder flitting along the bottom; now, when I snorkel these areas, I see none.

Of course now, with other fish gone, the big rage in fishing is catching bass and blue fish. When I was a lad, there were those who were devoted to surf casting for bass off Nauset Beach, but they were a few in number. Now everybody with a boat or beach buggy goes angling for bass and blues.

Moreover, although there are still a few draggers berthed in Rock Harbor, there are now countless charter fishing boats going out of Rock Harbor carrying groups intent on catching bass and blues. Starting when my two sons were in their early teens, I often arranged for four-hour charter trips out in Cape Cod Bay. In addition to my two sons, I usually invited along several friends from my law firm who liked to fish.

We have always gone on one of the older charter boats in the Harbor, the Empress, operated by my high school classmate, Stuart Finlay. Stuart, who was a teammate of mine on the baseball team, had been a shop teacher at the High School for many years. Stuart has all the fancy fishing gear for these trips, and we would troll along slowly, with lines out from four rods at all times, seeking bass or blue fish.

These earlier trips were always successful in terms of locating and catching blue fish and occasionally a bass. Both fish, when hooked, fight tenaciously and are fun to catch. Blue fish, however, seem feistier and when one is brought into the boat, you have to carefully avoid its razor sharp teeth as it thrashes around.

Several other times, Sam Sherman, who owned a house-boat which he kept in Beverly Harbor, would come across the Cape Cod Bay from Beverly, down to Rock Harbor on the Cape in his boat to stay for several weeks. We took excursions of friends out into the Bay for relaxation and a little fishing. Although we did throw out some lines into the water, I don't remember catching any fish, which did not diminish the fun of these trips.

In July 2001, I arranged another charter on the Empress for my son, Chris, his two daughters, and my nephew, Stephen Buckley, and his daughter Allison. Chris' daughters had been pressing him for some time to go out fishing in the Bay and they were very enthused about the forthcoming trip.

As it turned out, unfortunately, it was a bouncy and rolling ride throughout the journey, and sure enough, it was not long before the girls began to feel whoozy. Sure enough, ignoring my counseling, they soon curled up on the bunks below, groaning in their misery. Our fish production was also disappointing. Although we spent our time vigorously yanking the rods back and forth, jigging on the bottom, a tiring activity, we were only able to boat two bass.

Contrary to how a lot of people feel, I prefer the taste of blue fish to that of bass, which I find too bland. The blue fish is oily, but when cooked right, is delicious. I did discover, however, that the oiliness of the blue fish has advantages in other ways. When we were taking those fishing trips back in the Seventies, I was then living in Marblehead, and for a number of years, I maintained eight or ten lobster traps just outside Marblehead Harbor. I pulled the traps twice a week from my 20-foot Penn Yann.

Obtaining bait for my traps was always a problem, and I was continuously on the lookout for sources of fish parts to use in my traps. After one of our trips out of Rock Harbor, we had six blue fish which I cleaned and filleted, and I recognized at once that the heads would be good, durable bait for my traps. Hoping they would work well in attracting lobsters, I put two heads in two of the traps, saving the other four heads in the freezer.

Two days later, I pulled the first trap and there were 10 lobsters in the trap, eight of them large enough to keep. The trap was totally full of lobsters, crawling over one another. The second trap was also full, with about six lobsters as keepers. Not only that, the two heads were still fairly intact, and they attracted lobsters into those two traps for another week.

Apparently, the oily smell of the blue fish heads reached out through the waters to entice lobsters to crawl inside the trap even though there were already a lot of lobsters already there. After that, I used blue fish heads in my traps whenever I could get them.

Flounders may be gone, but blue fish just keep coming back year after year. Bass, too, are now very plentiful. And I was told that fluke, a large flat fish with abundant meat, similar in looks to the flounder, are now being caught in Stage Harbor, Chatham. So fishing out in the open waters of the Cape does go on, offering fun, relaxation and tasty dishes.

AN AUTOMOBILE: SYMBOL OF FREEDOM

Young men growing up on Cape Cod fifty years ago had various goals, but foremost among them was the acquisition of a car. The Cape was far more rural in those years, and since students from Brewster and Eastham attended Orleans High School, many of my friends (including especially those of the fair sex) lived miles away in those other towns. With friends scattered widely apart, the possession of your very own car meant independence, freedom of movement and enhanced social interaction, especially valued by teenagers.

The first step to obtain freedom of movement was learning to drive and securing a driver's license. Since Drivers Education did not exist in those years, teenagers, before they turned age 16, learned driving skills by operating borrowed cars in the family yard, on back roads, and in nearby fields.

When I was 15 years old, my Dad, who was an electrician (actually the first licensed electrician in Orleans) was using a small, secondhand telephone truck in his work. When he returned from work, I used the truck to practice, driving back and forth, turning and backing, up and down in the yard adjacent to our house. As with most vehicles in those days, the truck had a standard transmission which required careful coordination of the feet on the clutch and accelerator pedal. The clutch, I remember, was particularly sensitive and unpredictable, making my task even more challenging.

Apart from driving in the yard, I did take the truck onto the roads, along with my Dad as passenger, to obtain road-driving experience. In addition to the truck, we also had a 1938 gray Oldsmobile, rather ponderous in size and maneuverability. My training also included driving the big Oldsmobile on what were then the quiet, open roads of East Orleans. Traffic was very light in those days. Whereas now cars move along Tonset Road perhaps on the average of one every 30 seconds, in those days, a car might come along on average of one every 30 minutes.

As was true with most teenagers back then, when I turned age 16, we immediately filed the necessary papers with the Registry for me to apply for my driver's license. Equipped with all my driving experience, I had no difficulty passing the required testing, thus attaining the first step toward independence. (Could be, of course, that the inspectors were more casual and lenient in those times.)

I now had a driver's license, but this was only the first step on the road to full freedom. Step two was the acquisition of one's own car, and until that occurred, I was still dependent for my personal sojourns upon my parents to use the family car, the bulky Oldsmobile, comfortable, to be sure inside, but cumbersome to drive. And there were, of course, times when this car was not available. Full independence required ownership of one's own "set of wheels".

Although this was shortly after the end of World War II and Detroit did not get into full production of automobiles until the early Fifties, nevertheless, it was far easier for a teenager to acquire an automobile in those days than it would be today. There were no car inspections as we have now, and old cars, manufactured in the Thirties before World War II could be purchased for as little as $100. A young person today would have to save $2500 or more to purchase an acceptable car and have it ready for the road.

To be sure, the cars we bought often were in questionable condition, but if they ran, stopped when you applied the brakes, and were reasonably tight against the rain, that is all you needed to obtain that sense of independence. The first car I bought was a black Ford coupe, vintage around 1938, with a fairly dependable motor. It had a tight roof, but the floor had rusted out in places, and if you looked down while driving, you could see the road whizzing along beneath you. The car, nevertheless, seemed luxurious to me.

Dating was, of course, big in those days, and having a car greatly enhanced your ability to obtain dates. There were, moreover, various events and activities to which you could take your favorite female. Attending movies at the local theater, then operated by the Wilcox family and located in what is now the CVS store on Route 6A, was a standard dating event, but there were also record hops and square dances held regularly in the auditorium at the Eastham Town Hall. These were particularly popular, and it was there that I first developed what little dancing skills I may now have.

In leaving these dances at the end of the evening, however, we all had to be very careful to avoid Winnie Knowles, the zealous Eastham Police Chief who prowled in his cruiser, up and down Route 6 at night, bagging unsuspecting motorists who were exceeding the speed limits. Cars whiz along Route 6 almost non-stop now, but in those days, there were few cars moving along that road, and Winnie could, as he did, zero in on those he felt were even slightly over the limit.

Winnie, a small, feisty and energetic man, was not a cop to be trifled with. He not only handed out speeding tickets routinely, but also, if provoked, was known to seize and retain a driver's license plates. Often times, to avoid Winnie, I simply took the back road, over the Boat Meadow Creek Bridge, to return with my date to Orleans or Brewster, as the case may be, sometimes with a side trip to First Encounter Beach "to check out the submarines."

The only place you could get a bite-to-eat late at night in those times was the Reno Diner, which was located in the site now occupied by The Lobster Claw restaurant. The guys in our group, after dropping off their dates, would often go to the Diner for a snack and to recount events of the evening.

Reno Diner was often busy late at night, filled mostly with males, many of whom dropped by after the local bars had closed. And there were times when the interactions within this often-motley group did get out-of-hand.

At one point when I was still in High School, Sonny Walker and Leslie Quinn, who had a motor scooter and motor bike respectively, encouraged me to buy a motor scooter as a means of transportation. (I think Sonny had an old scooter he wanted to get rid of.) Anyway, I bought the thing, and the three of us chugged around the lower Cape together on our machines in our Levi pants and jackets...Orleans' version of the Hell's Angels.

I soon realized, however, that this form of transportation was restrictive in bad weather and not at all conducive to dating. The scooter and I soon parted. Sonny Walker later moved up to motorcycles, and even now, having retired as a barber in Chatham, still motors around on a large, fancy motorcycle, replete with chrome.

The most memorable means of transportation for me came about in the summer of 1952 following my sophomore year in college. My cousin, Steve, at that time, owned a large cream-colored Chrysler convertible, with leather seats, a radio and an automatic transmission, novel features for cars in those days. Steve was married in June that year, and he and his new bride, Cynthia, departed the Cape for an extended honeymoon trip, leaving Steve's impressive car in my care and custody.

With great respect, and I am sure, an unbridled sense of self-importance, I tooled around town, with the top down, fanaticizing that every young woman I passed was breathlessly pining to be invited to ride along with me. Cars do have a way, sometimes, in creating fantasies and self-delusion, even beyond teenage years. Friends of mine, now in their fifties and sixties, I have noted, even display these same tendencies in the cars they chose.

In 1953 I came into possession of a 1946 Ford wood-bodied stationwagon, popularly known as a "woody". This was a lovely, eye-catching car which my sister, Lucy Jane, had received in 1952 from my parents upon her graduation from Simmons College. Lucy Jane married the following year and moved to Connecticut, leaving the car for my use.

By then, I was junior at University of Massachusetts, Amherst, and there was distinction for me to have this car, so different from what other students were using on campus. I enjoyed the benefits of the wonderful "woody" up until I was drafted in September 1954 into the Army after graduating in June.

Over the years since those early times, I have owned a wide assortment of cars, moving from secondhand cars in the early lean years to the newer models in recent times. None of these automobiles, however, compare in my memory with those earlier cars, and clearly this is because those "wheels" of yesteryear afforded me independence, self-esteem and freedom of movement, so important to the development of a teenager.

SUMMER JOBS

Young boys growing up on the Cape 60 years ago were expected to earn money by working in part-time jobs. Starting as early as eight years old, we worked mowing lawns, delivering newspapers, cleaning leaves and brush, and in my case, working as assistant to the Shellfish Warden. An industrious lad could always find some part-time job, particularly in the warm months when summer people descended upon us, not in the hoards we have today, but still in pretty good numbers.

After grammar school, however, when we had reached ages 13 or 14, we were expected to take on a full-time job of some kind during the summer after school had recessed. Beginning when I was probably 14 years old, I joined the ranks of the full-time summer employed, and over the next nine years, up until I had graduated from college and was inducted into the Army, I held a wide variety of summer positions.

As best I can recall, my first full-time job was working for Bob Freeman who, using his large dump truck, operated a successful brush removal and rubbish pickup business. In later years, he was known as "Bushy" Freeman, but when I worked for him, he was just plain "Bob". I took on this job for two reasons: first, it paid well and was steady employment; and secondly, the job involved a lot of heavy lifting and I wanted to build up my muscles to improve my sports performances, an important goal for an aspiring athlete.

Indeed, as I soon discovered, there was a lot of heavy lifting. The cutting and removal of brush was tolerably strenuous, but what was really challenging was the garbage removal at the numerous summer camps which were in full swing on the Cape in those earlier years, Camp Viking, Camp Namequot, and Camp Monomoy, to name several. Bob Freeman seemed to have exclusive rights to remove disposable materials from these camps, and every afternoon we would go to each of the camps to remove rubbish and garbage.

For some reason, never clear to me, the garbage was placed in large steel trashcans, full of water, and weighing 200 pounds or more. Bob and I had to lift these heavy containers up approximately four feet off the ground to dump the contents over the tailgate of the truck. "Lift with you legs, not your back", Bob would say, as we raised the drum in unison up the required distance. My muscles did, indeed, get full workouts at these summer camps.

Every afternoon, after making the rounds of the camps in South Orleans, Bob and I would stop at the little store operated on Route 28, just north of Namequot Road, by one of the many Nickerson existing then. For me this was the highlight of the day. Behind the store were eight to ten small cottages, nestled in the trees, which were rented out in the summer, a typical form of accommodation for summer visitors in those years.

Amazingly, after all this time, those cottages are still there and are still being rented to tourists. Anyway, we would stop at the store, purchase a cold soft drink (I always had lemon and lime), and relax for 15 minutes as we quenched our thirst and chatted. This was always a welcomed respite from the strain and heat of our labors.

I can't remember now whether I worked at this job for one or two summers, but in any event, I moved on to other jobs. Probably, I had taken a look in the mirror, and decided I had had enough of muscle building and no longer needed to lift those enormously heavy steel garbage containers, full of water. Anyway, my next job was working in the fruit and vegetable department of the First National Store, which was located in the center of town in the building, which now houses the Bargain Shoe Store.

The display section for fruits and vegetable was on the left as you entered the store. Produce which was not on display was kept in crates in the cool basement below the display area, reached by a nearby stairway. There were usually two of us working in this department at any one time. I have trouble remembering whom I worked with, but I think one of the guys was Bob Kingsley, one of my classmates. While one of us worked below, readying produce to be brought upstairs, the other waited on customers, weighing and pricing purchases. In those days, produce was not pre-marked or weighed at the checkout registers, as they are today.

As far as I was concerned, this was a great job. I enjoyed greeting the customers, usually always women, chatting with them as I assisted them in their purchases, with banter, compliments, or humor as the situation seemed to warrant. But then, too, it was pleasant to escape to the cool solitude of the basement to move and sort out produce.

Occasionally, when we knew the manager was occupied elsewhere, we would launch into spontaneous fruit fights. Grabbing peaches which had become soft and overripe, we would hurl them at each other as we hid behind the crates or columns of the cellar. After a brief battle, we scurried around quickly picking up and discarding the battered peaches before the manager appeared on the scene. Fruit fights broke out about once a week, but I can't recall being caught or reprimanded once for our antics.

I'm not sure why, but although I liked the job a lot, I only worked that one summer at the First National. Maybe the manager knew about those fruit fights afterall. There was a period of time that I worked for my Dad as an electrician's helper. Dad's regular helper was Charlie Freeman, Bob's father, who lived nearby on Brick Hill Road, but Dad apparently had extra work this one summer and enlisted my services. This work involved stringing, snaking and stapling wire, mounting boxes for lights and outlets, and connecting plugs, switches or lights in those boxes.

When our work was on a new house under construction, as it often was, there was a sense of teamwork among the various tradesmen as they worked together, each dependent upon the other to a certain extent. Part of the feeling of camaraderie involved joking and good-natured ribbing between workers, with a carpenter, for example, telling the plumber that he was slow and holding everybody up, or vice versa.

Although I was young and new at this type of work, I did have the feeling of being part of an important, constructive enterprise, which was interlaced with humor and good will between those who participated in the complicated stages of building a house.

I did not work for Dad after that one summer, but I had learned some basic skills necessary to be a productive electrician's helper, and later, when I was about 18 years old, I worked for my uncle John Knowles who operated an electrical contracting business out of his home in Harwich. John had two electricians working for him then, Tommy Eagan, a small, energetic man with an impish wit, and my uncle Paul Knowles, John's younger brother. I was assigned to work with Paul.

Each morning we would all meet at John's house to receive his instructions as to where to go and what to do. Then we would select the materials we would need and disperse to our job assignments, Tommy going one way with his assistant, and Paul and I going off to another job. Probably because of his social contacts (e.g. he belonged to Eastward Ho), John seemed to have a lot of work to do. And yet, other than stopping by one of the jobs at the end of the day to check out the progress of the work, and occasionally estimating or bidding on a new job, John spent most of his time those summer months playing golf at Eastward Ho.

I thoroughly enjoyed working with Paul. He was conscientious, patient and hard working, and he was scrupulous about doing a job correctly, a basic trait of most Cape Codders in those years. Working in construction where you could often cut your finger, banged your thumb with a hammer, or hit your head on a pipe or floor joist, there were times when a workman would loudly curse or swear when such an event had befallen him. But never once, during the time I worked with him, did I hear Paul ever swear. The most he would say would be "goldarn" or "jeepers". I don't know how he could control himself so well. Unfortunately, I picked up the examples of the other, more profane workers.

I only worked that one summer for Uncle John. Paul had concluded he could no longer work for John and decided to develop a career in refrigeration and air conditioning. Eventually, he moved with his family to Texas where there were great opportunities in this growing field. I could not blame him for wanting to "get out from under" the dominating control of his older brother, who performed little "hands-on" work himself, but was quick to criticize the work Tommy and Paul performed.

When I was a sophomore in college, my mother arranged for me to take the one-week water safety and swimming instruction program which was offered in May, through the Red Cross, at a camp in Plymouth. Mother had always been supporter of the Red Cross, which was headquartered in Hyannis, and she worked constantly as a volunteer in various Red Cross programs over the years. She was an admirer and friend of Johnny Tulis who was then director of the Cape Chapter of the Red Cross, and I think that she had concluded that that a position such as that, and the work it entailed, would be perfect for me. In retrospect, I perceive that the participation my mother arranged for me at the training camp was the first step toward that goal.

The training camp presented challenging programs. Attendees learned life saving techniques, survival swimming, and methods for teaching others to swim. The air temperature the week we took those courses was cold and the water in the lake where we swam many hours a day was even colder. This, combined with the rigorous training, left participants in an exhausted condition at the end of each day. But I learned a lot, and later, I found it was well worth the time and effort.

After receiving this training and the certificate which went along with it, I applied for and was accepted for the position of lifeguard at Hardings Beach in Chatham. I was the only lifeguard on this beach, and although there were usually pretty good crowds at the beach, the water was shallow, with little wave action. Other than locating parents of a lost child once in awhile, I had little to do except scan the water constantly, back and forth, never once seeing any person in trouble. Being a lifeguard sounds like exciting, glamorous work, but I found the job, at least on that beach, to be a crashing bore.

The following summer, however, between my junior and senior year in college, I was able to make good use of the training I had received at the camp the year before. I was selected to be the Water Safety Director for the Lower Cape to provide life saving and swimming instruction in the programs which the Red Cross had established in several of the towns. As part of this work, I also set up recreational programs in two of the towns, which included my conducting baseball clinics for young people.

Each week, I would go to a different town and, depending upon who had enrolled, I would give lessons for beginner, intermediary, and advanced levels, as well as life saving instructions to interested advanced swimmers. This was challenging work, and it was rewarding to see the progress which many of the participants were able to achieve in only six days of instruction. There was also something very satisfying to drive up and park at the beach, get out of my car with my ever-present clipboard, and have the children run up and flock around me, their faces full of eagerness and expectations, waiting for their lesson to begin.

I enjoyed this work to the extent that I was seriously thinking, as I'm sure my mother hoped I would do, about ultimately going into Red Cross or recreational work, or into teaching. I was still thinking about these occupational areas when I graduated in 1954. As it turned out, however, my life's work was in the law, far removed from any of those fields. I never did ask my mother whether she was disappointed that I did not go into the Red Cross, as I am sure she had hoped back in those years, I would do.

I held this position the summer of 1953 and again in the summer of 1954 after I had graduated from University of Massachusetts and before going into the Army. The position was the perfect summer job. As already noted, it was very satisfying work, but in addition, the instructional programs concluded around 12:30, and after completing paper work and planning for up-coming programs, I usually completed my daily work by 2:30, and would normally spend the remaining afternoon hours playing golf on the nine-hole course of the Brewster Golf Club. Because of my Dad's earlier affiliation with the Club, I was able to play there free of charge.

I played a lot of golf the summer of 1954 and was able to shoot in the high eighties. But it's funny that later, after I had married and was raising a family, I hardly ever played golf. Now, in retirement, I have begun to play a little, although not with the constancy other retirees play. Still, golf takes a lot of the day to play, and I prefer racquetball in which you can get a good workout in an hour's time.

But I have digressed. Following the summer of 1954, I never again held what could be considered "a summer job". After military service, I worked in the Public Relations Department of John Hancock Insurance Company (boring and meaningless), began studying the law, and ultimately became a trial attorney. But like the part-time work I handled as a boy, those full-time summer jobs provided me with valuable experiences. Although those jobs were very diverse, one from another, each, in different ways, contributed to my development in those important, formative years.

THE COMEBACK KIDS

When upsets occur in sports, they are usually inspirational in nature and are often well received because the winners have beaten the odds by defeating superior teams. Impartial fans often root for underdogs and applaud when they are able to win against stronger opponents. There are always examples of this in both professional and amateur competitions.

Upsets will occur when ordinary players perform beyond their normal abilities, inspiring a higher level of performance from teammates. In addition, however, fate seems to take over, and for example, a ball will take a funny bounce to assist the underdog at a critical moment. It almost seems that a benevolent spirit, maybe something similar to a "genie", sometimes appears in response to the prayers of the underdog to engineer events leading to the creation of an upset.

The biggest upset in which I was fortunate enough to participate involved the 1950 Orleans High School baseball team and its drive to win the Cape Cod Championship against supposedly superior teams. Our High School at that time was smaller than most other schools in the Cape area. In 1950 there were only 12 boys in our senior class, and half of them were on the baseball team.

Our coach, Bud Davis, a courteous and genteel type, quietly motivated our players to give their best and never stop trying. The team had only one solid pitcher, Jimmy Buckley, who was called upon to pitch every game. Five players on our team could be called reliable hitters while usually performing well in the field. The others on the team were also decent defensive players, but they often went hitless at the plate. I played third base and was selected as captain of the team as we prepared for the 1950 season.

The Cape Cod League consisted of the Upper Cape Division, usually dominated by Barnstable, a much larger high school, with about 100 students in each class. The Lower Cape Division consisted of Harwich, Chatham, Orleans, Wellfleet and Provincetown. As we entered the 1950 season, Provincetown, which had a number of veterans back, was the favored team. And indeed, our team started its season in less than spectacular fashion, losing two of our first five games, while Provincetown won five straight games without a loss.

Going into the final three games of the season, the last game being with Provincetown on our field, it seemed unlikely that we would be able to overcome the lead that Provincetown had developed. But, quite unexpectedly, Provincetown lost its next two games to Harwich and Chatham, while we were able to win our two games. Suddenly, coming into the last game, we found ourselves in a tie with Provincetown for first place. In the meantime, Barnstable, considered to be a powerhouse, was breezing through its season in the Upper Cape League undefeated.

Our game with Provincetown which would decide who would be the Lower Cape champs, was played on June 2 1950 at Eldredge Park in Orleans. Jimmy Buckley, who had been pitching twice a week since the season began, started for Orleans, and Conrad Enos, a small but very competitive, hard-throwing lefthander, was on the mound for Provincetown.

The last game of the regular season could not have been closer or more tension packed. Games during the regular season were seven innings long. With both pitchers throwing well, there was no scoring during the first five innings. Enos, who had a way of causing batters to hit ground balls, had given up only a few hits and appeared very much in control. Jim Buckley had given up only a couple of hits while striking out seven batters.

In the sixth inning, however, Provincetown was able to push one run across, but in the bottom of the inning, we finally scored a run to tie up the game, going into the last inning. In the top of the seventh, Enos drove in one run with a long double to center field, and he then scored on a single. We entered the bottom of the last inning, for our last time at bat, trailing by two runs.

The scrappy Enos, who had been effective all afternoon, took the mound, ready to bear down to protect the two-run lead he had created. But such was not to be. The first three Orleans batters reached on an error, a single, and a bunt by Gordie Sylver. Barry Wilcox flied out to right field for the first out. And it was here that fate was to intervene. Stuart Finlay, who batted third, hit a ground ball, which took a bad bounce and went through the legs of the shortstop, allowing two runs to come in and tying the score 3-3. Now Bruce Peters, who batted fourth (I was the fifth batter), came up, with Gordie Sylver on third base. Bruce hit a grounder to Gaspa at third base, but Gordie was thrown out trying to score from third. Stuart moved along to third base.

Suddenly, I found myself thrust unexpectantly into the spotlight, as I moved into the batters box to face now an even more determined Conrad Enos, with two outs, the score tied, and the winning run on third base. In my three previous at-bats, I had walked, grounded out, and hit into a fielder's choice. Knowing that Enos could be difficult to hit, I had a brief sense of apprehension about letting my teammates down, but I quickly put those thoughts aside to concentrate on what would be thrown at me.

Working the count to three balls, two strikes, I then fouled off several pitches, as the excitement mounted among fans and players. By this time, it seemed I had been at the plate for a very long time. Finally, Enos came in with a pitch, which I was able to hit solidly, pulling it down the third base line, past the lunging third baseman. Stuart trotted home with the winning run, and I ran to first base where my teammates converged to pummel me as we celebrated a championship we thought we'd never realize.

High school sports were very popular on the Cape in those years, and the Sports Editor of the Cape Cod Standard Times, Ed Semprini, personally covered the more significant games. His descriptions of games were always vivid and detailed, as he tried to highlight the drama involved. And the story of the Provincetown game certainly reflected his ability to dramatize what had transpired, as he reported how Orleans, two games behind in it Division, had comeback to win, with two outs, in last inning of the final game. He soon began referring in his articles to Orleans as "the Comeback Kids".

But now we had to face all the talent of the Barnstable team, which had heavy hitters and several good pitchers. Indeed, their batters were described as having "the most murderous bats in schoolboy baseball." Two years before, Orleans had beaten Barnstable for the Cape Cod Championship, but the two teams at that time were considered to be more evenly matched. In 1950, Barnstable was considered by everybody to be an exceptional powerhouse, whereas we had barely been able to win in our Division, which was supposedly not as strong as the Upper Cape Division.

The game was played on Veteran's Field in Chatham, a well-kept diamond with huge outfields with no fences. This was the same field on which the two teams played each other in 1948. Bill Nicholas was on the mound for Barnstable. He was a veteran pitcher who had actually pitched in the 1948 championship game. Jimmy Buckley was again back to pitch for Orleans. Being the championship game, the contest was scheduled for nine innings, rather than seven.

Much to the surprise of most fans, Orleans jumped off to a 4-0 lead with a single run in the first on Bruce Peters' triple, another run in the second driven in by Jim Buckley, and two more in the third inning on three singles and a passed ball. In the fourth and fifth innings, Barnstable each time loaded the bases with only one out, but Jimmy was able to get out of those innings, allowing Barnstable only one run in each inning, while stranding a total of six runners.

With Jimmy tiring, however, Barnstable was able to push five runs across in the seventh inning to take the lead 7-4. The big blow was a bases-loaded single, scoring three runs. Orleans came up with one run at the bottom of the seventh, but Barnstable added two more runs in the top of the eighth inning to lead 9-5. Jimmy shut down Barnstable in the top of the ninth, and we went into the bottom of the ninth, for our last at-bat, down by four runs.

As Ed Semprini said, in reporting the game afterwards: "That last inning will long be remembered in Orleans. It was the inning the 'Comeback Kids' wrote another thrilling page in schoolboy baseball. They were with their backs to the wall when they came up for the last licks." We did, indeed, have "our backs to the wall." In fact, at the time, I noticed that a lot of Barnstable fans had left to head home, believing that we had no chance of coming back from a four run deficit to beat their team.

The last inning started out rather uneventfully. Gordie Sylver reached on an error, but Barry Wilcox struck out. We had a long way to go with only two outs remaining. But Stuart Finlay then hit a ball on to the bank in right field, so long that it ended among the cars parked there, but although Gordie scored, Stuart could only reach third base. But Bruce Peters then followed with a single scoring Stuart, and the score was now down to 9-7. I was the next batter, and hit a double to right center field. Unfortunately, Bruce, trying to score from first was thrown out at the plate on a fine relay throw.

Now there were two outs, with the bottom of our batting order coming up. Except for Jimmy Buckley, none of the four batters at the bottom of the order had had hits during the game. Bill Nicholas remained on the mound even though he had now given up 11 hits in the game (we were to end up with 14 hits, compared to eight hits by the "bombers" from Barnstable). Nicholas undoubtedly was tiring, but probably his coach figured that if he already had held the next three batters hitless, he surely could get one of them out, thus ending the game.

But this did not take into account how fate will intervene in creating upsets. First, Leslie Quinn came up with a single, sending me to third. Nicholas then made the major mistake of walking the weak-hitting Don Ohmann, loading the bases. The "genie of upsets" was clearly at work. Keeping this amazing rally alive. Scott Kelley, who had been hitless up until then, came through with a scratch single, scoring me with our eighth run.

Then, with the bases loaded, Jimmy, who had pitched so courageously all season long, came up with his third single of the game, scoring Leslie and Don Ohmann who slid ahead of the throw across the plate with the winning run. Jimmy was clearly the hero of the game, not as a result of his pitching, but rather of his hitting.

This was, without doubt, a major upset, involving "David against Goliath". Those on our team who normally could not provide offensive punch came through in the clutch with key hits and fine base running. Recognizing the significance of our victory, Ed Semprini carried the story, with his usual dramatic prose, on the front page of the Cape newspaper.

At the conclusion of his story, he observed that "Thus, another baseball championship banner flies over Orleans, and schoolboy fans on Cape Cod will remember for many years the sensational comeback of 'Orleans' Comeback Kids' of 1950." Yes, fate, or maybe the "genie of upsets" who grants the wishes of the downtrodden underdog, did look kindly upon the small, shorthanded team from Orleans in the final inning of that championship game.

BEACH PARTIES OF YESTERYEAR

With all the beautiful beaches in Orleans and adjoining towns, you can expect that groups of friends and family members will want to have parties on these beaches. Indeed, it is common these days for small convoys of four-wheel drive vehicles to travel across the sands to set up beach parties at remote points. Other partygoers reach their favorite spot on the outer beach by boat, while some simply walk to their chosen beach from the nearest parking area. Beach parties are definitely an important part of Cape Cod life.

My first memory of beach parties goes back to when I was about six years of age and attended family get-togethers on Nauset Beach with various uncles, aunts, and cousins. These beach parties were mostly on the Hopkins side of the family; the Knowles family, on my mother's side, usually held their family cookouts on the shores of Flax Pond in Nickerson Park.

The one thing that stands out most favorably in my memory of those early beach parties were the delicious hot dogs, cooked on an open fire, which were always included in the picnic menu. This gives you an idea of what is important to boys in that particular age group.

The "hay day" of beach parties, at least for my generation, was in the early fifties during our college years. Whereas we may now attend four beach parties each summer, celebrating such special events as The Fourth of July and Labor Day, back then, there were often four beach parties by our group each week. They were all at night and all at Nauset Beach.

There were no Town restrictions at that time on the use of beaches, and the "movers and shakers" in our group considered the beach to be a perfect, out-of-the-way place to hold the often loud and boisterous parties we organized on such a frequent basis.

These parties were always held around a small bonfire, which provided light and warmth on cool evenings. The total number of participants was approximately 20, but the average number attending any one party varied between eight and 12, depending on the weather, day of the week, and other factors. Included in our group were such local luminaries as Arnold Henson, Mayo Johnson, my cousin Steve Hopkins, Tommy Nickerson, Bobbie Howe, Jo Loebser, Charlotte Johnson, and Sally Wilcox, to name a few. Although there were some locals in the group, the members of this group were predominately from families who had been summering on the Cape for many years.

The parties featured a lot of good-natured bantering and spirited singing, mixed, of course with flagrant flirting and some serious courting. Most attendees, however, did not come with dates, but simply joined in to enjoy the ambience and camaraderie, and "to get away from it all". We didn't hang around street corners at night; we lolled around on blankets on the sand, under the stars, in the quiet beauty of Nauset Beach, with the surf making steady surging noises nearby.

Beer, of course, was the beverage of preference, and one of the favorite activities was a drinking game called "Prince". To play Prince, everybody in the circle around the fire had a different number, and player number one began the game by saying, "The Prince of Wales has lost his tails and number four [for example] knows where to find them". Player four responded "Not I sir" and number one then asked, "Then who sir?" to which number four replied, for example, "Number 10". Number ten then had to respond in kind, and this goes on until somebody either fails to respond or responds incorrectly. The miscreant then is required to take a swig of whatever beverage he or she was drinking at the time.

Over time, the introduction by number one became abbreviated to "Prince, Wales, tails, four". Also the clever and astute in our group developed tricks to lead other members into committing errors. Recognizing the gullibility of some in the circle, for example, the trickster, in responding, would answer "number eight", but in doing so would look and point at number six, who often became so flustered by the sudden attention focussed on her that she would immediately respond, "Not I sir", resulting in many hoots from those assembled. As you can see, it took little to keep us amused and occupied in those days.

Occasionally, we would have typical picnic foods at our beach parties, and often somebody would bring marshmallows to roast in the fire. But unlike today's beach parties, which usually feature a variety of delicious picnic dishes, food was not the prime interest at our parties. Hot dogs were then not as important to me, although I did welcome them when they were offered.

Singing, however, was a standard part of our parties. We regularly attempted to harmonize together such songs as "Blue Moon", "Wild Goose", "Slow Boat to China", and "Smoke Gets In Your Eyes". Then there was the old standby, always sung when we were disbanding for the night, "Good Night, Irene". Sometimes, somebody would bring and play a guitar or ukulele, which did help the less talented vocalists among us maintain some semblance of the rhythm of the song.

The parties always started after dark, around eight o'clock and usually ended around 11:30 or 12:00. Some nights, however, the party went on until 2:00 in the morning. Most of those in our group worked during the summer, and since parties were held during the week, it was not uncommon for participants to get home to sleep at 2:30 and get up at 6:30 to go to work the next day. Oh, the energy of youth!

But there were times during a workday, after a late party, when even I found my energy level was at a very low level. The job I had one of those summers was as an electrician's helper, working with my Uncle Paul Knowles. One of the typical jobs of an electrician's helper was to crawl under houses, passing along between floor joists, to string and staple wires from one point to another. These were times, I must admit, when having completed my task, I simply curled up on the cool earth under the floor and dozed off. This would last until Uncle Paul, wondering where I was, began calling for me.

I was not aware of anyone in our group getting in trouble with the police as a result of the many beach parties we held. Nor did I know of any complaints made to Town authorities concerning our nightly activities. We were, of course, careful to remove all debris from the area before departing for the night.

Under Town regulations today, the type of parties we had would not be allowed, and if such a party was held, I am sure the 911 number would be very busy with nearby residents lodging complaints. The Cape in the summer, however, is a very popular place for college students, and with the large number of people here now, in comparison to the fifties, there are good reasons for the regulations. Nauset Beach, otherwise, could be overwhelmed with beach parties.

In reading my description of those parties of yesteryear, I realize that some may ask, "What's the big appeal about sitting around on the damp sand, late at night, singing and exchanging jokes?" But there was, indeed, something compelling about walking across the beach in the darkness, with the stars bright overhead, feeling the sand in your toes and hearing the surf, moving along toward a group sitting around a fire in the distance, knowing that you will be welcomed into what we considered was a select group, to share in the warm friendship of your contemporaries.

I think back to the close ties we shared with those who participated in our parties, and yes, we did have a special type of bond, held together in a way, by those beach parties. I cannot help but visualize, for example, my cousin Steve, who first introduced me to the group, sitting across the campfire, with his curly black hair, jutting chin, and impish toothy smile, cracking a joke or singing loudly. Steve was several years older than I was, but we were always close friends. Steve unfortunately died in 1981 at age 54, but I do look back on my times with him fondly, particularly those beach parties.

After graduation from college, all of us became heavily involved pursuing careers and raising families. We tended to forget, during those busy times, the beach parties of yesteryear. Now that things have quieted down, I do pause, look back fifty-odd years with nostalgia, and acknowledge the special appeal of those beach parties. I also ask myself, "Fifty years, could it be that long ago?"

Now that I am retired, I have had opportunities to meet members from that original group, who have also now retired back to Orleans, some of whom I have not seen in all that time. My first impulse, upon seeing one of these old chums, is to shout out "Prince, Wales, tails, four."

Quickly realizing, however, that my friend of long ago may not view those earlier times in the same sentimental way I do, and might conclude I had turned daffy in my old age, I resist the impulse. Could it be, however, that he momentarily experienced the same urge and put it down for the same reasons? "Not I Sir!"

CHAPTER II. FACES AND PLACES.

As I am sure is true of most every person, when I look back on my life growing up on the Cape, I find myself thinking about certain people in the Orleans area who had particular significance to me. At different stages of my childhood and teenage years, my involvement with these individuals had special meaning, and they stand out in my memory.

Sometimes, a particular person was associated with a place, which in turn made the place special for me, and in other instances, the place had a prominence to me, on its own, unrelated to any person who may have been associated with it.

In the stories in this chapter, "Faces and Places", I describe those persons, who, aside from members of my family who will be discussed in another chapter, had special meaning in my life. In some instances, an individual played a special role in my life, although I could not recognize it at the time.

Insofar as there was a person or persons who enhanced the significance of the certain location, I describe and refer to them as well. Many of the "faces" in the stories and few of the "places", at least as we knew them back then, are no longer with us, and it is only through our memories, and in some instances, photographs, that they still exist. Through these stories, I have tried to bring them back, in each instance as honestly as I can.

NETTIE KNOWLES

I have no memory of the first "face" I want to tell you about in this Chapter, but she and the place with which she was associated played key roles in the most critical event which occurred in my life, namely my birth. I know about the role this person played from detailed reports on this event, which I have received over the years. The person was Nettie Knowles, the midwife who assisted me as I emerged into the world on April 25 1932.

This momentous event occurred in a small room in a wing attached to Mrs. Knowles' house, northerly of and immediately adjacent to the old Cove Burial Grounds on what is now Route 6 in South Eastham. Ironically, as I noted in the Introduction to the first Chapter, you could look out the windows of that room directly upon markers of the graves of Pilgrims in the cemetery, some no more than 20 feet away.

As you might imagine, there were many wry comments about the irony of births occurring next to a cemetery. And coincidentally, the closest stone to the birthing room was the large marker for Giles Hopkins, from whom I am descended, who arrived in Plymouth in 1620 at the age of 16 and settled later in 1646 at the head of the Orleans Town Cove.

Nettie Knowles, who was born at the end of the Civil War in 1865, began serving as a mid-wife in the Orleans-Eastham area in 1907. There was no hospital on the Cape at that time, and Nettie went, with the local doctor, to the house of the expectant mother to assist in the birth and to provide care to the mother and child after the birth.

In 1924, she added a small addition to the south side of the house, facing the cemetery, which she and her husband, James, owned. It was to serve as a birthing or lying-in room. Expectant mothers traveled to the Knowles house where she and one of the doctors in the local area, either Dr. White in Orleans or Dr. Bell in Wellfleet, attended the deliveries.

Although the Cape Cod Hospital opened in Hyannis in 1919, local ladies resisted going there because it was a long trip and some of them were suspicious of hospitals ("that's where you go to die"). Nettie, on the other hand, having been serving as a mid-wife for 17 years, was trusted to assist in the delivery of a child in a skillful manner and provide warm attentive care after the delivery to both mother and child.

Nettie's husband had become fatally ill, and after he died in 1925, Nettie had another room available in the house in which the expectant mother could stay. With the increase of births in the succeeding years, there were often times when there was double occupancy at the Knowles lying-in facility.

The work involved in caring for a mother and child was not easy. Cooking meals, cleaning, washing and ironing cloths and bed linens, and attending to the needs of her charges took a lot of strength and effort. Nettie delivered babies at her home up until early 1934 when she became ill and eventually passed away that year at the age of 69. During the period she operated her birthing facility, 83 babies were delivered at the Knowles house. The most delivered in one-year was in 1931 with the delivery of 17 babies.

The list of births during the 11 year span contains the names of many old Cape families in the area, such as Nickerson, Snow, Doane, Gould, Mayo, Richardson, Knowles, Sherman, Quinn, and of course, Hopkins. My sister was born in the room next to the cemetery in July 1930, and many of my classmates in school also were born there.

My mother, Lucy Hopkins, later told me that in those days a woman, after delivery, usually stayed at Nettie's house for two weeks before going home, the first week entirely in bed and the second week, sitting up part-time in a chair. Compare that with what typically occurs today.

There was no delivery room or delivery table in Nettie's home, and a baby was born in a bed, similar to home deliveries. If contractions were too hard, the attending doctor sometimes gave a small amount of gas or ether to the patient to ease the pain. Very different from what how deliveries are handled today.

In recent years, Nettie Knowles' house came into disrepair, and the owner was planning to tear it down rather than face the cost of renovation. Warren Quinn, who was born in the house in December of 1929, had other ideas. Warren recognized the historical significance of the building where so many of his fellow Cape Codders had been born.

For many years, he had been in the excavation and construction business, which included moving houses. And so he arranged with the owner of the Knowles property to have the building moved to a lot he had acquired one mile away and lined up a person to buy the resulting property for the cost of the lot and expenses, with the proviso that the new owner would renovate and maintain the building. In February 1999, the house was moved to this new lot where it was restored.

But the resulting property is missing one significant feature. It no longer has a view of the grave markers in the old Cove Burial Ground, upon which so many mothers looked as they rested, holding their babies, while they were convalescing in Nettie Knowles birthing room.

PIANO LESSONS

A year or so ago, I attended a concert sponsored by the Anguilla Community Foundation, which featured a talented young pianist, Anthony Molinaro, originally from Chicago. As I sat listening to him playing with power, precision and feeling the difficult musical compositions he had selected for his program, I could not help but think back to how my mother arranged piano lessons for me as a boy and how I failed to recognize the opportunity those lessons offered to me.

When I was growing up in Orleans, there was little in what we would call "culture" on the Cape. No symphony orchestra. No art galleries as we have now. There was a playhouse in Provincetown, but who would want to travel way down there? Oh, there were a few band concerts in the summer, to be sure, and the occasional appearance of a concert pianist in Hyannis to which my mother always shepherded my sister, Lucy Jane, and me. But other than that, Cape Cod offered little in the way of culture (pronounced by Cape Codders in those years as "cultcha").

Probably because of this lack of the arts, some of the mothers in our area, especially my mother, placed great emphasis on arranging lessons for their children. In our case, this involved first, dancing lessons and later, piano lessons. I began attending dance lessons when I was about seven years old. Lisa Farnham, sister of my Aunt Mona who was married to my Uncle John Knowles, operated a dance studio on Route 28 in Harwich, and for perhaps two years my mother drove my sister and me over to Harwich for dancing lessons at this studio.

I did not have fond memories of Harwich in those years. First of all, attending those dance classes where I had to stumble around with little girls as my dance partners, while attempting to display courtesy and manners, an integral part of the Studio's training, was an unnatural and uncomfortable chore for a seven year old boy. But even worse, farther down Route 28 easterly from the Studio, about two miles, was the office of our dentist, Dr. Doerr, and my trips to that location were even more painful than the dancing lessons. I dreaded those trips to the dentist.

But I am digressing. Back to the dancing lessons, I must admit that although I grumbled about taking these lessons at the time, when I was older and dancing with girls became a positive, even pleasurable, experience, the basic steps I had learned during those lessons gave me a confidence and the basis for leading my dance partner more smoothly around the dance-floor.

Our attendance at the dance studio stopped after a year or so, but in response to my mother's determination to provide us with "culture", I soon found myself, along with my sister, taking piano lessons from Mrs. Jeanne Richards at her home located on Tonset Road at the top of the hill from the intersection of Tonset and Main Street. These lessons were once a week during the school year, and I took them for about two years.

Mrs. Richards, I soon found out, was a strong disciplinarian. An attractive woman, she had long, sharp fingernails, and as she sat beside me while I attempted to hit the right notes, she would jab the nail of her index finger into my arm or wrist whenever I made a mistake, which seemed to be often. These training techniques only heightened my nervousness, resulting in my making even more mistakes.

By this time, baseball had become very important of my life and I thought it far more important that I be out on the diamond developing fielding and batting skills, rather than sitting on a hard bench, banging on a piano while being jabbed by this woman, pretty though she may be.

One day, to show Mrs. Richards that there were other important pursuits for me besides piano playing, I brought my baseball glove to the lesson and placed it prominently on the end of the piano. With great disdain Mrs. Richards quickly removed the glove and placed it on a chair, saying, "We cannot have these petty distractions". So much for showing her the importance of baseball.

Mother had earlier acquired an upright piano, which sat in our small living room, taking up a good deal of space. (In fact, after all these years, the piano is still in the same location, never having been moved, unused and covered with books and magazines, a sad relic from the past.) Under my mother's stern direction, my sister and I were required to practice our lessons on this piano at least 30 minutes a day. As I pecked away at the piano keys, I could only think of how I could be spending the same time sharpening my batting abilities.

Once a year, Mrs. Richards presented a recital at which her students would perform. While I was a student, these recitals were in the old Meeting House, across the street from the Town Hall on School Street, now owned by the Orleans Historical Society. There were approximately 12 students on average, and after they played, Mrs. Richards, with dramatic flourish, played several pieces, her favorite being Chopin's "The Polonaise." I often thought that the recitals were really set up to give her an audience before whom she could demonstrate her abilities, but I must say, she played well and I enjoyed the music. It was certainly an improvement over what her students were able to do.

In addition to playing one solo at each of these recitals, I also had to play a duet with my sister. Mrs. Richards, and I'm sure my mother as well, liked the idea of a brother and sister blending their music in harmony by playing duet. There were many hours of practice, and being two years older than I, my sister Lucy Jane naturally had to be "in charge".

Practicing the piece we were to play in duet was anything but harmonious (e.g. if she went faster than I, it was my fault for going too slow, or vice versa). Somehow, when the time came for us to perform our piece in front of all those parents staring up at us from the seats below, however, our fingers did move together in tandem, producing an acceptable rendition. I am sure that the impetus for this sudden improvement was the fear of public failure.

I was looking over the program for the recital which was presented in July 1942 in the old Meeting House on School Street. Besides myself and sister Lucy Jane, others who performed that night were Pricilla and Betsy Pond, Thomas and Connie Dill (Tommy also had to suffer through a duet with his sister), Ann Meads, Nancy Schofield, Scott Kelly, Barbara Walker, Ann Smith, and Harriett Goodspeed. The girls far outnumbered the boys. My sister and I played as a duet "Evening" by Low. My solo was "Folk Songs" by Adapted, whoever he was. I have no memory of either presentation. Mrs. Richards finished the program by playing "Hungarian Rhapsody No. 2" by Liszt.

After several years of lessons with Mrs. Richards, my mother arranged for me to take lessons from an older, more patient lady who lived on the corner of Main Street and Great Oak Road. This switch was undoubtedly the result of my complaints about Mrs. Richards's disciplinary techniques. Mother may have noted the scar marks on my wrist.

After that, thank heavens, there were no recitals (or duets). As time went on, however, and I became busier with sports and part-time jobs, my piano lessons slowed and than ended. Once the lessons stopped, my practicing on the piano ended as well, and except for being able to play a few simple melodies, whatever playing ability I had disappeared through lack of use.

It was not until years later that I recognized that having the ability to play the piano well, unlike baseball skills, was a rewarding and satisfying talent, which you could use throughout your life and into old age. To be sure, in your senior years, as many do, you can use the baseball abilities you developed as a young man in the Old Timers Softball League, but I know now that there would be far more satisfaction and enjoyment for me if I was able to play the piano with some amount of skill.

A good friend of mine in Marblehead, Will Perry (RIP), for example, was a well-respected radiologist at the Salem Hospital, but the one talent he had which I most admired was his ability to play the piano. Although he had this great talent, strangely, he did not like to play before other people, preferring to enjoy the music by playing alone.

Sometimes, when I visited his house, I could hear him playing inside as I headed to the front door. His wife Nancy would let me in and giving her a signal, I would go quietly to stand just outside the door to his music room and listen to the music pouring out of the piano, marveling at Will's ability to put together such wonderful sounds. And I realized that, if I had been as dedicated to my piano lessons as I was to improving my baseball talents, I could have eventually been able to play the piano, obviously not as well as Will, but at least in some reasonable way.

Yes, I give my mother credit. She always was a "doer and a shaker". To paraphrase an old expression, she led me to the piano, but I did not have enough foresight to take advantage of the opportunity she had created. She exposed me to a part of "cultcha" which could have given me life-long satisfaction and enjoyment, but I was too distracted by other activities I thought more important at the time to recognize the opportunity given to me.

Yes, when you get older, your views on what is important often change and you realize far too late what your parent was trying to do in your development.

VISITORS TO OUR HOME

Today, everybody goes to the super markets to obtain foods and household items. It is rare now for a vendor to visit homes to sell products from his truck. When I was small in the late Thirties, my parents shopped for food goods at small local markets, such as Lloyd Ellis', then located on Cove Road, but in addition, they purchased other products from vendors who stopped at our house on a regular basis.

Before we acquired a refrigerator, for example, the iceman visited our home, every two or three days, to carry what-to-me was a huge block of ice from his truck into the house, sliding the block into the bottom of the ice box in the kitchen. Ice was stored at the Ice House, which was located at that time one-half mile away, near the intersection of Champlain Road and Brick Hill Road, next to the Ice Pond. My Dad took me there once to show me the inside of the Ice House. It was packed with enormous squares of ice, stacked high in the dark, windowless building. And it seemed mighty cold inside.

As refrigeration developed in the late Thirties, however, the ice business, which had been so important for so many years, soon disappeared, and the old Ice House eventually was torn down. The last time the iceman made a delivery to our house was when I was about seven years old. For years thereafter, however, I persisted in referring to refrigerators as "ice boxes". Either I'm a slow learner, or this resulted from a basic nostalgia for the iceman who went away.

There were other vendors who visited our house regularly, some through the Forties and into the early Fifties. I remember a man who sold fish and shellfish from the back of his truck, stopping in front of the house at different times to ask my mother, Lucy, if she would like any of his products, "fresh out of the water." Sometimes, she would make a purchase.

There was, of course, the milkman who regularly delivered fresh milk, butter, cottage cheese and other dairy products. Milk routes hardly exist now, but they were extremely popular and prosperous in those earlier times, continuing well into the Sixties. Some of my college buddies spent their summers on the Cape, earning good money servicing milk routes.

The other door-to-door salesman who was successful for years was the Cushman Bakery Products man, who sold breads, cakes, cupcakes and other similar baked goods on his assigned routes in Orleans. Jimmy was the name of the man who visited our home with these baked products over a period of perhaps fifteen years. We knew him as Jimmy Cushman. I think, in retrospect, that his last name actually was Daley.

Jimmy, a good-looking, affable fellow neatly dressed in his Cushman uniform, was always well received by my sister and me, due mostly to the fact that usually, when he drove away, we were left with a box of chocolate cupcakes or some other tasty treat. Jimmy, who seemed to become almost a member of the family, stayed around for many years, but he, too, as with all the other door-to-door vendors, soon disappeared. I often wondered what happened to the ever-popular Jimmy "Cushman".

It was not as if we were isolated and did not have visitors back in those early years. I had countless uncles and cousins, for example, and one or more of them often came to visit and talk. But as a small lad, I was especially impressed with those men who came to our house, lugging in ice, selling fish, delivering milk, or dispensing baked goodies. They created special memories in my early childhood, reflecting a way of life that has now passed along, and I remember those visitors well.

But in thinking back about visitors to our house, one of the most memorable experiences related to a man who did not come to offer goods for sale, but rather appeared regularly over a period of time to fill his pails with water from the faucet outside the window where our kitchen table was located.

I was perhaps five years old when, while eating breakfast at the kitchen table, I looked up to see a small man, with a long flowing white beard and beady eyes, peering in the window at me. Although he had a quiet, benign expression, his sudden, unannounced appearance was startling. He seemed a cross between Santa Claus and one of Snow White's dwarfs, and for a five-year-old, this was a memorable event.

My father explained that this was Bill Ike Small, who lived just down the road on Hopkins Lane, with his brother, Fred. They were without water and until they restored their water, Bill Ike would be coming regularly to the house to obtain water from us, using the outside faucet. (In those days, everybody had their own wells, and sometimes they went dry, which apparently was what happened to the Small brothers.)

Indeed, Bill Ike for several years did appear almost daily after that to collect water in his pails. He never said anything. He simply peered around while his pails were filling with water, then picked them up, and trudged away home. I soon concluded, however, that he did not use any of the water for bathing purposes because it did not take me long to be able to recognize his arrival from the strong odor coming in through the open kitchen window.

Later, I heard reports that Bill Ike supposedly never slept. I had learned of this, probably, from hearing my parents talking. I did not realize until several years later that he had become somewhat famous for this alleged ability to stay awake to the extent that he was sought after by the national press.

There have been several stories about how our famous neighbor made news nationally on radio, and in magazines and newspapers for his supposedly non-sleeping powess. Even then the national press apparently was attracted to bizarre stories, regardless of how inaccurate they might be. Knowing that Bill Ike was a man of few words, I often wondered how those interviews went. Probably, a lot of questions by reporters, with a few "ayeps" once in awhile from Bill Ike in response.

Bill Ike died in 1939, but before he died, having heard this non-sleeping story, and being an inquisitive, enterprising boy, I went down the road to his house with an equally adventuresome playmate, and we surreptitiously crept up to the house and peered in the living room window. There was Bill Ike sitting in his chair, apparently deep asleep. And this was in the afternoon!

When I reported this to my Dad, we theorized that Bill Ike did not sleep in bed, which made his story partly correct. But he did sleep regularly, in his clothes, in a chair in the living room (perhaps contributing to his aroma). Not the first time the national press has been hoodwinked, this time by an eccentric old Cape Codder who only said "ayep".

Bill Ike was a true Cape Cod character. My Dad, of course, had known him for a long time, and even wrote a lengthy story about him, which appeared in a local newspaper in the early 1970's. Bill Ike, for example, was reputed to have been for years a habitual Peeping Tom. It was never clear, however, whether this was an aberration or simply represented a high degree of curiosity. As mentioned above, I, too, was the object of his peering.

As noted in the story in Chapter IV, native Cape Codders, particularly in those earlier years, were very accepting of the human foibles of fellow Cape Codders, and I am sure back in those times, they viewed Bill Ike's peeping habit as just being "his nature," pronounced nate-cha. But, for a six-year-old, he was a visitor to our home etched vividly in my memory.

THE ORLEANS MOVIE THEATER

The CVS Pharmacy in the center of Orleans occupies the entire space of a large building (by lower Cape standards), located next to the old graveyard at the intersection of Main Street and Route 6A. Back in the Forties and Fifties, however, and for some time thereafter, this building housed two businesses, which had special significance to young people in those times.

The main section of the building, all the way to the rear, with a center front entrance from the street, was a movie theater operated by Charlie Wilcox. To the right of the entrance was a drug store, which, as was so typical in those days, featured a soda fountain, with a counter, stools and five booths opposite the counter. It was called the Heath Pharmacy. There was another store on the other side of the center entrance to the theater, but I can't remember what kind of business it was. My friend Sam has told me it was a tire business.

Charlie Wilcox had four sons. The older three sons were all pretty good baseball players. The oldest, Stanley, was a hard-hitting leftie who played right field. Buzzy (his actual name, I believe, was Alan), about five years older than I, was a smooth shortstop and a good right-handed hitter. He had been in the Major League farm system for several years. Barry, who was in my class, was a catcher on our high school team which I captained my senior year, and since I knew him so well, I felt a sense of proprietary interest in the movie theater.

The drug store was a popular hangout, particularly after school. During my last three years in high school, most days after practice, whether basketball or baseball, my buddies and I walked up town from the high school (located next to the ball field on Route 28) to the drug store around 4:00 p.m. We would jam ourselves into one of the booths, each ordering a treat from the waitress, usually a friend, and discuss various subjects teenagers typically cover as we ate the delicacies put before us.

Our little group usually consisted of Jimmy Buckley, Leslie Quinn, and Barry Wilcox. We were very democratic, however, and sometimes let others join us, even when they were younger, like Sammy Sherman. Our bantering focused principally upon two subjects: girls and dating or sports. The discussions on girls typically went like this: "Hey, she's good looking so what does she see in him?" Or the discussion might take a 180 degree turn: "What can he like in that dog?" On the subject of sports, we usually talked about the next game we were scheduled to play: "You know when we're playing P-town in that little bandbox, we can't let that little Enos kid shoot from the corner."

Our favorite dish at the drug store was Boston cream pie, with a large scoop of vanilla ice cream. Usually, I would order a "black and white" frappe (chocolate and vanilla). There was one particular waitress, a student at the high school, who I think had a "crush" on one of the guys in our group. My memory is that Barry Wilcox, who considered himself a "ladies man", assumed that she had the "hots" for him.

In any event, she often would give us a check which would list two Boston cream pies, when in fact, we had had four. Those desserts were delicious, and the bargain prices were a definite factor in why our group liked the place so much. I'd dawdle there for perhaps an hour, chatting with my buddies and flirting with some of the girls who passed by until my father arrived up town to pick me up to head home (that is, if he remembered to pick me up).

We would also collect in the drug store after going to a movie next door, which brings me to the movie portion of this large building. The movie theater was relatively new in the early Forties and it featured most of the popular movies being released from Hollywood in those years. Other than the radio, there was little in the way of entertainment for teenagers in those times.

The typical movie show in those days presented, first of all, one or two animated cartoons, then a section giving us "News of the Day", which during the war years, consisted mainly of dramatic footage of our troops winning major victories, and then, finally, the main feature. Sometimes on Saturday afternoons, the theater would offer a double feature, two movies for the price of one. I never went to those events since I could not understand how anybody could sit that long, particularly when you could be outside playing ball.

There was something very appealing about the movie theater. It had, for example, a distinctive clean smell about it, both inside in the theater itself and in the lobby where the pleasant odor mingled with the smell of popcorn. There was a broad entrance within the building, approximately 50 feet long between the sidewalk and the lobby. The ticket booth was on the right, close to the sidewalk just inside the entrance. On the walls of this entrance were large posters describing coming attractions. Tickets were taken by the usher as you entered into the lobby.

There were usually shows at 7:00 and 9:00 p.m. Those who were waiting expectantly in line for the second show on the right-hand side of the entrance would carefully study the faces of the patrons who, at the end of the first show, would stream out to our left, in an attempt to figure out if those faces reflected pleasure, boredom, or disgust. Sometimes, when we saw somebody we knew, we'd ask, "how was it", and they would usually make some kind of hand-signal signifying what they thought.

Those who attended movies in those days almost always sat in the same section each time. There were two aisles running down to the front of the theater, with a large seating area in the middle and smaller areas on the outside of the aisles, next to the walls. The smaller kids liked to sit way down front where they had to look almost straight up at the screen. Being older, we viewed that area scornfully as the "peanut gallery" because of the size of those who occupied the seating.

Some others, who were older than we, sat on the left side near the wall, halfway down. My group tended to sit in the middle section, about half way down the left-hand aisle. Whenever I had a date, however, I kept away from that area, staying farther back, in order to avoid the inevitable wise cracks from my friends.

There was often some amusing event during a movie, other than what was depicted on the screen. Once, during the middle of a dramatic scene, a woman, presumably tracking down her husband, walked slowly down the left-hand aisle, yelling "Al, I know you're in here! You come out immediately!" Whether she thought he was in there with another woman or was supposed to be home working on something or other, I don't know. But

I didn't see anybody get up, and concluded that if Al was there, he had slipped down low in his seat, hiding from his avenging wife.

Of course, there always was some guy who, for example, during a romantic scene, as the audience waited with hushed expectation while the hero leaned closer and closer toward the heroine, would yell out loudly "Kiss her, you jerk". The women in the audience were always upset by these outbursts, but the guys always roared with laughter.

The manager of the Mayo Duck Farm, popularly known as "Ducky" Mayo, attended the movies regularly. But he often arrived after the movie had begun, held up we presume by his duties in making sure the ducks were bedded down properly. Like most adults, he sat in a particular place, which was on the right side of the middle section, half way down. And those sitting behind his favored spot could easily recognize him as he moved to his seat, silhouetted in the light from the projector. Several in the audience would inevitably say "quack, quack, quack" to herald his arrival. Ducky usually acknowledged this with a wave of his hand.

Rather routinely, some wise-guy kid in the front row would run up on the stage during the show to wave his arms as he was silhouetted in the bright light of the projector. When the ever-present and vigilant usher hustled down the aisle to discipline the miscreant, the kid would jump back down to his seat and the usher would then spend several minutes fruitlessly trying to single him out from the rest of the group of giggling boys.

Then, there was the time at the end of a show when one of the ladies in town, who was very large in the rear (in fact ponderous might be the correct word), could not pull herself out of the seat in which she had wedged herself and had to be yanked out of the seat by the ever-persevering, overworked usher.

During the war years, in the early Forties, the favorite movies for the boys were war stories which depicted our troops as brave and courageous and the enemy as cruel, sneaky and fanatical. The other favorites were western movies which featured the Lone Ranger, Tom Mix and Roy Rogers. There were also a number of lavish musicals in those years, which I avoided unless my date "just had to go to that movie".

Sometimes, my date was able to inveigle me to take her to one of those, to me, gushy extravaganzas, and I would sit there patiently more interested in my date, rather than the action on the screen. Later, in the early Fifties, there were some well-crafted movies featuring stars like Marlon Brando, Ray Milland, James Dean, Humphrey Bogart, Gary Cooper, and Cary Grant.

Yes, before the age of television, movie theaters were very popular, and the theater in Orleans was not exception. For a long period, the Orleans Theater, like most theaters, I'm sure, attracted patrons, young and old, who were looking to get out of the home and enjoy vicariously the loves and adventures depicted on the flickering screen, sometimes broken up by the humorous diversion of a vigilant wife looking for her wandering husband.

BASKETBALL COURTS OF YESTERYEAR

The basketball courts in the various towns on the Cape are now all regulation size. The court at Nauset Regional High School in Eastham, which encompasses five towns on the lower Cape, is housed in a spacious building by the standards we had when I was growing up in Orleans in the Forties. The courts we had back in those earlier days were small and anything but spacious, more like bandboxes.

The basketball court at Orleans High School in those times was situated in the auditorium of the high school building, which is now the Middle School in Orleans, located on Route 28 near the baseball field. The court was on the floor between the raised stage of the auditorium, where the player benches were located, and the raised balcony of permanent seats which consisted of ten rows, stepped up from front to rear. Whenever there was a school function, such as a play, folding seats were set up on the court floor, filling the entire auditorium with seating. Town meetings were also held in the school auditorium in those years.

The basketball court, however, was only about two-thirds the size of a regulation court. At each end, there was only about two feet of out-of-bound area between the end of the court and the wall. If you were running too hard toward the basket and did not brake properly, you would run flat-out into the wall. On either side of the court, there was only about a foot of out-of-bound area between the edge of the court and the stage on one side and the seating balcony on the other. What with the small court and the limited out-of-bound areas, there was a sense of confinement in playing games on the Orleans court. It took only several long dribbles, for example, to get from one end of the court to the other.

But Orleans was not alone in having a bandbox court. Other towns had equally small courts, and some were even more bizarre than the Orleans court. Barnstable High School, for example, which was located in the center of Hyannis in those times, had approximately 100 students in its senior class, compared to 25 students in my senior class. Its basketball court was also in the school's auditorium and was about the same size as our own court. Unlike our court, however, Barnstable's court was not located on the floor of the auditorium, but if you can believe it, on the stage, raised some four feet above the auditorium floor where the spectators were seated.

The locker rooms for the players were located under the stage, and players reached the floor by traversing up narrow circular stairs located at each end of the floor. At the beginning of each game, each team would run up those stairs and onto the court to the loud applause of the fans in the seats below. There was more out-of-bounds space around the edge of the floor, perhaps six feet on each of the four sides. But here again, if a player was running too fast toward the side, after an errant ball for example, and did not holdup in time, he could run off the edge of the stage onto the floor below. There was iron railing protecting the stairwell openings so that players would not fall down through those openings to the floor below, but there were no railings along the edge of the stage.

Because of the larger size of Barnstable High School, their teams in baseball and basketball were always hard to beat. The year I was a senior, for example, they had a center six feet, five inches tall and a forward almost as tall. Both were reasonably agile for their sizes. I played center on the Orleans team at just six feet in height, and I felt pretty small under the basket with these two towers looming over me, fighting for rebounds. We were, nevertheless, able to play Barnstable High School fairly evenly. We beat Barnstable handily in 1950 when we played on their court, hitting our shots from various angles, but lost to Barnstable in Orleans, in a fiercely played defensive struggle, which ended with a score of 29 to 28.

Harwich High School had a court about the same size as our court, but with fairly large out-of-bounds areas. The benches for the players were along the edge of the sideline of the court, more normal than being up on a stage. The Harwich teams, which we referred to, as "the hairleggers" (don't ask me where that came from) were always scrappy and competitive. Chatham's basketball court was in a field house which had been built fairly recently. After the confined space of the Orleans court, Chatham's larger, more open court, seemed palatial. Chatham's teams in those years, however, were not particularly strong.

The strangest, smallest court on the Cape, however, was at Provincetown High School, which in those years was our biggest rival. Our games with Provincetown were always hotly contested, and either Provincetown or our teams in Orleans would end up each season as lower Cape champions, and some times, as the Cape champion.

Sometimes our ball teams were invited to play in the State Tech Tournament against teams from other areas of the State. These games were played on the regulation-sized court at the Boston Garden. It was always difficult to adapt to playing on such a large court after all our games on the small courts of the Cape, and we never did particularly well in tournament play.

But I'm digressing. Getting back to Provincetown's basketball court, it was even shorter than the Orleans court, with smaller out-of-bounds areas. It was not located in an auditorium, and rumor has it that the place where the court existed was built originally for a swimming pool. It surely had that look about it. The court was located in the depressed "pool" section, some four feet below a small balcony on one side for seating.

The ceiling over the court, supported by large exposed steel beams running cross-court and parallel to the end lines, was very low. These beams were about 10 inches wide and two of them were located at each end of the court approximately five feet from the basket. If you took an arching shot from outside, 15 to 20 feet from the basket, you inevitably hit this girder. This was considered out-of-bounds, resulting in a turnover. I even hit the beam while taking a foul shot. Not only did you worry about an opposing player leaping to block your shot, you had to worry about those always present, immovable girders.

The only safe shot you could take from a 15 to 20 foot distance was from either corner. You could arch the ball from those spots, without hitting the beam, in the space between the girder and the basket. The offense of Provincetown basketball was designed to take advantage of the unusual features of its court. Their offense focussed upon speed and fastbreaks creating lay-ups, which avoided those menacing girders.

Cape-tip players never took shots from the outside, and whenever we were able to set up our tight zone defense, they would try to work the ball around to set up a shot from the corner. Provincetown always had at least one, sometimes two, players who were deadly with shots from the corner. It seemed clear that this was the only long shot they practiced.

The rivalry between our two teams was intense, and when we played in Provincetown, the local fans, packed into the seats in the raised balcony, were rabid in the vocal support of their heroes. Their cheers, shouts and taunts, coming from the low-ceilinged, confined space immediately next to the playing area, were loudly magnified, and as you ran down the court beside the raised seating area, some fans would stick their heads out over the court to yell right in you face as you passed by.

It was not a pleasant place for a visiting team to play and it was rare for us, or any other team for that matter, to be able to win a game there. When they came up with the term "home-court advantage", they had to have been thinking of the Provincetown court (a.k.a. "the swimming pool").

It seemed as though every year, in those times, we would lose in Provincetown, but win the games we played against them in Orleans. The big rivalry we had with them was fostered by fact that our games were so close, but beyond that, there surely was a challenge for us to play their teams on that basketball court ("pool") in Provincetown.

1950 basketball team, Orleans High School;
front row (left-right) Jimmy Buckley, Steve Hopkins, Leslie Quinn, Sam Sherman, and Stan Snow. Back row (left-right) Don Ohman, Scott Kelly, coach Bud Davis, Bruce Peters, and Bobby Richardson

CHAPTER III. CAPE COD CHARACTERS

One of the great influences upon a young person growing up are the characteristics and attitudes of the adults he or she typically comes in contact with in everyday life. In a small community such as Orleans, apart from family members, other adults I routinely had contacts with surely had an affect upon the views of life I was developing in those early years.

The one thing you could safely say about Cape Codders in those earlier times was that, on the whole, they were hardworking, good humored, conscientious workers who had the basic attitude of "doing it right or not doing it at all." Regardless of what type of work they performed, they all seemed intent on providing as perfect an end-result as possible. Even when I was small, I was aware of this, and as I grew older and began working myself, these positive attitudes toward work became even clearer to me.

In addition to these regular people, both men and women, whose attitudes had a positive influence upon me, there were other seasoned Cape Cod types I came to know, who, because of personal idyosynracies, rose to the level of being Cape Cod characters.

To be sure, they each had the same attitudes of hard, diligent work, but in addition, they had special attitudes, personality traits or patterns of behavior, which set them apart from the other locals. In the four stories, which follow, I have attempted to describe a few of these characters, most being from different generations.

CAPTAIN DAN, THE JACK-KNIFE MAN

Passing down Champlain Road in East Orleans, on the right-hand side between numbers 25 and 27 Champlain Road, you will see a small, somewhat run-down building, close to the street, hidden behind overgrown bushes. For many years, from the twenties into the early 1940's, this building served as the store operated by Daniel Benson Gould, who became known in his later years as "Captain Dan, the Jack-knife Man".

In those years, the store was neat and well maintained and Captain Dan kept it stocked with candy, crackers, soft drinks and bread for sale to his neighbors. In the earlier years, when few people had electricity, Dan also sold kerosene for as fuel for lanterns. In the forties, hanging over the front of the store was a colorful sign, carved by Captain Dan, which read "Old Carver's Shop."

In addition to selling food items, Dan also offered for sale pictures of ships and various carvings he made depicting ships and shorebirds which, of course, was the basis for his name. Living nearby on Hopkins Lane, I visited the Carver's Shop as a young lad to buy a candy bar and talk with Captain Dan. I remember him as a quiet, small man with a shock of white hair. Like many of the old-timers in those times, he was a man of few words, but on occasion, you could entice him into recounting one of his many sea adventures.

Daniel Gould was born on October 27 1963. Just before his birth, his father drowned in Nauset Inlet when his fishing boat capsized returning during a storm with a full load of fish. Growing up without a father, Dan developed a close relationship with Captain Willis Snow who was Wreck Master and the Boston Underwriting Agent for this area.

Captain Snow headed up a crew of men who were responsible for salvaging cargo from ships driven ashore and then refloating the ships, if possible, for the benefit of insurance underwriters. His crew had to respond quickly when a ship came ashore before others descended to grab portions of the cargo for themselves. Young Dan Gould, then in his teens, served as lookout during fogs and storms, and if he saw a ship, which appeared to be in distress, he would run to alert the wrecking crew.

In February 1886, Dan Gould married Selena Wiles. They settled down in their house on Champlain Road where they eventually raised nine children:

Grace, Ida, Lillian, Alice, Helen, Ralph, Herbert, Alvers and Willis. Lillian later married my uncle, Alfred Hopkins. Herbert, who was living in his nineties when this story was written, married Vera Eldridge in 1928, and they celebrated their 70th wedding anniversary several years back. As you might imagine, having started with such a large family, Dan Gould now has many grandchildren and great grandchildren, some living as far away as Paris, France.

Dan Gould served in the Coast Guard as a young man, thus continuing to deal with the many shipwrecks so common in those early years on the outer beaches of Cape Cod. Later, after leaving the Coast Guard, he captained several fishing boats out of Gloucester, fishing on the Grand Banks. As he grew older, he began fishing out of the harbor in Orleans, staying closer to shore and in the local bays and coves. Finally, in the 1920's, then in his sixties, he gave up his work at sea and operated his little store full time, concentrating on his carvings up until his death in 1949 at the age of 86.

According to those who knew him well, one of his proudest achievements was the advice and assistance he provided to the United States Navy shortly after World War I which resulted in the refloating of an American submarine which had gone ashore on Nauset Beach during a storm. The Navy had sent tugs and equipment to refloat the submarine, but even during high tides, they were unsuccessful. Finally, Captain Dan, who had been following the activities, approached the high ranking officer in charge and offered a simple suggestion which, upon implementation, freed the submarine from the grasp of the sand.

Captain Dan also liked to tell about the story of how the captain of a German ship landed headfirst onto our shore, a bruising introduction to American soil. According to this story, in the late 1870's, shortly after the Nauset Savings Station was built, the German bark Friederich ran ashore right in front of the new station during a heavy snow storm. The station lifesavers shot a line to the ship, rigged up a breeches buoy, and were able to remove all members of the ship's crew.

The German captain, who weighed 300 pounds, was the last to be removed and when he was over land, because of his girth, he could not get out of the harness. The captain of the station finally got so impatient he shouted, "Tumble him out!" The men manning the breeches buoy responded by flipping the lines, with the result that the good German skipper landed face first into a large snow bank below, somewhat bruised, but at least alive.

There are many other stories, which could be recounted, but these will give you an idea of the life and times of Captain Dan who spent a great portion of his life on and around the sea. What is especially noteworthy, having in mind Dan's many years of seafaring, was the fact that he could not swim. This seems hard to believe these days, but at that time it was not unusual. A good number of Cape Codders could not swim in those days.

Stewart Brooks, who taught history at Orleans High School from the Forties into the Sixties, had been friendly with Dan Gould for many years. In a story about Captain Dan, published in The Cape Codder newspaper 35 years ago, he reported that Dan, when asked about his inability to swim, answered "What's the use knowin how to swim? If you fell overboard, where would you swim to?" Well, I guess you could swim back to the boat, but I suppose Dan's excuse was as good as any others for being on Cape Cod and never learning to swim.

One time, when I was about 10 years old, I was passing along Champlain Road on my paper route when I noticed Captain Dan, bent over, sitting on his front lawn, next to his shop. It appeared that he was whittling away on the grass with his jack-knife. I asked somebody who happened along what Dan was doing, and was told that he was cutting his lawn. "What, with a jack-knife?" I exclaimed. But I accepted the story, thinking to myself, that "Afterall, he is Captain Dan, the Jack-knife Man."

THE MAYOR OF TONSET

Charles Moore, mayor of Tonset

Over the years, Orleans has had its share of interesting characters, but to me, one of the noteworthy ones was Charles Moore, Sr. Many of you knew or have heard of Charles Moore, Jr., who gave so generously to the town. Senior was, of course, the father of Junior.

Charles, Sr., was a somewhat stout gentleman with thick white hair who, back in the Forties, was probably in his late 70's. Born in Eastham, he eventually became Executive Vice President of the Burlington Scales

Company in Vermont. Charlie, as he was known to most people, lived his retirement years with his wife, a kind and gentle lady, in the beautiful old Cape at the end of the Ice Pond on Brick Hill Road in East Orleans.

In contrast to the tight-lipped Cape Codders, so typical back then, Charlie Moore was prone to expand at length, often in stentorian tones, on 'most any subject. People hereabouts were not used to this, and as a consequence, some referred to him affectionately as "Windy" Moore, never to his face, mind you.

Because of his work experience, Charlie for many years held the position of Sealer of Weights and Measures for the Town, and since this job entailed testing every device which was used to weigh and measure, a broad category of equipment, Charlie became known by a large number of people in town.

Even as a boy, I could see that Charlie, despite his propensity to pontificate, was generally viewed with humor and good will. As a result of his stature in the community, Charlie Moore was often referred to as the "Mayor of Tonset."

Charlie was a close friend of my father's oldest brother, Victor. Uncle Victor had traveled to many distant places and was able to exchange countless stories with Charlie...balanced I am sure equally between fact and fiction. The two of them during several summers arranged to take Charlie's grandson Jonathan and me to the Outermost House on North Beach where we spent a week swimming, fishing, clamming, and generally surviving in nature. As boys ten to twelve years old, we had many wonderful and funny experiences on these trips, and it gave me an opportunity to get to know Charlie Moore fairly well.

Charlie had a large black DeSoto back in those years which he kept clean and shiny at all times. Compared to other cars then, this was an impressive automobile. I remember him well, driving his black DeSoto with great dignity, slowly along Tonset Road, heading to town or back home...passing me by as I stood on the side of the road. I would spot his car coming, often on the left-hand side of the road, as I trudged along. Initially, I would turn to face him with every expectation that, knowing me as he did, he would stop to give me a ride. With head tilted up in his jaunty way (somewhat like FDR) and eyes straight ahead, he always passed right along. It became a joke. I am convinced, however, that deep in reverie, he simply did not see me.

As noted above, Charlie often drove on the left-hand side of the road. I had assumed at the time that, lost in thought, he simply drove on the left unintentionally, and it was not until sometime later that I learned that he actually drove on the left intentionally because of the theory he had developed relating to the wear of the tires of his car.

You see, back in those years, the roads were all crowned in the center so as to cause the rain water to run to the sides of the roads. Charlie felt that driving on the right caused greater weight on the tires on the right side of a car resulting in increased wear on those two tires, in contrast to the two tires on the left side of the car. In order to create uniformity of wear on all four tires, he intentionally drove on the left whenever he could see ahead that the road was clear. Thus, at least in his mind, there was "a method in his madness."

For a number of years, Charlie operated a small farm on his property, raising and selling asparagus, turnips, and cranberries which he grew in a small bog beside his house. The bog was maybe fifty yards long and thirty yards wide. I often visited his home as a boy, and Mrs. Moore always gave me a molasses cookie. This one time, while I was eating my cookie, Charlie was talking on the telephone with a friend in another state, as I was to learn later.

Charlie was explaining to his friend, in his usual resonant voice, that if he arrived on the Cape early enough, they could saddle up the horses and traverse the cranberry bog in a few hours to be back at the house for lunch. He made it sound as it the bog were a vast plantation, many miles in length. As he expounded to his friend, he turned to me and gave me a wink. Finally, after hanging up and seeing my puzzled expression, he explained that he knew his friend, because of the distance, would not be able to visit him, and he felt free, therefore, to "josh" him a bit.

It was pretty obvious that, as a consequence of his life experiences, Charlie Moore had developed a keen understanding of human nature and a knack for handling people. My dad was fairly friendly with Charlie, but one time Dad, while talking to Charlie on the telephone, got into a big argument with him over some matter. Dad was usually a quiet, peaceful guy, but on this occasion, he was as stirred up as I had ever seen him. He told Charlie that he was coming right over "to settle this," slammed down the phone, and charged out of the house. Off he went in a "big stew."

About an hour later, Dad came back, quiet and calm, and in response to my inquiry, Dad explained that when he went into Charlie's house to confront him, Charlie was talking on the telephone. Charlie smilingly waved Dad into the room, and while Dad furiously paced back and forth, Charlie calmly continued talking on the phone.

Eventually Dad's pacing began to slow, and Dad finally sat down in a chair Charlie had pointed to. After a few minutes, as Dad quieted down, Charlie briskly concluded his conversation on the phone, hung up, and asked, "Now, Reuben, what can I do for you?" They then discussed their differences calmly and resolved whatever problem had developed. Dad said that as he was driving back home, although Charlie had been talking on the phone all that time, he began to suspect that there was actually nobody on the other end of the line. Months later, Charlie confirmed that what Dad had suspected was true. In later years, I used the same technique successfully myself in several potentially tense situations.

Yes, the "Mayor of Tonset" was indeed a character, but in my mind, with some people today overly serious, with little humor, often contentious and ready to take offense, there really ought to be a few more Charlie Moores in our midst.

YESTERDAY'S BASEBALL PLAYERS

The teams of the Cape Cod Baseball League today are made up exclusively of star players from colleges across the country, but back in the forties and fifties, the League was made up of town teams composed of local players. The players ranged in age from 18 to 50, but on the whole, they were talented and dedicated, and the games were good quality, entertaining and competitive. Moreover, for local fans, there was the added bonus that the players were from the community and they knew most of them.

The Orleans Cardinals, in those years, always had winning seasons and often won the Cape championship. Having played with the team for two years after graduating from High School, I got to know the players well, and they were, in every sense, an exceedingly diverse bunch of guys, some of them being memorable characters.

Several of them stand out in my mind, such as Johnny Linnell, who played center field. Johnny, a strong competitor who said very little, was a short slight man then in his late forties, with a gimpy leg. When he ran, he had a limping hitch in his stride, but he was amazing in the area he could cover to haul down balls hit anywhere close to him. The glove he used was vintage 1935. Unlike the large "scoops" used by today's players, Johnny's glove had no webbing and little padding. Essentially, he caught those hard-hit balls in the palm of his hand.

Another player you could not forget was Dave Bremner, who played shortstop. Dave, a tall rangy guy with a hound-dog face, was also a fierce competitor, but unlike Johnny Linnell, Dave was prone to speak his mind, making pointed comments to anybody he thought was "dogging it". In many respects, he was the leader of the team.

Dave hated to lose. One time after a particularly disappointing loss, a frustrated Dave Bremner, believing that Stuart Finley, who was playing right field, was smiling, angrily accused him of thinking the loss was funny or trivial. Even when Roy Bruninghaus, the team's fireball pitcher who had played pro-ball, told Dave that Stuart's "smile" was really a facial grimace he had when he was nervous or upset, Dave retorted that "OK, but he still shouldn't be smiling about it".

There were a number of other memorable characters: Mac McCray, a tall, lanky hard-throwing sidearm pitcher; Minot Reynolds, a somewhat rotund outfielder; Stan Wilcox, an unpredictable but powerful left-hand hitter; and Junior Lee, the big, silent hard-hitting leftfielder.

Several of the players on the team were hard-drinking types, and it was not uncommon for one or more to show up for a game "somewhat relaxed" shall we say. It did not seem to inhibit their abilities on the field, and indeed, in some case, appeared even to enhance their performances.

The one player who stands out most in my mind, however, is Red Eldredge, the veteran catcher for the team in those championship years. Red now leads a quiet, retiring life, but in those years, he was anything but peaceful and restrained. He was a tall, strongly built, good-looking man, with a thatch of bright red hair, reflective of his fiery play on the field and the basis of his name.

Being the catcher is one of the better positions to play. Unlike other positions where you seldom handle the ball, you are constantly involved on every pitch. In calling signals on pitches, catchers study and learn the weaknesses of a batter and try to outwit him. Apart from being a good hitter, Red handled these catcher chores well.

But catchers also are positioned right in front of the balls and strikes umpire, and this created a unique situation for Red, which he could not resist utilizing when the occasion warranted. If Red felt the umpire, for example, was overly restrictive on the strike zone, he would voice his displeasure in a low growl, but if that did not work, he used another technique. As he waited in his crouch for the next pitch, with his mitt poised as the target, he used his free hand unobtrusively to flip dust and dirt onto the umpire's shoes. Usually, the umpire, waiting intently for the pitch, did not notice what Red was doing, later wondering how his shiny black shoes had suddenly become all dirty.

One time, when Red thought the umpire had made a particularly bad call, Red called for a high fast ball and, just before the pitch arrived, he pulled his mitt down slightly and the high fast one hit the umpire's mask squarely and solidly. What could Red do? The pitch got away from him. The umpire, I noticed, was far more careful after that in the calls he made.

There are other similar type stories, each displaying in its own way the unique character and competitive fire in those town-team players of yesteryear. There was something great about seeing a player close to 50 years old run down a flyball, wheel and throw on a line to cut down the runner who unwisely tried to move up after the catch.

Those old players may not, as a group, have had the level of skill of the college stars who play in the Cape Cod League have today, but they were surely fun to watch and they did indeed give it their all.

OYAM, THE PAINTER OF SURREALISM

When I was growing up, my parents were friendly with Cecil Mayo and his wife, Charlotte, and we often visited them and their daughter Florence at their home on Tonset Road during the forties. I remember Cecil as a quiet, somewhat debonair man, with a well-trimmed mustache, unusual in those days.

Cecil was born in 1899, and served in the Marines during World War I. After that, he married and joined the New England Telephone Company as a linesman, working his way up eventually to supervisory positions.

Over the years, however, he developed a sign painting business on the side, working out of his garage. The signs he painted, I remember, were neat, colorful and professionally done. Cecil's mother was Ethyl Baker Mayo, a well-known creative painter during that period, who lived a short distance down from Cecil's house. Although Cecil dabbled in creative painting, mainly of ships and the sea, he was far better known for his sign painting.

67

When Cecil retired from the Telephone Company in 1964, he was able to apply more time to sign painting. In addition, however, known only to a few, he also became a surrealistic painter whose works were well received among fans of modernistic art who visited here in the summer.

Cecil used a nom de guerre on his creations, and the art aficionados did not realize that it was Cecil Mayo, the sign painter, whose paintings they so admired. And certainly, these devotees did not know that Cecil's talents in surrealism developed unknowingly, purely by chance, as a result of the methods Cecil used in cleaning his brushes in the course of painting signs. Now reported for the first time is the secret behind the development of Cecil's remarkable artistic talent.

After completing painting a particular color on a sign, Cecil would soak his brush in paint thinner, in a can, and then work the paint out of the brush by painting on a plywood board, his cleaning board. Other times, he would let the brush sit in the can, and later, splatter paint residue from the brush onto the cleaning board.

Over time, Cecil's cleaning board built up a wide variety of colors in assorted stripes, splatters and blotches...weird and unusual in appearance. During the 1970's, surrealism had become popular in the modernistic art world, particularly in New York City. As a consequence, some of our summer tourists were especially receptive to painting of these types, seeking out surrealistic paintings at the art shows organized locally.

Cecil's friends often visited Cecil at his garage while he worked on his signs, and one day two of them, studying Cecil's cleaning board in the corner, pointed out that it was a perfect example of surrealistic art, as good, if not better, than what they had seen at the shows they had attended. Knowing that another art show for local painters was to be held again in several weeks, it was decided that Cecil should enter the cleaning board as a surrealistic painting in the up-coming show.

Cecil did not, however, want to enter the "painting" under his real name because local people would recognize the name to be a sign painter. Something impressive and trendy was required, and so they came up with the name Oyam (Mayo spelled backwards). Cecil carefully wrote in the lower corner of the board "Oyam", in precise script, framed the board fittingly and entered the painting in the show.

Reports have it that some of the attendees were especially enamored with the cleaning board (oops, I meant painting) commenting, with ohs and ahs, about the depth of feeling, the collage of bright colors, and the broad scope of the imagery reflected in the work. Some wondered if Oyam was a spiritual leader from India or some other exotic place. I never learned what price Oyam asked for the painting, but I understand it sold very quickly at the show.

After that, I was told that Cecil became even more vigorous in cleaning his brushes, thus producing more paintings for entry in local shows, and that these, too, were also bought up by those able to discern the special qualities inherent in these productions.

Cecil always aspired to be a creative painter, like his famous mother. And indeed, although his technique of production was unconventional, to say the least, he did become known and popular for his "paintings" in a way he never envisioned.

Cecil Mayo, right, with his friend, Louis Eldredge, at Brewster golf club.

THE MISPLACED CAPE CODDER

During the time my stories were being published in the Cape Codder, there also appeared in the newspaper, on a regular basis, letters to the editor written by Sam Sherman, one of my childhood buddies. They seemed to pop up almost as frequently as my stories. In these letters, Sam, in his inimitable style, often made critically scornful observations about my stories. This is typical of Sam, however, and his criticisms did not bother me.

Sam's letters often described, in a humorous way, life in Orleans in earlier years, and a reader would naturally conclude that Sam was, and is, a true Cape Codder. Yet, if you looked at the address on his letters as they appeared several years ago, you would have seen that he actually lived in Groveland, Massachusetts. Where, you may ask, is Groveland? It is a little burg located next to Haverhill near the New Hampshire border.

Sam had taught for many years in Marblehead, actually at a time when I was living there. Unlike myself, however, when he retired from teaching some 15 years ago, rather than returning to the Cape, he stayed on in Salem, and then moved to Groveland, of all places.

And yet, as reflected in his letters, he is fundamentally a Cape Cod character. To be a Cape character, the individual must be a Cape Cod native, but also have special, additional traits or characteristics setting them apart from the rest of us. Sam definitely satisfies this definition. And he will continue to be a Cape character even though it seemed that he could not find his way back to the area where he grew up.

The stories I have written about Cape characters have been about personalities who are no longer with us. Various people have urged me to write a story about Sam. At first, I resisted. One good reason I have focussed upon people who have departed is that they cannot now contest my memory of past events. After further reflection, however, and recognizing that Sam is an unusual personality, I have decided to write a story about him.

Sam's full name is George Samuel Sherman Jr. He grew up with three older sisters, which may have been a factor in his personality development. They may, for example, have laughed at his antics as a little boy, thus encouraging these traits as he grew older. His sisters did teach him to

71

dance, and over the years, he has become a smooth and accomplished dancer, unusual for a man of his size. After his Dad died, Sam seemed to try using the name, George, but it never caught on, and he continues to be known as Sam.

One of my first encounters with Sam was when I was about nine years old (and he was seven). I often visited Leslie Quinn, a classmate, after school at the Quinn home on Main Street, next to the cemetery and across from the road going into the Legion Hall. Leslie was the youngest of four brothers, and there was usually always some adventure or risky activity in the offing, especially if Warren was around. One challenge, for example, was to ride on a small wagon down the long, steep road, from the top of the cemetery to Main Street below. I often wondered how we all survived those hazardous trips onto a road where cars passed back and forth.

Anyway, Sammy (when he was younger, he was known as Sammy, moving along to Sam as he aged) appeared this one-day at the Quinn house to participate in our escapades. He was then a skinny redhead, with jug ears, buck teeth, and what was obviously a mischievous disposition. Since he was younger than I was, I knew him only casually at that point.

When it was time to head home, Leslie offered his bike for us to use going home, but I discovered that Sammy had taken the bike and was peddling along in the direction I was planning to go, looking back over his shoulder with an impish grin. I chased him, but he speeded up as I approached and outdistanced me. I stopped and walked, then charged again, without success. This game went on for about a mile, with me getting more incensed as we moved along, which only added to Sammy's amusement.

Finally, feigning disinterest to lower his attention, I was able to catch him near a briar patch on Hopkins Lane, and after a good thrashing, threw him into the briar patch, retrieved the bike, and rode home. (Since Sam eventually grew to six feet, five inches, outweighing me by 40 to 50 pounds, I would not attempt to repeat this feat today.)

This was not the most auspicious way to begin relationship, but after that, we gradually became friends and as we grew up, we participated in a lot of activities together. We worked for the Shellfish Warden together; we played Army in the woods and went swimming with our buddies; we played various sports, both together as teammates or against each other; and we double-dated. For some reason, we often did not have dates New Years Eve, and found ourselves driving around town, looking for something to do while we groused about unreasonable restrictions our mothers sought to impose and about the female gender in general.

So with this background, here are a few stories, which should give insights into Sam's personality. In some instances, these events will also demonstrate traits, which are commonly found in Cape Cod types. One such occurrence happened shortly after the briar patch incident.

The driver of the school bus which Sammy and I used to get to school, then located in our present Town Hall, encouraged one of the older high school girls to sit in the seat directly behind him where the two of them could converse in whispers. I noticed this, but since the last place I would want to sit was behind the driver, I could have cared less.

Sammy, on the other hand, considered this a major injustice. In his mind, every unoccupied seat should be available to any student regardless of age or sex (sex and age discrimination in earlier years). Since he boarded the bus before the "chosen one", Sammy this one morning plunked himself down in the seat directly behind the driver, who promptly told him to move to the back of the bus. When Sammy refused to budge, the driver, who shall remain nameless, grabbed Sammy by the collar, marched him off the bus, re-boarded and drove along his route. Sammy was left forlornly at the side of the road to walk to school.

Not an admirable performance by the driver, but most illustrative of how far Sammy would go to stand up to an authority figure for what he perceived was wrong and unjust, often something the rest of us would have dismissed as simply a "that's life" issue.

This trait has served as an integral part of Sam's personality throughout his life. Over the years, he has often, as a minority voice, taken on establishment types in the military, in education, and in local government for what he perceives are inequities. Standing up for right and justice is a Cape Cod tradition, although Sam pursued these issues further than the rest of us would.

The other Sam Sherman trait, particularly early on, was his propensity for mischief. The briar patch incident is one example and the letters he sent to the editor reflect his propensity toward mischief. Another example occurred when Sammy, Jonathan Moore and I worked for Elmer Darling, the Shellfish Warden, picking up moon-snails on the flats of the Town Cove at low tide.

73

Since we were required to work approximately four hours, up until the time the tide came in up to our knees, Sammy came up with the bright idea of our getting down on our knees when the tide had come in up to our ankles so that Elmer, seeing us waving as he looked out from the distant shore, would think is was time for us to knock off. This ruse worked the first time, and we giggled and punched each other in the back of Elmer's car as he drove us home. When we tried this again, Elmer simply waved us off.

There are other similar "mischief" stories, including the story how he and Stan Snow, hidden in bushes beside Tonset Road, fired musket blanks as two local damsels were passing sedately in their pony-wagon along Tonset Road, thus panicking the pony to gallop away wildly. Space does not, however, allow for a description of the stories.

Finally, the other characteristic, which sets Sam apart, making him in my book, a character, is his finely developed ability to heckle. Again, this trait is also reflected in the letters he composes to the editor. The ability to heckle usually has little practical usefulness, but in Sam's case, it did heighten his value as a member of the Town's baseball team in the early Fifties.

Sam had become one of the team's regular pitchers, but when he was not pitching, he was assigned to the third base coach's position. There, with his loud, sharp voice, he would yell a mixture of insults, jibes and humorous comments at the opposing pitcher. Being only a short distance away, the pitcher could not long ignore this heckling.

Often times, you could plainly see that after awhile, they became so flustered or furious by the steady stream of comments that they simply fell apart, walking batters, throwing wild pitchers, or committing balks, thus allowing unearned runs to score. Sam should have gone into the Big Leagues as a third base coach. (Can you imagine him yelling across at that self-important Roger Clemens, the man with the enormous rabbit ears?)

Sam has many admirable qualities. Like most Cape Codders, he will drop everything to help someone in need, without thought of reward; he displays a keen sense of humor and, as you will see in Chapter V, he is able to tell funny stories with certain embellishments. Sam also has respect and understanding of our earlier times on Cape Cod and what the Cape is truly all about.

He surely has those traits which place him in the category of a "Cape Cod character". And he will always maintain this distinction even though he may continue to live in Groveland, of all places. But then, with Sam, we would expect nothing else. He ain't going to change simply because he's off somewhere else. (Postscript: Since this story was written, Sam, the "displaced Cape Codder", in May of 2003, returned to the Cape and is now living permanently in Eastham: the Cape Codder returns.)

CHAPTER IV. FAMILY INFLUENCES

Family members have the potential of creating a significant influence upon a child's development. This is not limited to the parents of the child, whose influence could be the greatest, but in some situations, involves the extended family, grandparents, aunts, uncles and cousins.

My mother was from a family of seven siblings, reared in Eastham, consisting of three sisters and four brothers. Most of them lived on the lower Cape when I was growing up and I had considerable contacts with these aunts and uncles, and their children, my cousins, in my early years.

Dad was from a family of 10 siblings, seven boys and three girls. With one exception, all of the brothers lived in East Orleans during my childhood, and since I saw them on a regular basis as well, they, too, I am sure, had subtle influences upon my development.

The biggest influence upon me as I was moving along from childhood into my teens, the person with whom I had the closest relationship, was my father, who, over the years, became my closest friend. In honor of my Dad's memory, I have written a Portrait of Dad, which will describe the type of man he was and my relationship to him.

Before going on with my stories under this Chapter, however, I did want to point out that, apart from the many aunts, uncles, and cousins I had, I also raised a large family of my own. It consists of four natural children, in order of age, Christopher, Joshua, Jessica and Bethany, and four adopted children, Juliana, Victoria, Jocelyn and Minh. Each has now moved into mature adulthood and each, in his or her own way, was been able to attain established goals. They are a diverse group, but they get along reasonably well, and I am very proud of each of them for the responsible way they have developed, each in his or hers individual way.

The stories in this Chapter do not focus upon my children. With eight children, it would be very difficult to write a full and fair assessment of each. Rather, the stories deal either with my childhood contacts with certain family members having special meanings to me and about general family traits and traditional activities. These stories will also reflect, in varying degrees, the overall effect which Cape Cod life has had upon my family's development.

PORTRAIT OF DAD

The author with his father, off Snow Shore, circa 1950.

My Dad, Reuben S. B. Hopkins, died in 1974 at the age of 80. He and I were very close, and I often think of him fondly. There are reminders of my Dad in various parts of our house: his old tools, for example, which I still use, such as handsaws, a plain, a level, a square, and other similar items. Then there are the family artifacts, passed along to me for safekeeping: a Culpaper medical book, circa 1670; an old musket from around 1820; a top hat and silk vest, both circa 1815; and various family records, photographs, and letters.

We also have photographs, of course, of Dad, although unfortunately, not too many. They show a man, at different ages, rather handsome in appearance, looking quietly at the camera. Although these pictures reflect images of Dad, they tell little about his character, disposition, intellect, aptitudes or physical capabilities. This is a brief essay intended to provide a verbal picture of my Dad, as I remember him.

Dad was about five feet, seven inches tall, with a thick "bull" neck, and barrel chest, atop thin, bandy legs. He had a large round head, which, as a boy, earned him the nickname, "Reuben Roundhead".

The one thing that stands out in my mind about his physical condition, more than any other, was his hands. The fingers, particularly the thumbs, were large and overlaid with thick calluses, the result of working with his hands for many years as an electrician. He often had small cuts and crack in the callous, but because of its thickness, these never seemed to bother him. Although his fingers were large and thick, he could, however, use them in very nimble ways, holding and manipulating small screws and nuts, for example, while working.

Although he had a barrel-chest on short, spindly legs, he could, nevertheless, run surprisingly fast. He played baseball as a youth and was a reasonably good hitter and fielder, which as noted below, helped in my development as a ball player. Dad was a strong and avid swimmer. He never became involved in hunting, but he did enjoy clamming and fishing.

Dad played golf beginning in the early 1930's and was still an active player when he died in 1974. I often was able to play golf with Dad at the Brewster Golf Club, where he had a lifetime membership. We were well matched, both usually scoring in the low 90's. Although I could outdrive him by 50 yards, he always evened the score with his shots around the green and his putting. As with everything he did, he played the game in a quiet, modest, good-humored way.

Dad remained vigorous even into his sixties and seventies. It was not uncommon, for example, to see him sprint from his car to the front door to conserve the time involved in walking the same distance. My mother, Lucy, when she saw him making these sprints, would often reproach him for "overtaxing his heart". This was, of course, long before medical opinion had developed that regular exercise, even in advanced years, was beneficial in maintaining a strong circulatory system.

As with most Cape Codders of his generation, Dad typically was a man of few words, not prone to "small talk". If there was nothing important to say, he said nothing, comfortable in his own silence and inner thoughts. It was not unusual for the two of us to sit together, either at home or in the car, for long periods of mutual silence, and yet, it was never awkward.

One time, when I was about 10 years old, we were sitting together in the old Oldsmobile, up-town, waiting for my mother to complete her shopping. This meant her going from store to store, comparing prices and quality of products. We were sitting silently, when Dad turned to me and in all seriousness, grabbed my arm and said, "Son, I'd rather have a good beating than go shopping with your mother." Dad was a stoic in many ways, but thinking about "a good beating", I was amazed by his firm pronouncement. It was not until many years later, when I was trailing around behind a wife on a shopping mission that I fully understood what he meant.

During World War One, Dad served in the Coast Guard, stationed at the station, which was then based in Orleans on Nauset Beach, near the end of Pochet. As an historical footnote, he may have been the only serviceman to have been fired upon during "The Great War", while on United States soil. See the "German Submarine Attack" in Chapter X.

After his discharge from the Coast Guard, Dad eventually became involved in electrical work. Few houses on the Cape had electricity in the 1920's, and Dad was one of the first, if not the first, local electrician in Orleans. As a consequence, he installed wiring in many of the old houses in Town, which meant snaking wires carefully through existing walls and over ceilings, avoiding any outward signs of damage.

Often, as we drove together through the Town, Dad would proudly point out the various houses he had originally wired back in the 1920's and 1930's. Sometimes, he would say that the house-owner still owed him money for his work, but he said this without rancor and in a matter-of-fact way, and apparently, thinking the owner would pay if he could afford to do so, he never pressured to obtain payment.

When I became a teenager, I sometimes worked with Dad as a helper, crawling under floors, climbing up ladders, and traversing attics, to string wire from plug to switch to light. We typically used romax as wire in those years, and Dad was a fanatic about having the wire flat and perfectly straight, upon the beam or joist before it was fastened down by staples. He took great pride in the neatness of his work, pointing out that other tradesmen, when they observed the wiring, would know that this was a "Reuben Hopkins job."

Beyond electrical work, Dad over the years also built several houses on his own. The first was a small cottage he built in 1948 near the mill-run on the Mill Pond, which became known as "Red Shutters". This was one of the first buildings in this area. When I was available to do so, I worked with Dad, helping in the construction of the cottage.

The cottage was to become a summer retreat for me and my family, as it grew, and now, 50 years later, my children, in turn, with their children, enjoy vacation time during the summer at Red Shutters and the shores of the Mill Pond.

Dad also built another cottage, next to Red Shutters, which was called, as you may have guessed, "Blue Shutters". When not used by family members, the two cottages were rented to summer tenants, some of whom (i.e. the Flathers) have been summer renters for nearly 50 years. In 1968, as part of a settlement in Dad's divorce, Dad conveyed Blue Shutters to my mother and sister, Lucy Jane, and Red Shutters to my mother and me. Dad also built a house on Captain Curtis Way in the late 1960's, living in it several years prior to and after his divorce. He later sold this house.

Dad was always hopeful that the two cottages would remain in the family, for use by future generations. In the early 1970's, however, Blue Shutters was sold to raise money for mother and Sister Lucy, but although I have been offered as much as $400,000 for Red Shutters, I never gave a thought to selling this cottage. When I later obtained full title to Red Shutters, moreover, I set up a family trust to assure the retention and availability of the cottage for future generations, just as Dad had visualized.

But Dad had aptitudes and interests far beyond those required to be an electrician and builder. He was exceedingly bright and well read. He followed the news carefully and regularly read books, particularly on history, including all of the Churchill volumes, and could discuss issues and trends in a clear and intelligent manner. We always had supper together as a family, and often discussed together world, national and local issues. The interest which I later developed in history, and world, national and local issues, can be traced directly to Dad's interests and influence.

When Dad graduated from Orleans High School in 1913, he was qualified for college, but with nine other siblings and parents of modest means, this was not financially possible, particularly when his younger brother, George, had the chance and was planning to go to MIT. So, as was common in those days, Dad stayed at home, helping on the farm, and several years later, joined the Coast Guard.

Yet, he always had a desire, over the years, to improve his knowledge, through reading, which, looking back now, I realize is unusual. Many people who did have the benefit of college, I have observed, never opened a book after graduation simply to improve their overall knowledge of world and national affairs. Yet, Dad did this routinely.

Dad was also a dedicated chess player. He played with several local players, including Charlie Freeman, who was Dad's helper for many years. I became interested in chess in my early teens, and sometimes played with Dad, with little success. I found Charlie to be more my speed. Dad had various books on chess, which outlined tactics and strategies, and he studied those books closely, seeking to improve his game. He also maintained games with several players by mail. Whenever he received a letter from an opponent, setting forth his move, Dad would immediately get out the board, taking great care in choosing his counter-move before mailing it along.

Like many people on the Cape in those times, Dad was a staunch, Yankee Republican who believed in self-reliance and freedom from governmental intrusion. Although the Depression of the 30's created financial stress upon our family, as it did for many other families, Dad opposed what he considered to be programs for government handouts developed by Franklin Roosevelt's administrations. (He had little use for FDR, but did admire Harry Truman for his courage and honesty.)

On the other hand, after World War Two, Dad recognized the need for zoning in order to limit uncontrolled growth on the Cape, even though many of his contemporaries opposed those regulations as an infringement upon their person freedoms. These opponents did not realize that the value of their properties, in the long run, would be greatly enhanced by larger lots, space between building, and controls on building development. The preservation of the Cape as it is today can be attributed in large part to the adoption of zoning in those early years.

Dad also was one of the few old-time natives who supported the creation of the National Seashore. Many of his friends felt that this, too, would limit private rights and did not recognize the positive, long-term benefits which the preservation of the vast open spaces on the lower Cape would have in maintaining the beauties of the area, thus enhancing real estate values in the entire area.

Dad served the Town in various ways. He was a member of the Zoning Board shortly after zoning was enacted. He later was a member of the Town's Finance Committee and served on various other study committees over the years. He was one of the founders of the Orleans Historical Society and supported its work in developing and preserving historical artifacts and materials.

Dad was proud of the fact that he was a direct descendent of Stephen Hopkins, who, with his family, survived the arduous journey of the Mayflower across the ocean and the difficulties, disease, and hardships which existed in the Pilgrim settlement in the early years. He carefully verified the development of our family tree and was able to establish through his records that he traced back to five other Mayflower passenger, including William Brewster. Since there were so few families in the Plymouth Settlement in those early years, it is easy to understand that there necessarily would have been marriages between progeny of many of the Mayflower passengers.

Dad spent a lot of time in what we would describe as fatherly responsibilities. I remember early on, as a small boy, listening keenly as Dad told stories to my sister and me. The stories ranged around, but the most popular ones had to do with the adventures of "Oscar, the Penguin", who had a magic umbrella which he used to avoid the terrible dangers which always confronted him.

In those early years, he also took us swimming, often at Crystal Lake. One time, when I was about five, I was running after him as he swam through the water with Sister Lucy on his back, and inadvertently moved out over the edge of a deep drop-off beyond my depth. Fortunately, he saw me struggling underwater just in time to haul me out after I had gone down for the third time.

As I grew older and learned to swim, swimming excursions with Dad became a regular routine. Dad would arrive home from work around 5:30, and I would be waiting, usually with a friend or two, for Dad to change clothes and drive with us down to Boat Meadow Creek to swim in the fast currents on the river. This is where the family tradition of underwater swimming first began. (See "Underwater Swimming, A Family Tradition".)

Apart from swimming, Dad also spent many hours with me in the front yard, practicing baseball, playing pass, and hitting fly balls and grounders to me. These sessions took place either on weekends or after Dad had returned from work at the end of the day, with me waiting expectantly with ball bat and glove. I am sure there were many times when Dad must have been tired from work and would have preferred to sit down quietly with his newspaper, but I do not recall that he ever refused my request to practice with me.

There are many other things Dad did with me, which represented learning experiences...golf, baseball, swimming, chess, and reading, as noted above. But also, clamming, fishing, carpentry, masonry...numerous activities which provided me with opportunities to learn and develop additional skills and confidence in my ability to learn. And always, regardless of what activity was involved, he always displayed good humor, patience and perseverance.

Later, I was to assume the role as father to eight children, each very different in interest, physical ability and temperament. With my Dad serving as role model, I instinctively, without conscious effort, tried to deal with each of my children in the same way he dealt with me, namely, trying to participate in their activities and including them in mine, while attempting to treat them with warmth, courtesy, respect and patience. Hopefully, a little of Dad's fatherly qualities did rub off on me to help in my effort, and in turn, those same qualities have been passed along to my children for use in their child-rearing.

In July 1974, while I was living in Marblehead, I received a call that Dad had died suddenly while clamming on the clam flats off Snow Shore. He had been in good health and I was stunned by the news. Yet, I realized that if you had to go, there was no better way than suddenly in the midst of an activity you enjoyed while surrounded by the quiet beauty of the waters and the marsh.

This description of my Dad, I hope, will provide a portrait which reflects what he was like and why I look back upon him with such fondness. Shortly after his death, a friend of mine came to our house in Marblehead to offer me his sympathy. He had not been very close to his own father, and expressed the view to me that although I may have had difficulties with my Dad, I should think of the good times I had had with him, not the bad. I replied, much to his amazement, that I had never once exchanged a harsh word with my Dad, and to me, he was the greatest guy I had known. And he was.

UNCLE VICTOR AND THE CABIN ON OUTER BEACH

My Dad's oldest brother, Victor Hopkins, had spent his earlier years travelling off to faraway places, but in the late Thirties, when I was a small boy, he had returned to his birthplace in Orleans to settle down. He and his wife, Willa, a soft-spoken, pleasant lady, lived in various houses in East Orleans, and it was not until later, when I was older, that I learned that he bought those houses, improved them, and sold them for a profit, as a source of income.

Looking back at how fascinated I was with Uncle Victor and how much fun I had with him, I realized that he had an innate understanding of small boys and how to treat them. I remember, for example, how, using his jackknife, he turned an ordinary piece of shingle into the shape of an arrow, with a point on the thick end and a large fin on the narrow end. Then using a string with a knot on the end, attached to a rod, he placed the knot into a notch on the heavier top of the arrow, and then thrust the rod upward to propel the little projectile high into the air. Guided by the fins cut into the rear of the arrow, it would move straight up into the air, and finally turn, shooting back to earth. I soon learned from him how to propel the devise into space and craft my own arrows, in different sizes and widths, from shingles I could find. I spent many hours making and firing these missiles into the air.

But that was simply one of many activities in which Uncle Victor got me involved as a small boy. He taught me other games to play, as well, but his real talent in dealing with boys was his ability to create intriguing "make-believe" scenarios. Uncle Victor had a small cranberry bog right next to Hopkins Lane about 100 yards easterly of our house. There were no other houses in that area at that time. He spent a lot of time working to improve his bog. Now, trees and bushes have grown in the bog, totally concealing it.

There was a batch of small pine trees on the westerly side of the bog, and I soon discovered that I could crawl up through those trees, I thought unseen, to spy on Uncle Victor as he worked in the bog. He always seemed to know I was there, however, because, much to my delight, he would suddenly look around frantically, feigning fright while yelling that Indians were surrounding him. I would then happily join in the charade by making loud "warcries", ducking down giggling after each outcry.

For a seven year-old, this kind of playing was real adventure and he and I replayed different versions of this game many times. Uncle Victor, to his credit, was always ready to indulge the imagination and fantasies of a young boy in games such as this.

The best part of my relationship with Uncle Victor, however, was when he arranged to me to participate in trips he and his close friend, Charley Moore, made to a weather-beaten cabin tucked away in the dunes near Coast Guard Beach in Eastham. I was about ten years old when we had our first trip there for a week's stay.

Charley Moore was the grandfather of Jonathan Moore who had been coming down to Orleans to spend summers for many years. Jonathan, who was my age, lived in a cottage on the Town Cove, not far from Hopkins Lane, but before this first trip to the outer beach, I had not met him. Our trips to the cabin, which were repeated for several summers thereafter, were wonderfully great adventures. And my introduction to Jonathan turned into a lifelong friendship. Even now, he and I talk about those trips to the outer beach and how Uncle Victor created such fun and excitement for us.

In many respects, those trips were lessons in perseverance and self-reliance. We lived in the dunes with basic provisions, relying mostly upon the fish we could catch and the shellfish we were able to dig up. The cabin did have water, which we had to pump up from a pipe driven deep into the sand. Life was fundamental and primitive, and although I had not read Henry Thoreau's essays at that age, I later realized that our activities on our trips were patterned after the style of living he extolled.

Jonathan and I were exposed on our very first trip to the need for hard work and self-reliance even before we reached the cabin on the outer beach. Outboard motors were rare in those days, and we could only reach the outer beach by rowing from Snow Shore. Jonathan and I were designated to do the rowing, and although we had just met, we did reasonably well, each manning an oar, in rowing with some semblance of coordination.

We went smoothly across the channel from Snow Shore, but then, in passing into the channel which ran up between two marshes and on to our destination, we discovered the tide was running strongly against us. With encouragement from the adult members of our crew, we rowed and rowed valiantly, but when we looked at the marsh to check our position, it seemed like we had moved hardly at all. Neither of us was willing to acknowledge defeat, however, and we simply kept rowing.

Finally, we reached a sandbar in the middle of the channel and Charlie Moore, looking down, calculated that the water was shallow enough for Jonathan and me to get out of the boat and pull it along over the large bar which extended a good distance up the channel. (Charley was good at giving directions, but seldom provided the work necessary for accomplishing the tasks he had set.) Indeed, the water did look to me shallow enough for us to walk through easily.

So out we jumped only to discover that the water was actually up to our necks. I thought for a moment that the boat was going to be pulled by the tide from our grasps and drift away with our cargo, leaving us alone in the middle of the channel.

Somehow, we held on, got ourselves situated and began pulling on the bow of the boat against the tide. Even with two of us pulling, it was not an easy task because we had to reach up over our heads and with little leverage, pull this large boat, laden as it was with two large men and the provisions we were taking for a week's stay, through the rushing tidal waters. Somehow we managed, and eventually found ourselves in shallower water on the bar.

We had stocked up with the typical provision for "living in nature": hot dogs, hamburger, bread, milk, soft drinks, butter, etc. I'm not certain how we kept the perishables cool. There may have been a cold cellar at the cabin. To a great extent, however, our meals revolved around what we could catch or collect. Soft-shelled steamer clams, which I loved, were very plentiful. With guidance from our two elders, we also were able to dig quahogs out of the slough holes in the marsh and catch flounder to vary our menu.

Jonathan and I spent time each day collecting driftwood from the beach in order to make a fire each night. When we were not digging clams, fishing or collecting firewood, we either swam in the nearby waters or took long walks exploring the beach, checking out what the tides and waves had brought ashore.

After eating each evening, we typically spent an hour or so sitting around the fire, toasting marshmallows while Uncle Victor and Charley Moore regaled us with stories. We would then fall into our bunks, worn out by the activities of the day, and drift off to sleep, lulled by the surf crashing on the nearby shore.

These trips to the outer beach were truly memorable and made me recognize even better the unique natural qualities of the Cape. Uncle Victor has long since gone, but I am able to recognize and appreciate now the wonderful qualities he had in entertaining and creating adventures for young boys.

THAT'S NOT SUCH A BAD FAULT

Native Cape Codders, particularly in earlier years, were typically disdainful of tourists and "wash-ashores", and even though it was recognized that our summer visitors were vital to the Cape's economy, the locals still tended to be critical and somewhat intolerant of what they perceived were the shortcomings and limitations of the off-Capers in our midst.

In contrast to these attitudes, however, most native Cape Codders were remarkably tolerant and accepting of the weaknesses, misadventures and character flaws of their own kind. A fellow native might be a habitual drunk or a nagging shrew, but it was common for others who knew them, in discussing their flaws, to say, "Well, that's not so bad...there are worse faults."

A man might be prone to brawling or a confirmed peeping Tom, but their contemporaries often simply observed, "That's just his nature" (pronounced "nate-cha"). I was never sure whether this attitude of acceptance was to be admired of criticized, but it was a definite trait among native Cape Codders in earlier years, and to a certain extent, even today.

And this brings me to the heart of this story which involves a foible which, I must acknowledge, seems to be inherent in the Hopkins family, passed along from generation to generation, like some kind of regressive gene.

There have been suggestions by some outside the family, some veiled, others more direct, commenting on this, but I think it time that a family member should step forward bravely, admit the problem exists, and rely upon the fundamentally tolerant nature of my fellow townsmen (at least toward another local) that this fault will be accepted as simply part of our "nature". Yes, we Hopkins' have a weakness: namely we are forgetful, or absent-minded, if you will.

When I was still a young lad, my Dad, Reuben, sort of off-handedly, informed me that being forgetful, or absent-minded, was a family trait. At first, this meant little to me...afterall, what could a seven-year-old forget which would be of any significance? But as time went on, and stories of this family characteristic mounted, Dad's observation became more real, and worse, more personal.

A few examples will illustrate what we Hopkins' have had to cope with over the years. My Uncle Alfred operated a fishing boat out of Rock Harbor for many years back in the forties. For some reason, never clear to me, he was called Captain Dick, not his given name. Well, Uncle Alfred (a.k.a. Captain Dick), when he returned to port from his fishing excursions, always went to the head of the harbor where he gassed up, turned around, came back and tied up to the dock on the port side, facing out, ready to go the following day.

Alfred "captain Dick" Hopkins, on his boat in Rock Harbor

This one day, he was in a hurry because he wanted to get to Brownie's service station before it closed in order to have the boat's battery charged, and so he skipped the turn-around and simply hitched the boat to the dock, facing in. He quickly disconnected the battery, grabbed it up, and headed to the port side to step onto the dock, as he always did, and stepped off instead into the open water. Down he went to the bottom, some 12 feet deep, clutching the heavy battery tightly to his chest.

Realizing that if he were to avoid becoming a permanent fixture at the bottom of the harbor, he would have to relinquish the battery, he finally dropped it, swam up to the surface, and eventually pulled himself from the water...another victim of the dreaded Hopkins trait of absentmindedness.

Very much himself a Hopkins, my Dad also displayed episodes of forgetfulness. Various times during my teenage years, he was supposed to pick me up uptown, after team practice, only to drive along home, leaving me with a two-mile walk. Charlie Freeman, who worked with Dad in his electrical business, often grumbled to me that he, too, had been left at some job site because Dad had forgotten to pick him up, as promised. There were always good reasons for these oversights...his one-track mind was focussed intently on the job he had to do the following day, or some other important matter.

The best story had to do with a trip my Dad made to Boston to visit his sister, Winnie. Usually, he took the train for these trips, but this one time, because he was carrying a table to her, he went to Boston in his car. After a pleasant visit, and again dwelling upon some matter of importance, he walked to the train station, as he did so often, and returned by train, only to discover when he reached the end of the line that his car was back in Boston. The Hopkins gene strikes again.

But I, too, must confess to falling under the absentminded spell. When I lived in Marblehead on the North Shore, I usually took the Blue Line subway from the Wonderland Station in Revere into Boston where my office was located. On occasion, however, I had to have my car in-town, and OK, I must acknowledge that, more than once, I ended up at Wonderland, having left my car in Boston. There have been other similar incidents, but I won't go into those.

You must understand, however, that in each of these episodes, I was concentrating intensely upon important matters, and simply forgot the mundane details of commuting home...the Hopkins gene at work in another generation. Have I seen these symptoms in my children? Yes, indeed. When I saw symptoms among my sons, I concluded that the gene was passed along through the males of the family. But this theory was debunked recently when my oldest daughter, who attained a Doctor's degree in psychology and now consults in Providence, confessed that she also has the requisite symptoms.

Now I know that some of you who belong to the so-called "senior" age group will say, "That's not a big deal...I tend to forget things too." Since I now belong to this age category, I can understand such a reaction. But you must remember that my Dad and I were in our thirties and forties when we were having these difficulties, and we cannot, therefore, claim that forgetfulness of older age is the contributing factor.

I am not certain how well known this family foible is outside of the family. Since some of my contemporaries have made note of it occasionally, maybe a public acknowledgment such as this is not necessary. There is, however, a sense of expiation in composing this confession, particularly when I know that among native Cape Codders, they will simply smile and say, "That's their nature, and it isn't such a bad fault".

MY COUSIN STEVE

With fifteen aunts and uncles, most of whom lived on the lower Cape, there necessarily was also a large number of cousins with whom I had regular contacts during my formative years. Some of those, namely the four children of Aunt Ester, my mother's sister, lived in Eastham next door to my grandparents, Abbott and Flora Knowles, and I saw these cousins almost every Sunday when we visited my grandparents at their home. Other cousins, however, I saw only on an infrequent basis.

The one cousin I had the closest relationship with was Stephen Hopkins, the youngest son of my Uncle George. Although George worked as a geologist for the government in Washington, D.C., the family owned a small cottage off Freeman's Lane in East Orleans, and they spent most of the summer months each year at that cottage. My father was very close to his brother George, and I have memories, commencing when I was fairly small, perhaps five or six years old, of visiting with Uncle George, his wife Frances, and their three children at their summer cottage.

Cousin Steve was four years older than I was, but he always made an effort to include me in the children's activities and games. George's children, for example, had a small clubhouse next to the cottage, which they called "the Rinky Dink Club," and in his good-natured way, Steve readily acknowledged me as a member of this exclusive club, truly an honor for an impressionable young boy. Early on, Cousin Steve reflected a kindness and understanding which, as I was later to recognize, was an integral part of his personality which he showed throughout his life.

Uncle George's cottage was located near the farmhouse and barn owned by Freeman Snow, a well-known local personality. A large hay field, belonging to Freemy, as he was known, separated the two properties. When Steve and I were young lads, Freemy, a short slight man with a small white beard, was probably in his mid-seventies. He was a devoted church-goer, and I have a vivid memory of attending services at the Federated Church and listening in amazement to Freemy bellowing at the top of his lungs, as he fervently sang, considerably off-key, the hymns of the day. For those who knew him, Freemy was a kind and gentle man, and Steve and his siblings enjoyed his company and spent considerable time with him as he went about the chores of his farm.

Unfortunately, Steve's keen interest in Freemy Snow and his desire to share activities with him resulted in an accident which caused Steve a very serious injury. Freemy was cutting hay in the nearby hay field, riding on a machine which had a cutting bar about ten feet long which sliced through the hay as Freemy moved around the field. Fascinated by this procedure, Steve went out onto the field to watch, and Freemy, not fully aware he was there, came too close to Steve, and the blades of the cutting bar almost completely severed Steve's foot. The foot was ultimately saved, but the bones, muscles, and tendons of that foot were forever scarred and misshapened. This physical disability prevented Steve from moving about freely and must have caused him pain and discomfort throughout his life. He was very accepting of his infirmity, however, and the fact that he was always so cheerful and good-natured was even more remarkable.

As we both grew older, I continued to see Steve intermittently during the summer months. This socializing increased significantly, however, when I began attending college and Steve, four years older, was spending the entire summer months working the Cape. Steve, for example, organized parties, both at his parents' place and at Nauset Beach, and he was good enough to invite me to those events. In this way, I got to know and appreciate him better, while having the chance to meet his friends, an interesting and fun-loving group. Steve had a great sense of humor and an infectious grin, and he was a popular and respected leader of this band of friends.

After graduating from the University of Maryland, Steve married Cynthia Chase in a ceremony on the Cape in June 1952. I served as an usher for this event, and when the newlyweds went off on a two-week honeymoon trip,

Steve entrusted me with the care and custody of the large yellow Chrysler convertible he owned at the time, a truly sterling automobile. This was a demonstration of infinite trust, and I drove the car carefully and with pride around the town, thinking of course that I was greatly impressing the local damsels.

In getting to know Steve better, I soon realized that beyond being a nice guy, he was an exceptional individual in other ways. Just as when we were small, he continued to be kind, generous and good-natured. Beyond this, however, he was a man of many talents and skills. Even at a young age, he was a master mechanic who, during a number of summers, worked overhauling and repairing engines at Judah Eldredge's garage on Route 6A in Orleans, where Nauset Marine is now located. He could listen to an engine running and know at once if it was malfunctioning and the cause of the problem. I had seen him demonstrate this skill once when he was checking out the engine in an old car I had, and another time when I asked him to look at my outboard motor which had been running poorly. To me, this was an amazing attribute.

These mechanical aptitudes were not limited, however, to combustion engines. When he was older, Steve began inventing various contraptions for domestic use, including the trash compactor, for which he received a patent. Unfortunately, as it turned out, the patent was not properly descriptive of his invention, and Sears Roebuck was able to get around the patent and began successfully manufacturing and marketing knockouts of Steve's trash compactor, making huge profits over the years. Sad to say, large corporations have often been able to usurp the inventions of creative persons such as Steve.

Steve's mechanical talents and inventive ways were merely a side activity, or hobby, for him. His primary vocation was education in the science area. After graduating from the University of Maryland, Steve spent a year at Harvard, earning a master's degree in education. He then became a science teacher in the public school system of Washington D.C., and eventually, became chairman of the Science Department for the entire city system.

Steve had settled down with his wife in a modest home in a nice neighborhood near Washington, and over the years they had five daughters. Maintaining the Hopkins line had always been a concern in our family (my dad often mentioned to me the need to keep the family name going), and although Steve never talked openly to me about it, I knew he had been hoping to have a son among those five offspring. Although Steve and his family lived in Washington, they did build a small cottage on land they had bought on Tonset Road and spent their summer months at this cottage.

Steve, like his older brother, Buddy, developed arteriolosclerosis and coronary heart disease in his forties, and when he was about forty-eight years old, he underwent a triple by-pass operation because of serious blockages in his arteries. After the operation, he seemed much improved and was physically active for several years, but in July 1981, at the age of 54, while he was making a drink and talking to Cynthia in the kitchen of their little cottage, Steve suddenly, without a word, keeled over and died.

During his brief lifetime, Steve was able to do many worthwhile things and he touched in positive way the lives of family, friends, and the many students, I am sure, with whom he worked. Still, for a man with his numerous and varied talents and his wonderful personality, his passing was much too premature.

UNDERWATER SWIMMING, A FAMILY TRADITION

Some families participate in competitive events which, over the years, have taken on special meaning for family members when they get together in the summer. This may involve contests in such diverse sports as tennis, volleyball, badminton, croquet, or sailing, but whatever the contest, these activities have often introduced into family gatherings competition of historical significance.

Members of the Hopkins family were not, as a group, big in terms of tennis, croquet, or badminton, but beginning when I was about 14 years of age, we have engaged in one unique competition, namely, underwater swimming contests. As with many things, this competition began in a haphazard fashion, with the initial participants having no idea that 50 years later these contests would remain the family's traditional sporting event.

When I was in my early teens, I waited patiently at the end of the day during the summer for my Dad to come home from work so he could take me swimming. He no sooner arrived home, driving his old telephone truck into the driveway, when I and other boys from the neighborhood who were also looking for a swim, would urge him to take us swimming. He almost always obliged, and looking back, I now realize there must have been days when he would have preferred to rest.

Instead of the sandy beaches of Skaket or Crystal Lake, our favorite spot for swimming, I was never sure why, was Boat Meadow Creek, not at the beach end but further up into the marsh. Reaching our spot required us to journey across the wide expanse of spiky marsh grass, and we found the best way to do it was to run across the grass as fast as we could. This resulted in foot races between whoever was in the group that day, including Dad. But once there, it was great fun because we could dive off the banks of the creek into the water, and swim along with the strong tide, which always was either going in or out of the river.

After many trips to the creek, Dad, looking for more to do, came up with the idea of having contests to see who could swim the furthest underwater. Everybody joined in these contests, and what made it especially satisfying was the fact that swimming with the swift current, we could, at least in our minds, go incredible distances underwater. Dad could hold his breath for a long time, and he inevitably won those early contests.

Thus began what was to become a family tradition of underwater swimming which has passed down through generations and is still flourishing today. Dad and I competed initially, joined in the early years by various cousins and uncles. Eventually, I could beat Dad, but even in his seventies, he continued competing in races with me, my sons, Chris and Josh, and younger brother, Richard. Just as Dad was able to surpass me early on, I was able to outdistance my sons up to a certain age, when they, too, began to edge me out.

The number one star in the family, however, when she was an active swimmer, was my daughter, Jolie, who at age eight, came from Vietnam to join our family. By age 13, Jolie had become dedicated to swimming training at the YMCA in Marblehead where we were then living. The hardships she had suffered in Vietnam had given her determination and perseverance, and she soon became a strong and accomplished swimmer. Although small and still young, having witnessed the underwater contests between older members of our family, she wanted not only to participate in this competition, but also to win.

The first few times I raced with Jolie in the pool at the YMCA, I was able to outdistance her, but not by much. Jolie continued swimming at the pool almost daily, and several months later, she challenged me to another match. This time, I went first, and pushing myself to the limit, swam two full lengths of the pool, up and down. The pool was approximately 45 feet long.

Jolie then dove in, and with fast, strong strokes, she quickly covered two lengths of the pool, and turning again, she amazingly returned underwater to complete a third length. Having in mind her size and age, this was an incredible feat. No member of the family has ever been able to equal this distance. Jolie later lost interest in swimming and did not retain her swimming strengths, but she continues to hold the family record for underwater swimming.

There are two basic concepts, which one must recognize for success as an underwater swimmer. First, you must breath long and deeply for a period of time before your swim in order to generate excess oxygen in your blood stream. Anybody watching one of our contests will see the participants huffing and puffing vigorously before plunging into the water.

The second theory of success has to do with the fact that each swimmer is able to cover a certain distance with one stroke, and to measure your performance and know whether you are improving in comparison to others, you have to count not only the number of strokes you take as you swim, but also the number of strokes others are taking. Swimmer A might go 15 strokes to cover 30 yards while swimmer B might take 12 strokes to cover the same distance. In order to outdistance swimmer A, swimmer B will strive to increase his strokes to 15. Counting strokes, therefore, is very important to improvement and for practicing alone.

Another important point: colder waters, such as inside Nauset Inlet, can quickly sap the energy of a swimmer and the distances recorded in these colder waters are always less than those who are swimming in warm waters. Recognizing this, most of the family contests took place off the docks in the warmer waters of Pilgrim Lake. There we would dive off one dock, swim underwater by the parallel dock, and often end up in the pond lilies beyond. Swimming in the warm waters of the Caribbean is even more rewarding, especially so in those long winter months.

While I was in Anquilla, I spend a lot of time in the water, and this gives me a chance to work on my underwater swimming. Getting ready for summer competition, I increased my strokes from 10 to 15. Last summer, Nicholas Denis, son of my cousin Carol, participated in the family underwater swimming contests with great enthusiasm. The Denis live in Paris, but spend each summer at their family home on Nauset Heights on Cape Cod.

During one recent winter, I sent an email to him, telling him I was swimming regularly underwater and was up to 15 strokes. He immediately responded that he would be practicing underwater swimming all winter in the pool because he was determined to beat me in the summer.

Such is how these family contests keep growing and expanding into healthy, enjoyable competition, not only between members of different generations, but even from different countries. And who knows, maybe if I keep practicing, I will be able to get up to 20 strokes and break Jolie's record. Realistically, it ain't likely, but, hey, we have to keep trying.

Jocelyn holds swimming record

CHAPTER V. SAM'S STORIES

As you would know from reading stories about my boyhood in Orleans, ever since I was about nine years old, I have had an on-going friendship with George S. Sherman Jr., better known as Sam Sherman, or in the early days, Sammy.

Several of the stories in the earlier chapters focused upon Sammy. Indeed, one of those stories, entitled "The Misplaced Cape Codder" described, from my perspective, the personality and character of Sam. (Sam, of course, may view the story as character assassination.) As those who know him recognize, Sam is one-of-a-kind, direct, outspoken, but always humorous, a character in all respects.

Anyway, prior to my writing any stories, Sam would, from time to time, become aroused about some issue and shoot off a letter-to-the-editor, usually an unfortunate official at The Cape Codder, a local newspaper, commenting in a jocular way as only he can do about this or that.

After I began writing stories, a number of which were printed in The Cape Codder, Sam, apart from a few more letters-to-the-editor, began writing stories himself about growing up in Orleans. Although Sam chided me for writing stories in my retirement, story telling easily can become contagious, and having time on his hands and apparently having forgotten his comments about my writings, he too soon succumbed to the bug.

Sam always did have a prodigious memory for names, places and events, remembering persons and events from those earlier years growing up on Cape Cod, which I either was not involved with or have totally forgotten.

He also has an acute sense of humor and tends to remember the funny stories he has heard. Here are some of Sam's stories, which are different, as you will see, from mine. I think you will enjoy them.

Sam Sherman, 2003

WHY I WANTED TO BE A FIREMAN

I enjoy going back and re-reading articles in the Cape Codder newspaper during its fledging years because there were often stories about the activities of the Orleans Fire Department. You see, when I was a youngster, I had a secret aspiration to become a fireman when I became an adult, a goal that slowly faded away as I got older.

Back in those years, the Fire Department, apart from a few regulars, consisted of volunteer firemen who worked in a variety of regular jobs, but responded when the existence of a fire was signaled. Everyone in town had a little card near the phone. The cards listed the meaning of various blasts from the fire siren, located in the center of town on top of what was then the Cummings Building where the Land Ho pub is now located.

One blast indicated the fire was in the center of town; two blasts were for East Orleans, a wide area, to be sure; and one short and one long blast indicated some other part of town. One long blast was the signal that the fire was out. These signals made it possible for the on-call firemen, if they didn't have time to get to the fire station before the trucks left, to go directly to that section of town the fire signal had designated. How they knew what part of East Orleans to go to, for example, is still a mystery.

At that time, the fire station was located easterly just beyond the traffic light on Main Street in the building currently occupied by the Community Building. The building just westerly of the station was the old telephone building, now occupied by the clothing store, Soft As A Grape. When a fire was called into the telephone office, the operator, usually Betty Childs, would call out the area of town and the fire siren would be activated. Being an avid fan of the firemen, whenever I heard the siren, if I was free to do so, I would hurry to the fire station to see how the firemen responded.

When the siren sounded, the volunteer fireman, working their regular jobs, would drop what they were doing and rush to the station if they were close enough. Lloyd Ellis would come running to the station from his grocery store on what is now Cove Road, through the field that is now the parking lot of the Cape Cod Bank and Trust. Lester Quinn wouldn't be far behind as he dashed (if you want to call it that) out of Ellis' Liquor Store where Brownie's Garage now stands today.

Judah Eldredge would leave his auto repair garage, now Nauset Marine, and head for the station in his wrecker. Bud Penniman would leave his work at the French Cable Station. Nate Ellis would shut down his bulldozer and head either for the station or the area designated, depending on where he was working. In short, they'd all be coming at the same time from the four winds.

Al Brown lived above the station. He doubled at night as the clean-up guy and ticket taker at the nearby movie theater. Al was missing several fingers on the hand he used to take tickets from patrons. Seeing the hand as he took our tickets was an eerie experience for us kids.

Anyway, when the fire signal was given, Al would rush downstairs, open up the large doors on the front of the station, and start the engines of the trucks. After starting each engine, he put the shift gear into low-low gear and let the truck kind of mosey out of the station. Then he'd rush to the next truck and do the same thing, and so on, until there were four fire trucks creeping along heading slowly toward the street, unmanned!

There was a vacant area across the street from the fire station and our dedicated firemen would park their vehicles in that area, by throwing the shift into second gear, shutting off the key, and letting the cars come to a "coughing" halt haphazardly in the vacant lot. It was really comical to see these grown men rolling out of their vehicles and going full tilt, actually running, for the trucks. In those days, you never ever saw middle-aged men running. Apparently, there was something undignified, or maybe it was considered unhealthy, for the typical pot-bellied older person to move along at a pace greater than sedate walking.

I soon began to realize, however, that there were good reasons for their haste: you see whoever got to one of those slowly moving trucks first was entitled to drive the truck to the fire, a cherished and challenging honor.

Watching all of these men scurrying around excitedly, and thinking about driving those trucks to the fire and then joining the efforts to fight the fire, created in my mind the dream of someday becoming myself an Orleans fireman, dramatically fighting fires on behalf of my town. That dream, alas, soon faded away and never did actually materialize.

A BENEFIT OF BEING A BOY SCOUT

In the mid-Forties, the American Legion Post 308 in Orleans met every other Monday at 7:00 P.M. on Cove Road, then known as Bakeshop Road. The Boy Scouts, under the guidance of Alaric Coffin, father of Oliver Coffin, used to meet at the same time in a building next-door, just right of what is now the Left Bank Gallery, formerly L.R. Ellis' grocery store.

Being a faithful member of the Boy Scouts, I would ride uptown with my father George, a member of Post 308, and we would separate and go to our respective meetings. After the Boy Scout meeting, it was my custom to walk next door, enter the back of the Legion Hall, and quietly take a seat to watch while their meeting progressed to a conclusion.

On one occasion, the formal part of the Legion meeting had ended early. It seems that a rather progressive member of the Post, a guy, who I recall as "Kid" Baker ("Kid" evolved from the fact that he had done some amateur boxing), had recently returned from a trip to New York City where he had obtained what was then referred to as an "artistic" film featuring attractive nude women posing for "artistic" purposes. Knowing that many of the Legionnaires were interested in art and culture, he brought the film to the meeting for a showing.

When I entered the back of the hall, the lights were out, the film was running, and members of the Post were keenly enjoying the art displayed on the screen. I quietly sat down in the back, scrunching down in my seat and marveling at what was being shown. Nobody knew that a twelve-year old was sitting in the back of the room. As the film proceeded, the Legionnaires along the way made "critical" remarks about the artistry displayed before them.

The film ended, everyone got up, turned to leave by the rear door, and then saw me sitting low in my seat in the rear. Most, if not all, of the so-called prominent men in town were members of Post 308, and it seemed that they were all there for this showing.

When they noted my presence, there were some priceless expressions on their faces. Confusion reigned, as varied thoughts ran through their minds. How was the principal of the High School going to explain his presence? How would the Police Chief defend himself before the selectmen, some of whom were also in attendance? What would one of my teachers have to say to me tomorrow in school?

My father gathered me up quickly and we went out to his car for the ride home. On the way, he explained that I need not tell anybody what I had seen, especially emphasizing that I should say nothing to my mother. And up until the preparation of this story, I followed his instructions to the letter. But that was one great Boy Scout meeting!

MY NEIGHBORHOOD FRIEND, STAN SNOW

I go way back with Stan Snow of Snow's Home and Garden fame. His family had a summer house, the one Stanley and Bonnie now occupy, on Gibson Road, overlooking the Cove. As you turn off Tonset Road onto Gibson Road, you must bow your head in reverence as you pass the first and second houses on the left, the ones my family built and occupied when I was growing up.

Stan and his brothers, Bill and Bobby, were "friends" of mine during the summer months when they stayed at their cottage. We had plenty of fights over the years, but that was all resolved by the time we reached high school. The Snow boys were not usually involved in athletics, but they were very fast runners, especially Stanley who had long, strong legs.

In his junior year, much to our surprise, Stanley decided to try out for the basketball team. He couldn't shoot very well and couldn't dribble worth a hoot, but oh, how he could jump. He played guard which placed him under the basket in the zone defense we employed, and we all noticed after a time that when the other team shot the ball and missed, Stanley would often end up with the rebound.

Stanley just seemed to know how the ball was going to bounce off the rim or backboard and would leap like a deer, over the outstretched hands of everybody else. Many times when the ball was coming to me and as I closed my hands on it, the ball would suddenly disappear as Stanley grabbed it away. Since he had trouble dribbling, he would quickly pass the ball up to Steve Hopkins, our center, or a forward on the side to start a fast break. He also was a great threat to any opponent who dared to shoot anywhere near him. He would crouch low as the unsuspecting opponent approached and began his shot, then fly up and bat the ball away in midair, often down upon the head of the startled shooter.

Anyway, we became good friends in those days, but we did raise a bit of deviltry. Stanley always seemed quiet and serious, particularly around adults, but he did have a mischievous side. (And everybody who knows me realizes that I ordinarily am not like that.) I shall share with you one event in which we engaged when we were about age ten to demonstrate. Stanley had a lot of toys, mostly derived from his father's store. But he also had an old musket and powder horn. I, too, had a musket of my own, and the two of us decided that it was our responsibility to guard the "Snow woods", as they were called, located between Gibson Road and Tonset Road.

With his unbelievable resources, Stanley had a bunch of metal caps that one could put on a spot where the hammer of the musket would strike when the trigger was pulled, resulting in a loud "BANG". No other boy in town had any comparable weaponry, not even Steve Hopkins.

Well, as we were patrolling the perimeter of the woods, we heard the unmistakable "trit-trot" of either a horse or pony advancing along Tonset Road. We stuck our heads out and saw a pony pulling a cart heading out way. This was an unforgivable intrusion of the territory we had vowed to protect, and something surely had to be done and we readied our weapons.

What we did not realize in our haste was that the pony, which belonged to Garfield Freeman, was not used to war games and might react in a frightened way to our defensive actions. The pony cart was occupied by two local maidens, Elaine Mayo, daughter of "Hot-mix" Freddie Mayo, the town's road surveyor, and Harriet Freeman, daughter of Charlie Freeman, who worked as Reuben Hopkins' helper, well-known for his long walks home from a job because Reuben had forgotten to pick him up at the end of the day.

We later learned that Garfield Freeman, Harriet's uncle, had let the two girls take the pony for a WALK around the loop of Hopkins Lane and Tonset Road. He had given them strict instructions not to run the pony because it was springtime and the pony had not had any exercise all winter and should not be pushed, especially not galloped. But how did we, the saviors of the Snow woods, know that.

Well camouflaged in the bushes, we waited for them to come into closer range, and then, with muskets loaded and cocked, we leaped from our hiding place and let go with two near-deafening blasts, surprising even ourselves with the noise we created and the success of our attack. The pony, not to mention the girls, did not join in the spirit of the event, and whinnying and snorted in total fright, reared back, almost tipping the cart over backwards, and took off as if his backside was aflame, the girls being completely unable to regain control. As later reported, the pony galloped helltilarup (an old Cape expression) for the barn, about a mile away.

Our sense of victory slowly faded as we realized the gravity of what had happened. Harriet and Elaine conveyed to us their displeasure in colorful language the next day in school, recounting the "talking-to" that Uncle "Garf" had given them upon their earlier then-expected return to the barn.

I bumped into Harriet a couple of years ago at the Eastham Post Office, and before even asking me how I was, she lit into me again about what a couple of jerks Stanley and I were on that occasion. And I guess we were. So, speaking for Stanley, as well as myself, we apologize and promise never to do it again.

MY BRIEF CAREER IN RAILROADING

Back when I was a kid, there was a rail line running through the center of Orleans, which traveled north down to Provincetown. This was an important form of transportation in those days and freight trains regularly moved up and down on this rail line transporting cargo and commodities. The only evidence of this rail line today is the open pathway now used as a bike trail as it comes into Orleans, next to what was Nickerson Lumber Yard, now Mid-Cape Home Center, across from Snow's.

But when those trains were operating regularly through the center of Orleans, dropping off freight cargo, they represented a source of intense fascination for boys such as myself. As I recount here, I was fortunate enough to be able to experience firsthand as a young boy, the thrills and excitement involved in the operation of a freight train as it delivered cars to commercial sites in the town.

Back in those days, when I was about ten years old, the whistle of the on-coming freight train could be heard pretty far away, in other parts of the Town, as it pulled into Depot Square. Often, when I heard it, I would rush up to the center of Town to see the train. Jack Walsh, a tall thin man with graying hair, ran the freight office in Depot Square in those early years. The freight office was northerly of what is now Captain Elmer's Restaurant. I was too young to know exactly what Jack Walsh did. All we knew was that he worked at the station, and when a train arrived, he was there to deal with it in some fashion.

Actually, we really didn't care what Mr. Walsh did because we were more interested in who the engineer on the train was and what he did. We soon learned that if it was the "old fella", we had a good chance of being invited into the cab of the engine while it was in Orleans. The younger engineers, on the other hand, seemed impatient and grouchy, which seemed strange to us since, for us, it was usually the older people who were the grouchy types.

When the "old fella" was there, we'd approach the cab of the train and ask him very politely, "Can we help ya to run the train today?" Sometimes, seeing our eager faces, he would invite us aboard with a grin on his face, saying "Sure, come aboard, but don't forget the rules."

We knew the rules better than we knew how to add and subtract, and although, as young boys, we were not known for following other rules given to us, we were careful to follow the rules laid down by our mentor while in the cab of the train. My memory was that Bruce Peters, who lived near the center of Town, was often with me when we were attempting to become members of the train crew.

"You stand over there, hold onto that bar and don't let go", he'd say to Bruce. "And you jump up into the seat and take your turn first", he'd say to me. We were quick to comply. Usually, we had a lot to do. There was Harry Snow's coal to deliver and we often had to drop some cars full of lumber for Josh Nickerson's yard. We had to be very careful at Nickerson's because if we didn't leave the cars in just the right spot, Grover Chandler, who was one of those old grouchy types, would have to use his push stick to move the car to where he wanted it, something he preferred to avoid.

Before delivering cars to Nickerson's and Snows, the engineer would uncouple the cars used for general freight next to the freight office, and presumably various people, under Jack Walsh's supervision, would unload the ordinary freight items. Now we were ready to deliver the cars to the side spurs.

"Sound the whistle a few times", I was told. I would use my left hand for that because that way, I could lean farther out of the engineer's cab, looking back and forth ostensibly for safety purposes, but really with the hope that other kids, standing in awe outside, would see me at the controls.

"Now open the valve slow". And as I did so, "boff, boff, boff" sounded the steam as it pushed the big piston on one side, and than, on the other side of the engine. If you opened the steam valve just right, you'd release just enough steam so that the engine would creep forward slowly, gripping the tracks without slipping. If you did it too fast, however, the wheels would spin, and the stoker who was in the cab with us, would give first the engineer "that look" for letting us kids on, and then to us, for having lost so much steam going nowhere. We learned fast how to operate that valve.

Down a short distance toward Eastham we would go, hanging out the window looking back for the flagman to give us the signal that the end of the train had passed the switch on the line to the Nickerson Yard. Our friend and mentor would then tell us to "shut her down and pull up the brake." Now the other kid, usually Bruce as I remember, would join in and help pull on that large long brake handle.

Actually two kids were needed for this because the pull was hard and we didn't weigh much in those days. "Clak, clak, clak," the brake handle sounded as it passed each cog, with us pulling frantically on the handle. The tons of steel of the train would then come to a rattling halt, with each car banging into the car ahead, taking up the slack between them.

Then we would stop and watch until the flagman had signaled that he had thrown the switch. When he flagged us again, we were told, "Release the brake, and let's back her up and see if we can keep old Grover happy". This part sounded easy, but the brake release required perfect timing. The handle was at a 45 degree angle so the two of us would grab hold, jump on the count of three, squeeze the handle, and use all our weight to release each cog, moving the brake forward to full release status. That was the hardest part, and the "old fella', knowing we wanted to do it alone, never would help us.

We then begin the process of backing the train, with some trepidation, onto the line going into Grover's domain. "Open up that other valve and back er up" The same "boff, boff, boff" would sound, as we slowly crept backwards into Nickerson's Lumber Yard, where we would brake again, with the two cars hopefully in the position where Grover wanted them to be. The cars would then be uncoupled.

Next we had to move forward onto the rail spur going into Harry Snow's coal yard to pick up the empty and drop off the car full of coal. The Snows spur was connected to the main track on the Eastham side of Main Street. We would go back onto the main track, moving toward Eastham, and once beyond the switch for the Snow's spur, the flagman would throw the switch, signal us, and we would begin backing onto the spur, with the car full of coal at the end of the train.

The train would push the coal car back until it came in contact with the empty car already on the spur. After coupling that car to the full car, the train would move forward back onto the main track, until the empty car was clear of the spur, on the main track. The switch was again thrown so that the train could move straight back toward the freight office.

The train would then go backward in a southern direction until the empty car came in contact with the freight cars waiting at the freight office. The empty coal car was coupled to the nearest freight car and uncoupled from the train. The train then moved forward on the main track until it cleared the Snow's spur. The switch was again thrown, and the train would back the full coal car onto the spur, leaving it in the same position as the empty car had been.

Forward again the train jogged onto the main track. The switch for the spur was thrown, allowing the train to back up to the cars waiting at the freight office to be recoupled to the train. Once all cars were coupled together again and cargo for Orleans taken out of the freight cars, the train would take off toward the freight office in Eastham. Although I would have been happy to travel down to Eastham, the "old fella" would politely ask us to hop off before he took off, commending us, however, for our diligent work.

We soon the process down pat. As we were told what to do, we took turns in handling the different functions. Release the brake. Pull the brake. Back and forth. Forward and back. Jump on the brake. Open the valve slowly. No slippage. Back and forth. Forward and back. Under the tutelage of our mentor, we were learning fast how to become a trainman.

For a number of years, I had a vision of someday becoming an engineer, moving those monster trains up and down the tracks, with all the noise associated with those movements. Alas, it was not to be. Freight trains to Orleans became fewer and fewer in number, soon disappearing. My interest in railroading waned, as I became interested in other pursuits. I ended up being a teacher of foreign languages, somewhat different from railroading, you might say.

CONTROLLING A DUMP FIRE

Back in the Forties, the Orleans Town Dump was located at what is now the entrance to Finley Road. The dump keeper in those years was Leslie R. Chase, who was commonly called "Lightning", a nickname he had acquired not for his speed, but rather the lack thereof. Lightning lived with his brother, Dirty Paws, the derivation of which is not clear, in a small bungalow on Route 28 near the entrance to the dump.

Lightning was a slow, deliberate type fellow, but when he was called Lightning, he was quick to respond by saying, "My name is Leslie R. Chase!" He walked from his house to the dump everyday to oversee the disposal operations. It was an old-fashioned dump, in that you simply backed your vehicle up to what was already there and dumped whatever you had, no matter what it was. There were none of the elaborate rules, which exist today. About once a week, Lightning would start a fire and burn off most of what had been amassed, making room for more disposal.

Back in those years, almost everybody had a cesspool, which had to be pumped on a regular basis. Two local entrepreneurs, Charlie Young and Ralph Mayo, had a monopoly on these operations, commonly referred to as the "Honey Wagon" business. Using large hoses, they pumped out the cesspools of their customers when they had become filled, carrying the contents in large tanks affixed to their trucks, up to the dump where they discharged, by reversing the pumps, their goods into a pit located next to the regular dump area.

One day, Charlie Young was approaching the dump area when he saw Lightning, more or less running up the hill, headed for the main road. Now Lightning was never seen running, and so Charlie stopped and inquired, "What's going on?" With little breath left, Lightning was able to convey that he had started the usual fire to burn off debris, but the fire had gotten away from him and was creeping into the nearby scrub pines. He had to get to a telephone and call the fire department.

The Fire Department in those days was strictly volunteer, and knowing the amount of time it would take for them to assemble and come to the scene, Charlie said, "That will take too long. Get right in here, and we'll take care of that fire ourselves." After Lightning had jumped into the truck, Charlie drove around the edge of the dump, close to where the fire was working its way into the scrub pines. "You just put the truck in low-low and creep along the edge of those trees," Charlie instructed.

Lightning jumped behind the wheel and began following Charlie's directions, while Charlie started up the rear pump, putting it up to full speed, and trained the large hose high up on the tops of the trees. It wasn't long before the fires succumbed to the liquid blasts trained upon them, but the stench resulting from this novel form of fire control, as it blended with the fires, was overwhelming.

More dramatic, large quantities of toilet paper and other "things" were left hanging in festoons from the upper branches of the trees. For days thereafter, poor Lightning, in addition to his other duties, had to explain to patrons of the dump what the odor wafting around the dumping area was and explain how all those white decorations had gotten onto the nearby pine trees.

DEER SLAYERS

Years ago, brothers Chet and Irving Higgins, along with Harry Hunt and Lester Young, went deer hunting up in South Orleans, near Pleasant Bay. They were all rough-cut, hardy Cape Codders who were fishermen, hunters, and trappers, as a supplement to what each did regularly for a living. They were driving deer toward Little Pleasant Bay, thinking that they would catch up with some deer on the shore, resulting in each having some venison for the up-coming winter.

Well, they got a good-sized buck pinned between them and the water. They were about to shoot, when the big deer jumped into the water and began to swim for one of the nearby islands, leaving the bewildered hunters on the shore, looking longingly at their quarry as it seemed to slip away.

Luckily, just a short distance away was Earl Chase's brand new skiff, with its shiny new engine, which he had left up on the shore while Earl waded out hip deep to scratch for quahogs. Of course, Earl had seen what was going on, and so when Chet yelled to him from the shore that they wanted to borrow his boat, he waved the okay sign, although with some trepidation.

Off the valiant hunters went, chugging along, gaining gradually on the deer as he swam frantically for safety. They caught up to him about mid-way across the channel. Suddenly they realized the problem they faced as to what to do with the deer once they came up to him.

Harry Hunt came up with the idea for a bloodless method of getting the deer. "Let's drown him," he said. So Harry, who was strong and hefty, leaned over the side, grabbed the deer by the horns, and held his head under water. After an appropriate amount of time, the deer ceased to struggle and the hunters pulled him into the boat and stuffed him under the middle seat.

Not much time went by, however, when the deer woke up—and actually got up, breaking through the middle seat of Earl's new skiff and knocking the two Higgins boys into the water, high boots, shotguns and all. Lester Young tried to get control by grabbing the big buck by the tail, but all he got for his efforts was a good hoof to the mouth, which sent him into the brink with his two buddies.

This left Harry high in the bow, face to face with the deer. Harry quickly drew his hunting knife, offering a mano-a-mano fight to the death. The big buck made short work of that invitation with a good butt to Harry's chest, knocking him into the chilly waters, bringing the deer's average to a perfect four-for-four.

The boat, still in gear, proceeded sedately along toward the distant island. Imagine the look of despair on Earl Chase's face as he saw his new boat heading out into larger waters, the deer standing as if at the helm, with an expression of satisfaction and freedom.

We don't know what the four intrepid hunters said to Earl when they finally reached shore, but we sure can guess that Earl had some choice words for them to describe his displeasure.

Some old-timers say that on the anniversary of that fateful day around midnight you can see what seems to be the silhouette of a shadowy boat moving along through the Narrows, with a deer standing tall in the rear, as if passing in victorious review.

KNOWING WHAT'S COMING

In many ways, I have been lucky in life. No great disasters have befallen me. I have found that I lived in a time experienced by few who grew up in other eras. I had personal resources available that I could tap for important information. For example, I had three older sisters who would come home from school and tell me all about how school functioned.

When I entered the first grade (there was no kindergarten in those years), I knew all there was to know about how to go to school. Be at the bus stop five minutes before the bus was to arrive. Get on the bus, put your lunch bucket on the floor next to the driver (Rudolph Hopkins early on), sit in any vacant seat (there supposedly was no saving of seats), go single file into the school located on School Street, raise your hand if you wanted to answer or go to the bathroom, and so on.

Another source of information for me was Stephen Hopkins. Although he does not know it, and I never admitted it to him, he had a hand in shaping my life and making me the great success I was throughout the years. You see, he was, still is, two years older than I. Because there were so few kids in town in those years, one could stretch up or down a couple of years in order to have playmates and buddies.

Being taller and more athletic than my peers, I was able to stretch up several years and got to play and socialize with bigger boys such as Steve, Leslie Quinn, Barry Wilcox, Jimmy Buckley, John Hathorne, and others. Steve lived close by just through the woods on Hopkins Lane, and we could reach each other's homes in about ten minutes by running through the sapling pitch pines between our two houses. Steve and I spent a lot of time together enjoying what Cape Cod in those years offered to your men trying to learn the ways of life.

One of the great things that came our way was the creation of a Sea Scout Troop in Orleans. It was just after WW II, so we were able to get some navy-like uniforms from some of the veterans who were then returning home. Most of us had some semblance of proper wear, in that one would have a Navy blouse, another a pair of thirteen-button pants, while another might have a coveted pea jacket. We all had a white seaman's Navy hat.

Among the many things that we learned in the Sea Scouts was close-order drills, or how to march in a military fashion. We all were required to march in formation, and each of us had the opportunity to lead the formations, barking orders which the others had to obey; "Forward hutch"! "To the right flank hutch!" "Platoon halt!" "Order arms!" And so forth.

Mon Cochrane and Stan Boynton, our regular leaders in those years, aided by Bernard "Junie" Collins and Elmer "Dah" Darling, taught us the rules of the road for boating, how to plot a course, how to find our way by locating the North Star, and general survival skills. But the thing that was to serve me the best later was knowing close-order drill and the manual of arms.

As we got older, Steve went off to college, while I stayed behind to finish my last two years of high school. But when Steve came home on vacation or for the summer, he would tell me all about college life and what it was like. Just as it was with the first grade, when it was time for me to go off to Tufts in 1952, I had the advantage of prior knowledge.

As I progressed through college, Steve finished and began his draft stint in the Army in 1954. When I had graduated from college and was ready for the draft myself, Steve had mustered out and came home to the Cape in 1956. Among other leg-up information I received from Steve was to remain unobtrusive and never to volunteer unless you were certain that what you would be doing would favorable to you. But if a sergeant asked if anyone had experience in a particular area, and you knew that it would be something beneficial to you, it was OK to step forward and even exaggerate your experience.

They sent me to Fort Riley, Kansas, for eight weeks of basic training. I soon discovered that the cadre was in need of trainees with some military leadership experience to assist in the basic training. Those selected would be given temporary sergeant stripes and would not have to pull KP, walk guard duty or fill any other similar detail. I recognized immediately that this was for me.

"Does anyone here have any previous military experience?" asked the sergeant. Up went my hand in a flash. "What is your experience?" I didn't want to be laughed back to the barracks by saying I had received training in the Sea Scouts, and so I gave it an old Cape Cod stretch. "I had four years of R.O.T.C. in college," I said, sensing my mother's presence behind me. "But I turned down the commission."

That afternoon, and for the rest of my basic training, I wore temporary master sergeant stripes, and marched the 27 men in my platoon back and forth from one exercise to another, shouting out: "Hup, two, three four!"

SAIL BOAT RACES IN THE FORTIES

Situated at the head of the Orleans Town Cove is a stylish building which houses the Orleans Yacht Club. There are certain people in Orleans these days who pine to become members of what they perceive to be a prestigious club, and the waiting list for membership is long. But back in my days as a young boy, the Yacht Club was a bare bones operation with sail boats, to be sure (Town Class), but nothing in the way of facilities as exist today. Yet the races in those days were rough and hard fought, I suspect not at all like the genteel competition now in vogue.

In addition to the few sail boats which got together for regular races on the Town Cover in those earlier years, they had a power boat that they used to carry judges. That boat moseyed around the middle of the Cove, mostly to help in case anyone swamped. These judges did not seem to like to become involved in disputes between boats because a decision was bound to be viewed with disfavor by one or more parties.

I lived with my family on Gibson Road, on a bluff overlooking the Cove, and we could see the sailboat races from our living room. We all knew all the boats and their owners, all mostly local people: Doctor Radin (the Town's dentist), Alton and Carlton Smith (the famous "Smith Boys" who ran the hardware store), a Mr. Winslow, George Ellis, a Mr. Jones, and Jared Blodgett, to name a few.

As these men began to get along in years, they noticed that there were no young people to take their places, and so they decided to invite some of the kids to join them as members of their crews. The Town Class boats were really built for two people, but three could fit, one on the tiller, one on the main sheet, and a kid on the jib. Every boat managed to take on a jib kid. But I was lucky in that George Ellis, a wily old veteran of many a race, lived next door to me, and he invited me to join his crew as the jib kid.

Step by step, George Ellis taught me not only how to sail, but, even more important, how to race. He let me sail the boat from the mooring to the head of the Cove where the races always began. And eventually, he let me plan the maneuvers before the final starting gun so that we were on the starboard tack, which had right of way privileges over boats on the opposite tack, and crossing the finish line first, with billowing sail. He would ask me what route I would take as we reached for the first buoy, then he'd offer his opinion as to where we ought to go, an opinion which I soon learned to respect as it always seemed to put us into a good position to win.

As time went on, however, I noticed that we would lose out unnecessarily on the last leg of the race. And each time, as we began to lag behind, Hamish Gravem, a jib kid on another boat with Rita Winship and her brother, would give me a nod and a smug "gotcha" look, as they overtook and passed us. This really irritated me. I asked Doc Radin about this, and he told me that George Ellis had won plenty of trophies over the years, and that his primary goal at present was to make sure the Jarrett Blodgett didn't win.

I soon learned from George that he did not like Blodgett, considering him to be a showoff and "bigmouth", personal traits most Cape Codders abhorred. After hearing this, I began to notice that half way around the course in a race, George would have his eye out for Blodgett and try to pull up beside him in order to steal his wind and cause him to fall back. Of course, that made us fall out of the pack as well, but that didn't matter to George since he considered it a victory if he made Bldogett come in last, the worst of all fates.

One Sunday, George pulled a major coup. It was a brisk wind from the south, and on the last leg, we had to tack back and forth, beating our way against the wind toward the finish at the head of the Cove. Suddenly, and for apparent reason, George tacked and headed easterly away from Blodgett's boat, going to the opposite side of the Cove. I noticed that all during this tack, George kept looking back to see where Blodgett was heading. Just as Blodgett tacked on the west side of the Cove, we tacked as well over on our easterly side. We were then on a collision course with "Mr. Bigmouth", though still quite distant from each other.

George, almost drooling in anticipation, had planned to put us right-of-way tack (starboard) with Blodgett on the opposite tack. The plan seemed to be for us to keep our heading until we got close, and then demand our right-of-way, which would mean that Blodgett would have to fall off and go behind us or tack down below us. As this was unfolding, I thought that George wanted Blodgett to tack because, in that way we would be able to "lay on top of him" and run him onto the shore if we had to. But I was wrong. George, always the wily one, had another plan entirely.

In a strong breeze, all three crew members would be way up on the upper side of the boat, using our weight to counterbalance the boat against the wind. But, in this instance, as the moment of truth approached, George told me to climb down to the leeward, or downside, of the boat, and told me, "When I tell you, Sammy, I want you to bang the side of the boat just as hard as you can with your fist." Blodgett wasn't going to give way except in a last desperate moment, so George just kept bearing down upon him. Closer and closer we came until there were only a few feet between us.

"Right of way", George bellowed, and Blodgett finally decided to give it up and tack away about five feet from us. "Bang the boat," George yelled, and I immediately pounded the side of the boat hard, as instructed. We were not that near the judge's boat, and the officials could not see me due to the angle of the boat, as George had planned, and so nobody, other than Blodgett, saw me whack the side of the boat.

"Foul", yelled George, as he stood up, waving his arms at the judge's boat. Reluctantly, the judge's directed their boat over toward us, and after hearing the story from George, and being mindful of the noise they had heard, they disqualified Mr. Blodgett for what appeared to have been contact of his boat with ours, causing George to smile broadly with satisfaction.

A few years later, George sold his boat to the Down's family who lived a short distance up the Cove. I guess Connie Downs, an attractive brunette a few years older than I, had expressed an interest in sailing, which she perceived as a genteel sport, and so her father bought the boat for her, and she became the first woman and youngest captain in the club at the time. Because I had been with the boat for several years, Mr. Downs asked me if I would stay as a crew member for the up-coming season. Connie had a girl friend, Barbara Patten, a nice looking blond, who became the mate, while I, with far more experience, remained the jib kid.

Our first race of the season found us in a nice breeze straight down the Cove, headed for Hopkins Island. So, the first leg of the race was "running free" with the wind coming behind us and pushing, with the sail and jib at right angles to the boat. The first buoy was right opposite "Cubby" Collins', and we were supposed to go around the left side of the buoy, pull the sail tight, and head for the other side of the Cove, where they had placed the second buoy.

117

The problem was that as we neared the first buoy, our sail was on the starboard (right) side so, at some point, we would have to jibe (swing the sail from way on one side way to the other side), a tricky maneuver since it is possible that the wind will catch the sail as it comes around and push the nose of the boat into the water, resulting in a swamping, the worse thing that can occur in a sailing race.

Although only the jib kid, I audaciously advised Connie that, although we would lose a little speed, it would be far better to attempt the jibe movement before reaching the buoy because not only would it be difficult to do, but even more difficult while turning around a buoy with a bunch of other boats closing in on the same buoy along with our boat.

Here was Connie, dolled out in her yachting cap, v-necked sweater to match, sunglasses, fancy boat shoes, and shiny new stop watch, in all her authority as captain of the ship, and there was I, barefoot, torn-off short pants, no shirt, hardly the image of anything but a jib kid, and she was not about to listen to me, and so on we went toward the buoy. Knowing that we were in for a bad experience, I hinted to Barbara, the mate, that when he sail came around, she should catch it amidships and let it go out gradually as we made the turn around the buoy, and then gather it is to the "close-haul", as we began the run for the second buoy.

Barbara heard the first part and caught the sail amidships, but then froze, holding the sail there as we made the turn, the wind knocked us right down, and in no time, we were swamped. As the boat went over, I kept climbing for the high side, staying high and dry. As I looked toward the other boats moving by, I saw Hamish Gravem go by, with that same smug smile and "the look". Unfortunately, both girls were on the down side of the boat and were dumped unceremoniously into the water. It was a sad sight to see, the two of them drenched to the skin with their starched finery clinging to them and their carefully coiffed hair wet and in disarray.

After we finally got ourselves righted and the boat was towed back to the head of the Cove, I decided that I had had enough of race sailing. Instead, I took up tennis as a supplement to my baseball endeavors.

MEETING THE TENDER TENDER

After my discharge from the Army in 1959, I obtained a job for the summer at the Goose Hummock Shop, a well-known sporting goods store overlooking the Town Cove in Orleans. Bobby Bremner, who had played second base on the Town team, worked there at the same time. Freddie MacFarlane, a pleasant, good-humored guy, managed the Shop.

When things were quiet in the store, Bob and I would look out the back window of the Shop and watch the water skiers go whizzing by. (I noted recently that they are doing the same thing today.) Both Bobby and I became interested in learning the sport, thinking that surely we could do as well as those guys. And so we engaged Roger Gill, whose father, Mert, had a fast speed boat, with all the necessary paraphernalia for water skiing, to assist us in our training.

There was a birds-eye view of the Cove from the back of the Shop, and when one of us was out on the water, learning how to get up on the skis, the other had an eye out the back window to check on how he was doing. Slowly, and I do mean s-l-o-w-l-y, each of us was able to master getting up from a dead stop in the water, then the next challenge of popping off a float to a standing position, to move across the water. Soon, we were able to go back and forth over the wake of the boat, and finally, dropping one ski to perform slalom movements.

Being avid competitors, Bob and I would challenge each other with new tricks. After a while, however, we ran out of new things to do, and so I decided to come up with a novel maneuver, raising the ante you might say.

At the time, Goose Hummock had a fleet of rowboats at anchor right behind the Shop. An old wooden tender, in very fragile condition, was used to tow the rowboats to shore for customers to use. It was moored out in the water, some fifty yards away from shore, and would be pulled in on a lanyard rope so we could then row out to obtain a rowboat when the need arose.

Looking at the tender floating there, I came up with the idea of jumping over the small boat while skiing. After all, I had found that it was easy to jump into the air, while snow skiing, and thought it would be equally easy to jump high in the skis while on the water so as to clear the tender.

I told Roger what I was planning to do, and so roaring down from the head of the Cove, I swung out to the left of the wake, heading straight for the tender, as it bounced gently up and down on its tether. I could see that I had an audience looking out the back window of the Shop. They had learned about what I intended to do. Bending my knees in preparation, I timed the jump with perfect precision (at least for a snow jump).

Alas, I quickly learned that what you can do in snow-skiing, does not apply to water skiing. When I jumped, the skis hardly got off the water and the tips hit solidly against the side of the tender. I found myself in mid-air heading for the opposite interior-side of the boat. As I came down, I had the good sense of lowering my right shoulder just as it was about to smash into the inside of the tender.

The force of this crash, however, ripped the whole side off the boat as I finished my spill, with my skis pin-wheeling off my feet and over my head. Dazed, I came up in the water, spitting out water, but except for a bruised shoulder, pretty much in one piece. The tender, however, was demolished.

When I swam ashore, I was greeted by a bunch of guys on the shore, hooting with laughter. Freddie MacFarlane, who had been in the audience for this performance, had to acknowledge that it was a pretty good show. He also admitted that he had been meaning to replace the little tender for some time.

CHAPTER VI. COLLEGE LIFE

When I journeyed out to Amherst in September 1950 to enter my freshman year at University of Massachusetts in Amherst, I was not really prepared to handle the demands of a college education. It was not so much that I did not acquire in high school the fundamental skills and knowledge necessary as a foundation for college. Rather, I had not, during my years in the Orleans school system, developed work-study habits which, in college, you must have to respond effectively to the challenges of college learning.

My failure to develop good study habits resulted from two factors: first, I was able to obtain what might be called "gentleman's grades" in high school with little effort; and two, my primary focus had been upon sports, dating and other extracurricular activities. When I suddenly was thrust into college life, my attention, as before, became directed toward these same areas, and I fully expected that the basic approach I had used in the past in my courses would get me through.

And indeed, this was true to a certain extent. Again, with poor study habits, I was able to get by in the courses which were required in the first two years at UMass, but unfortunately, unlike in high school, where my marks were A's and B's, my marks at UMass in my freshman and sophomore years were fair to poor. Part of this, to be sure, had to do with the fact that I had little interest in some of the courses which all student were required to take during the first two years, such as math, science and foreign language. Academically, I was performing in an uninspired and mediocre way.

Mt first two years were spent in dormitories with a roommate whose entire goal in life was athletics. Dick Norman ultimately was on the varsity basketball and baseball teams, as well as a member of the UMass tennis team. He planned to major in physical education, and indeed, Dick later in life became the Athletic Director of a major high school. Dick was a great guy, but the fact was that in my two years as his roommate, there was little or no discussion between us about issues in the fields I was interested in, namely history and the social sciences.

Fortunately, this turned around in my third year at college when I began living at the fraternity house of QTV, which I had joined the prior year. QTV was a Latin fraternity, the only one on campus, which was established many years earlier when UMass was the Massachusetts Agricultural College, known as Mass Aggie. There were approximately seven other fraternities at UMass in the early fifties, all Greek fraternities with national affiliations, and QTV stood out as a one-of-a-kind organization.

QTV was made up of a diverse group of guys from various parts of Massachusetts and other states. They represented a wide range of personality types and ethnic origins, with such names as Bresnahan, Butler, Dean, Dennis, Johnson, Kenney, Letourneau, Maxie, Masseschi, Melley, Midten, Ott, Rosa, Scarfoni and Walker. We came together in September 1952 knowing little about each other, but by the time I graduated in June 1954, we had become a close, cohesive group, truly together as fraternal brothers.

Our house was a three-story, old Victorian structure, located off campus on the main road into the college. There were two large living rooms on the first floor in the front, with a kitchen and dinning room in the back. The second floor consisted of individual rooms assigned to specific members for studying and socializing activities. The third floor was a large, open room, with beds, much like a barracks, where everybody slept. I was assigned one of the front rooms on the second floor, along with Victor Johnson, a senior, and Mel Walker, a junior.

My social and extra curricular activities increased significantly after joining QTV, what with beer parties, dances we sponsored in-house, and the usual competitions between fraternities, particularly in athletics. The fraternity leagues were highly competitive, and the games we had in touch-football, basketball and softball were hotly contested. I became Athletic Director for our fraternity, and during my two-year tenure, we finished first in touch-football and second or third in the basketball and softball leagues. We also did well in the Winter Carnival ice sculptures and the chorale competitions.

QTV did, however, have a reputation on campus as a somewhat unruly irreverent bunch. Nothing really serious in nature; rather more on the mischievous side. Our antics did, at times, result in frowns and admonitions from the school administration. For example, each year the ROTC sponsored a large parade down the main street in Amherst and onto the campus. This was a very serious event, with all members of the ROTC expected to be in sparkling uniforms and ready to march precisely and solemnly.

The parade passed right in front of our fraternity house, and one of our members, Frosty Deans, who as student-colonel took his ROTC responsibilities very seriously, was slated to lead a regiment in the parade. A group of us decided that we should act as a reviewing stand for the parade, replete with costumes, seats, and an American flag. As the ROTC members began passing by us, the head of each group was faced with the question of whether to acknowledge and salute the flag and the motley group sitting there, or to simply ignore us and proceed along. I can't remember what colonel Dean did when his regiment passed, but he was obviously horrified by what he encountered.

The Dean of Students must have received an earful from the Army and Air Force officers who ran the ROTC program. A week after the event, our fraternity officers were summonsed by the Dean for disciplinary action against QTV, and all members of the fraternity, including those who marched in the parade, were required to attend four lecture sessions, conducted by the regular officers of the ROTC program, as to the proper respect for the flag, how it was to be displayed, handled, etc. One can only assume that this was what the ROTC leaders had recommended to the Dean. Looking back at those sessions, I wonder how the ROTC officers were able to fill four hours of time describing how to display the flag.

But the really significant change in my college life as a result of my staying at the fraternity was not the heightened social life. There were approximately 40 members of the fraternity housed in our frat house, and among these members were some who were, like me, majoring in history and social studies.

Although they enjoyed a good time, they also approached their studies in a far more serious way. This was especially true of my roommates, Vic and Mel. Each night during the school week, they would sit down at their desks at 8:00 and study their lessons diligently until 11:00. If there was an important exam the next day, some often stayed up until 2:00 A.M. in preparing for it.

In my third year, I was now able to take elective courses in my major and did not, therefore, have to face those uninteresting courses mandated by the school as part of the curriculum for the first two years. With my two roommates and others in the fraternity sharing my major, I soon became involved with them in lengthy debates about historical trends and political issues, something which was lacking before. More important, I became impressed with the disciplines they showed in their study habits.

The real clincher in my academic rehabilitation occurred in December of my junior year. I woke up one morning with acute pains in my abdomen. I at first attributed this to something I ate the night before. Finally, however, I went to the college infirmary, and after a simple blood test, I was rushed to the Cooley Dickenson Hospital in Northhampton where I was operated on for removal of a very inflamed appendix.

As I was recuperating from the operation over the next five days, mostly in bed, I began to think about how college offered me a great opportunity to learn, and the more I learned, the better off I would be in later life, something I had not really focussed on before this. This new attitude, coupled with the examples of my history-oriented frat brothers, resulted in me buckling down over the next year and a half, spending my evening studying hard, researching and carefully writing essays, reports and term papers.

Moreover, working with the elective courses I enjoyed, I found the entire process exciting and intellectually stimulating. As I became more dedicated to study, my marks increased correspondingly.

I did not know what I wanted to do after college. One minute I thought I might like to become a history teacher. Other times, I wondered about joining the State Department or other similar work. I did not give a thought to the possibility of becoming a lawyer, but later, after two years in the Army, I did end up going to law school, and the positive studying habits I finally was able to develop at UMass carried over to help me later through the challenges and travails of law school studies.

QTV did have a reputation in those years as a wild and woolly fraternity, but behind that façade were serious students who worked hard and were conscientious about their studies. Indeed, many of them went on to attain advanced degrees in different fields of endeavor. Fortunately, those positive attitudes toward schooling eventually rubbed off on me, and for that, and for the laughs, good times, and camaraderie we had together as fraternity brothers, I shall be forever grateful.

CHAPTER VII. LIFE IN THE MILITARY

I was in the seventh grade when World War II ended in 1945. The United States was not involved in any armed conflict when I was a senior at Orleans High School in 1950. The Soviet Union, under Joseph Stalin, was, however, aggressively pursuing expansionist goals in various areas of the world, thus creating the so-called Cold War. Faced with international tensions, our government had retained the selective service system, better known as the draft, so as to be prepared militarily for possible open conflict.

Young men in high school, such as myself, recognized that the draft lurked in the background, but did not dwell on it especially since, at that point in time, our country was not engaged in warfare. All that quickly changed when armed divisions from North Korea, well equipped and encouraged by the Soviet Union and China, invaded South Korea on June 24 1950, one week after I had graduated from high school.

Faced with the prospect of North Korean troops wiping out all of the United States troops then stationed in South Korea and taking over this strategic peninsula, President Harry Truman realized that a large number of American ground soldiers had to be dispatched quickly to Korea to prevent communist forces from seizing territory through this naked act of aggression. Since this necessarily required the induction of many new recruits to beef up our military, the draft suddenly loomed large in the lives of young men who were then coming out of high school.

A person enrolled in and actively attending college, however, was granted a deferment from the draft. Since I was accepted at UMass-Amherst to begin classes in September 1950, I received a deferment which carried forward for the four years I attended the University. High school friends and classmates, who did not go onto college, either enlisted in other branches of the military or were drafted into the Army, and some of those in the latter group did eventually engage in harrowing combat in Korea.

When I graduated from UMass in June 1954, there were signs that the war in Korea (always carefully labeled as a "police action through the United Nations" by the administration) might be winding down. I recognized that my deferment would end and I would soon become subject to the draft, basic training and possible assignment to Korea. I did not object to the idea of the draft. Indeed, as I went through college, I had concluded that our country, for its own well-being, even in peacetime, should have a system of universal service, by which high school graduates would provide service, either through the military or through other agencies, to the nation for a period of one year.

Wanting to have some control over my destiny, I volunteered to be inducted in September, thus affording me the summer months on Cape Cod where I was working as the Red Cross Water Safety Director for the lower Cape area. Sometime in early October 1954, pursuant to orders from the Draft Board, I appeared, along with other Cape Cod youths, in Hyannis, for a bus ride to the Boston Army Base for induction. Once there, we met with other groups delivered to the Base from other areas of Massachusetts. As it turned out, in what was now a group of approximately 100 men, a large percentage were college graduates, like myself, whose deferments had also lapsed.

We all underwent physical examinations and aptitude and IQ testing. They also had psychiatric testing which, I discovered, consisted of a bored professional asking a few questions such as "Do you like girls?" This was all preliminary to our military training, which would consist of eight weeks basic training (boot camp), and eight weeks of advanced training. Most of us had heard stories about what military training was like, but we really were not prepared for the reality of what was to come.

Mind you, as college graduates, for four years, we had been trained through our education to identify and resolve issues, question the positions of others, and seek solution on these matters in a logical way. The military does not function in this way, and indeed, because of the Army's basic mission, cannot function in a manner designed to raise questions or promote independent thinking.

127

Detailed rules and regulations exist and are rigidly enforced. There is a chain of command, and you are expected to accept orders and discipline from your superior regardless of how illogical they may seem. Orders, which are issued above, and passed along below, are to be obeyed, without question or analysis. Not easy for somebody fresh out of college.

After the initial processing stage at the Boston Army Base, we were all shipped down to Fort Dix in New Jersey. Everybody in our group was found to be sufficiently sound, physically and mentally, to become soldiers. After several days at Fort Dix, during which time we received inoculations and our Army gear, we were flown down in two-engine Curtis Commando planes to Camp Chafee, Arkansas, for eight weeks of basic training which would involve long marches with full packs, calisthenics, camping in the field, obstacle courses, firing various weapons, and simulated warfare.

I was not concerned about the physical demands of the Army training. In fact, being in reasonably good shape, this was one aspect of the military I did welcome because I saw it as an opportunity to get in better shape. Although I knew it would be arduous, I did look forward to the challenges of the long marches, the gunnery, obstacle course, and all. Indeed, with eight weeks of training, I trimmed down and was, without doubt, in the best physical conditions I had ever been, about 165 pounds, lean and mean.

But there were aspects of training wholly disagreeable. This involved the manner in which the cadre directed and supervised our activities. Ever present were orders, inspection, discipline and punishments for minor infractions. This was to be expected. It was part of instilling military discipline. But the cadre, composed of seasoned NCO's, were excessively mean, arrogant and petty. Their antagonism, moreover, seemed to be directed more to the college graduates in our ranks. "So you think you're smart, Mr. college grad", and similar gibes, were routine.

Every week, we had barracks inspection. Beds had to be tightly made so a quarter could bounce off the blanket. All items in our footlocker had to be arranged in perfect regularity. But most important, we soon learned that the boards in our barracks floor had to be washed with water and Clorox to the point of being bleached white in color.

The Company Commander, a captain who we never saw otherwise, would appear at the door of our floor, followed by a retinue of cadre NCO's, who would yell "tenshun" as they entered. We all leaped to stand at ridged attention by our cots as the entourage moved imperiously down one side of the barracks and up the other, checking our uniforms and appearances, examining footlockers, and checking the bounce of the blankets.

Reprimands or punishments were handed out for individual infractions, but invariably, after the inspection party left, the Master Sergeant would return to inform us that the floor was not clean enough. We would then spend the next hour, with Clorox and water, trying to make the boards even whiter. The smell of Clorox always permeated the air of our barracks, and even now, when I smell it, I think of those inspections.

The manner in which the cadre dealt with us may very well have been purposely calculated to unite into a close and unified force what otherwise was a very diverse group of individuals. We had in our platoon young men from very different backgrounds. The guy in the bunk next to me was a small, slim Italian from Brooklyn, who I suspect had not graduated from high school.

When I received a package from home, it contained tollhouse cookies, which I offered to him. When he received a package, it always contained a highly aromatic salami, portions of which he would always offer me. We also had the Swedish sons of farm families in Iowa, big, strapping men with blond hair and Swedish accents. Although the recruits in our platoon were diverse in many ways, faced as we were by a common foe, namely the arrogant cadre, we became melded together as close and loyal.

The majority of us made it through basic training and we moved along to advanced training. There were several members in our group, however, who we recognized were having great difficulty dealing with the physical rigors and discipline of training, and as the weeks passed, they quietly disappeared from our ranks. It was later reported, for example, that one person I remember as a bright, intense graduate of Harvard Law School, who surely would have had a bright future in civilian life, had suffered a complete nervous breakdown and was confined to the mental ward at the local infirmary. We never knew how he made out.

Advanced training was basically in four areas: advanced infantry; artillery; quartermaster work; and clerk typist school. Anybody assigned to the first two categories could very well find themselves eventually replacing soldiers in the front lines of Korea where there was still fighting. We all waiting anxiously to learn our new training assignment. As it turned out, I was assigned to clerk typist school.

The eight weeks attending this school, also located at Camp Chafee, passed rapidly and uneventfully. My biggest achievement at the school was to learn to type and increase my typing speed to 80 words a minute. As our advanced training reached its conclusion, we now began to focus upon where our final assignment would be. Soldiers with a clerk typist MOS, at that time, could be assigned to Korea, to work in field offices. There was also a chance of being assigned to an Army base in Europe where large numbers of American troops were still stationed.

When I had graduated from college, knowing I would be inducted into the Army, I said to myself that if I could be assigned to a base in Germany, the military experience would be more than worthwhile because it would afford me an opportunity to see Europe firsthand. Many of my history courses in college involved studies of modern European history, events leading to the rise of fascism and communism, and this enhanced my desire to see Europe. As it turned out, my wishes were granted: I was assigned to the Troop Information and Education Section (TI&E) at Seventh Army Headquarters, located near Stuttgart, Germany.

Our trip to Germany involved a two-week voyage on a troop ship across the North Atlantic in stormy March of 1955. We did not have winter cloths and if we stayed on the deck, we suffered the pangs of the cold temperatures. If we stayed below in the rough seas, however, many soon became seasick. I elected to stay on deck as much as possible and was able to avoid seasickness, but some of my friends stayed below and they were sick the entire trip, totally unable to eat. The trip for them was harrowing. Some lost 25 pounds and when they left the ship in Bremerhaven, they were gaunt, thin and weak.

From Bremerhaven, I traveled south on a slow train, finally arriving in Stuttgart for my new assignment. I wondered what I would be doing as a clerk typist: probably filling out routine forms and shuffling papers. As it turned out, I ended up with a great assignment as an editor and writer for the Seventh Army Sentinel, which was a weekly newspaper for the Seventh Army. Two other enlisted men also worked on the newspaper: Dick Hoyt, a graduate of Tufts College who had gone through basic training with me, and David Lighthill, a Harvard Law School graduate, who had been working on the paper for a year and was editor-in-chief when I arrived.

We worked well together, completely on our own, in a separate office on the base, writing and collecting stories and photographs, setting up pages and headlines, and overseeing the printing of each issue of the newspaper which was performed at a local German printing shop off base. Part of my job was covering sports events within Seventh Army, and this required me to travel to other bases in Germany for boxing tournaments or important basketball games. For these trips, I used sedans or jeeps, which I was able to requisition from the motor pool. I also used my leave time to take trips to Rome, Copenhagen, Paris, Southern France, Barcelona, Vienna and London, and wrote feature articles about some of the places I visited.

Working on the newspaper was the ideal assignment for somebody, like myself, who wanted to see Europe. Moreover, the three of us, working alone in putting out the newspaper, recognized that our positions were more civilian in nature, rather than military. Every month or so, we did have inspections and guard duty to remind us that we were still soldiers, but this was a far cry from what basic training was like.

We also had unannounced "scrambles" whereby soldiers in all units on the base loaded equipment onto trucks and moved into the nearby woods where we set up tents and equipment to function, supposedly, as we would at the base. This was meant to simulate what would happen, and what we would do, if the "balloon went up", meaning if the Soviets attacked into Western Germany. (This term may have had to do with raising observation balloons at the front in World War I when the enemy launched an attack.)

When Soviet forces invaded Czechoslovakia in 1957 and used its tanks to put down in a brutal way a display of independence there, the possibility of United States forces in Germany being in armed conflict with the Soviets became all too real. As it turned out, although the United States ordered partial mobilization and we were put on high alert, the Soviets confined their assaults to Czechoslovakia and the President chose not to intervene.

I worked on the newspaper from April 1955 until early September 1956 when I was scheduled to return to the United States for discharge in early October, the end of my two years of service. Although the trip back was again on a troop ship, the weather was much better and the trip across the Atlantic was so uneventful that I hardly remember what happened.

As I went through the process of being mustered out of the Army, back at Fort Dix where it all began, I realized how truly fortunate I had been to have had the opportunity to travel around Europe, as I had done, and to have been able to work on a newspaper, writing and editing.

After my discharge from the Army, I did consider a career in journalism and even seriously entertained an offer from the New Bedford Standard Times to join its Sports Department. Ultimately, however, after a stint working for John Hancock Insurance Company in the Public Relations Department, I chose to go to law school, and eventually became a trial attorney, which I discuss in the next chapter.

My brief stint as journalist in the Army, however, was a rewarding and useful experience, one to which, in my retirement, I find myself now being inexorably drawn.

CHAPTER VIII. A TRIAL PRACTICE

Growing up on Cape Cod, it never crossed my mind that some day, I would become a lawyer, let alone a trial attorney. My focus in those years was upon fun and games with my buddies, sports such as baseball and basketball, and later in high school, dates with girls. I did get decent marks in school, with minimum effort, but going on for a college education was not a high priority.

I always did reasonably well on standardized tests, and in the fall of my senior year at Orleans High, after having taken a battery of these tests, the guidance teacher took me aside to say that I should be thinking about college. She went on to point out that my aptitude scores reflected that I had the skills and abilities to become an attorney. Well, college was one thing I could visualize, but some day becoming a lawyer was far beyond my comprehension.

Of course, the rest is history. I went on to obtain a Bachelor of Arts Degree from the University of Massachusetts (Amherst) in 1954, and after two years in the Army, I began attending Law School at Boston College nights, while working days as an administrative assistant in the United States Attorney's office, married and with a young son, Chris who later became a trial attorney. When I began law school, I quickly realized that the law, and all it involved, fit in perfectly with my aptitudes, interests and abilities. The guidance teacher, some 10 years before, was entirely correct.

After graduating from law school in 1961, I worked for a year as law clerk to Judge Andrew Caffrey in the Federal District Court in Boston. When I first began the practice of law in 1962, as an associate at the Boston law firm, Sherburne, Powers and Needham, my goal was to specialize in trial work.

As a law clerk in the Federal District Court, I sat in on major trials and had a chance to study the trial techniques used by leading trial attorneys in Boston as they handled the trials of cases. For me, the courtroom was where the action was. This was where the edge of the law was cut. This was where you could develop and test your skills against your opposition within a competitive framework.

Fortunately, Timothy Donohue, the senior trial attorney in the firm when I first joined it, represented a number of insurance companies, and this generated a constant stream of trials of cases, big and small, in various courts in Massachusetts. In my early years, for example, it was not uncommon for me to handle two, sometimes three, trials a week.

The pace was frenetic, but I loved the work. Matching wits with opponents. Being required to assess a witness quickly and know how to handle them, whether on direct examination or cross. Dealing with judges, both good and bad. Thinking on your feet. These experiences offered great opportunities to develop trial skills.

I enjoyed sifting through evidence, developing a foundation of facts, and determining how the law applied to those facts. I liked meeting with clients and witnesses, assessing their strengths and weaknesses, while trying to bolster their confidence in preparation for trial.

All of this, of course, was done in a competitive framework, which required you to grapple with opposing counsel, assessing his strengths and weaknesses. Having enjoyed the competition of sports for many years, the challenge of winning in the courtroom, within the applicable rules, was a major motivating factor.

As time went on, however, Tim Donohue left the firm and I found myself, at a relatively young age, the firm's senior trial attorney. Younger attorneys then in our office were assigned the smaller cases, and I began handling larger, more complicated cases. I had fewer trials, but when they came along, they often were two or three weeks in duration.

By the time I retired from Sherburne Powers and Needham in April 1998, I had tried more than 300 cases. When I first joined the firm in 1962, we had a total of 14 attorneys, three of whom were trial attorneys. By the time of my retirement, the firm had a total of 80 attorneys, of which 35 were in litigation. The trial department represented the fastest growing portion of the firm.

Now into my retirement years, and looking back on my career, I have written a series of stories which describe the types of trials I handled, beginning with one in which I was involved in the early years at the District Court level (non jury). I then present a story of my first jury trial, followed by stories describing other jury trials I handled later. I also describe my last trial before retiring.

The cases I describe are all civil actions. I handled only a few criminal cases during my career. In choosing cases for these stories, I have attempted to present (1) a full variety of the types of cases I worked on; and (2) cases which were unusual, I hope with more human-interest value for the average reader.

Toward the end of this series, there is an article entitled "Courtroom Tactics" which describes a few of the techniques attorneys have used during the trial of a case. And at the conclusion of the series, I have an article entitled "Looking Back", which sets forth my observations on how trial practice has changed in recent years and my concerns about those changes.

Be forewarned that these stories will not read like a Perry Mason presentation, but they are "for real" and should offer insights as to what the trial and settlement of cases is all about. I do hope you find the stories to be interesting and informative.

Stephen A. Hopkins

THE BUS THAT MOVED SIDEWAYS

The law firm in Boston I joined in 1962, Sherburne Powers and Needham, represented a number of insurance companies, and in those years, before "no fault" insurance had been adopted, the firm was involved in defending a large volume of small personal injury cases arising out of auto accidents.

Tim Donohue, an experienced veteran trial attorney, was responsible for handling these cases, and he immediately enlisted me to assist him on the smaller cases. As a consequence, during those years, I was trying two or three cases a week in courts in Boston and surrounding areas. Trials of these cases usually lasted three to four hours, and I often received the file on a case the day before the trial was to take place.

These cases typically involved a plaintiff who claimed to have been injured in a "fender bender" type auto accident. The injuries alleged were often of the whiplash variety, almost always involving two weeks total disability, three weeks partial disability, and four visits to the doctor.

These cases were filed in the district courts of Massachusetts (or in Boston, the Boston Municipal Court), and if they did go to trial, the judge, rather than a jury, would determine whether the plaintiff had proven that he or she was injured as a result of the negligence of the defendant, and if so, the amount the plaintiff should recover as damages.

Many of the district court judges back then were politically connected locally, and tended to favor the plaintiffs (and the local attorneys who represented them) in their decisions. Attorneys who were defending the claims, therefore, had to present compelling evidence to obtain decisions in their favor.

Other than obtaining written answers from the plaintiff to questions which were submitted to them, plus whatever evidence the insurance company investigators could develop, there was little available to use in preparing for trial. Thus, and attorney essentially had to be able to "wing it" as the testimony and evidence was presented during the trial. These cases, and the volume of them, did afford young attorneys great opportunities, however, to develop trial skills and instincts.

One of our clients in those years was Transit Insurance Company, which insured various bus lines in the area. There was one bus line case I had,

136

pending in the Boston Municipal Court, which I thought would be a clear victory for the defendant. No way could the plaintiff succeed in this one.

The plaintiff, you see, had asserted in his answers to interrogatories, that on a cold day in February, as he was passing along one of Boston's main streets in his station wagon, a transit bus, which had been parked at the curb, suddenly pulled out and clipped the right front of his car. He was claiming the usual whiplash injury, with two weeks total and three weeks partial disability.

The information from our driver was that he had parked the bus, shut off the motor, and was visiting the rest room of the nearby gas station when the incident occurred. Since the gas station manager, who was available as a witness at the trial confirmed this, I figured the plaintiff could not possibly win and offered nothing in settlement.

The plaintiff's attorney, however, recognized from the defendant's interrogatory answers what our position would be at trial and the fact we had a third-party witness, and when he put his client on the stand, this is how his testimony went: "I was driving my station wagon along the street. The street was narrower than usual because of the large mounds of snow on either side of the street. As I came opposite the transit bus, and was passing it, the front of the bus slid sideways to the left off a mound of ice the front tires were on, hitting the right front of my car."

Plaintiff's attorney was then to argue that the driver was negligent in parking his bus on the mound of ice, an amazing somersault. Naturally enough, in my cross-examination, I had a great deal of fun using the earlier statement the plaintiff had given in his interrogatory answers as to how the accident had occurred. Since the trial was before old Judge Riley, who was hard of hearing and had trouble paying attention, I was not certain whether the good Judge recognized how preposterous this new version of the accident was.

Certainly, I attempted to make our point to the Judge in the loudest possible voice, but he sat back in his chair, eyes half closed, with a totally blank expression on his face. Every so often, the Judge did slowly bend forward in his chair and his head disappeared under the bench. Slowly he would return to his sitting position, with the same blank expression.

I could not imagine what he was doing, and after awhile, when I saw him begin his slow bending motion, I edged up beside the bench, as I was asking questions of a witness, to see what he was doing. It turned out that he was chewing tobacco, and when the juice had built up in his mouth, he bent over his wastebasket to spit some out. He seemed more intent upon this activity than the evidence being presented, and I became concerned as to what the result might be.

One week after the trial, however, I received notice from the Court that Judge Riley had found in favor of the defendant. With all his chewing, he did hear and understand the evidence after all.

As the years passed, I began to handle fewer, bigger cases before juries in Superior Court, and trials on these cases often lasted two to three weeks. But I always missed the pace of those early years, and the variety of characters I met, claimants, witnesses, attorneys and judges. I also recognized just how much the experiences of the work had helped me to understand the intricacies of a trial, and how testimony can twist and turn, and yes, even slide sideward.

DEFENDING A CLAIM BY "JACKIE KENNEDY"

Appearing as counsel for a party in a trial before a jury is the biggest challenge a trial lawyer can face. Not only do you have to deal with the judge, carefully assessing his reactions, but you must constantly monitor members of the jury as the trial proceeds, trying to determine how your evidence is affecting them.

You are always "on stage" as the jurors watch silently, often without any expressions, viewing what you are doing and saying. In some ways, you are both actor and director in what is played out during the trial. While you are attempting to present your story in the best light possible, opposing counsel is seeking to obstruct you at every turn through objections and other tactics.

For a young attorney, the first jury trial has great significance. I had been working at Sherburne Powers and Needham for about a year when I was thrust into my first jury trial, with little advanced warning. Tim Donohue, the senior trial attorney in the firm, had two jury trials scheduled in two different courts the same day. One of the cases involved a plaintiff who had sued the Bradford Hotel, claiming that an elevator operator had assaulted her. The trial was scheduled in Courtroom 3A in Suffolk Superior Court at 10:00 a.m. before Judge Francis Swift.

Tim gave me the file for the case two hours before the trial was to start, explaining to me that he had arranged with the Hotel to have Stanley, the elevator operator, at court at 11:00. Trials typically begin at 10:00. I quickly skimmed through the reports and pleadings in the file, and soon discovered that the case had already been tried before a single justice of the Boston Municipal Court where a finding for the plaintiff for $2500 had been entered.

The Hotel had removed the case to Superior Court to assert its right to jury trial. When this occurs, the lower court's finding can be entered by the plaintiff's attorney into evidence in her favor, and I would then have the burden of overcoming that finding. Filled with concern and trepidation, and wondering how I could win this case, I headed over to court for my first jury trial.

Judge Swift, in appearance, was all you would expect a judge to look like. He was tall, dignified, with white hair and spectacles. But alas, he was in his eighties and so badly incapacitated by arthritis that he had to be helped by court officers into his chair on the bench where he sat, glaring down at the attorneys. Clearly, he was anything but in a good mood this particular morning.

Plaintiff's attorney, a veteran who knew his way around, had appeared before Judge Swift on many occasions, while I, a young lawyer, had never been before him. As the trial began, Judge Swift directed his ire toward me, in part I am sure, with the hope of pressuring me to settle the claim so that he could return to the comfort of his chambers.

The jury was promptly empanelled and after openings by counsel, my opponent read into evidence the finding of the lower court, and then called the plaintiff to the stand. Jackie Kennedy was then First Lady in the White House and exceedingly popular in Boston in those years. The plaintiff, who was attractive with a hair style exactly like Jackie's, had a striking resemblance to the First Lady.

In quiet lady-like tones, she described, in response to the gentle questions of her attorney, how she entered the elevator from the lounge on the top floor of the Hotel, with her girl friend, to go to the lobby, and the elevator man, during the ride down, had accosted and abused her to the point that she suffered extreme emotional upset and had to be treated by her physician for bruises on her arms.

The file had indicated that the plaintiff had been a cocktail hostess at a lounge in Revere for five years, and on cross examination, I highlighted this, as well as the fact that she and her friend had been drinking at the Bradford lounge for some three hours before the elevator ride. She could not remember how many drinks she and her friend had had that night.

As her testimony on cross-examination continued, the lady-like qualities she displayed when she was responding to the questions of her counsel disappeared, and she began to come across as rude and belligerent. The friend who was with her at the time, a rather hardened type, did, however, provide testimony, which supported the plaintiff's story.

While this was occurring, and the clock on the wall had moved along to 11:30, I kept looking to the back of the courtroom, wondering if my elevator man had arrived. Since I had never met him, I could not be sure if he was in the courtroom or not. At about 11:45, when the plaintiff's counsel announced that he was resting, I asked the Judge "respectfully, you Honor, may I have a brief recess?" "No, counselor", growled Judge Swift, "you will proceed, if you can."

Just about then, the door in the back of the courtroom opened, and a small, timid-looking young man, in what was obviously an elevator's uniform, far too big for him, walked in to the back. He peered around in a shy, apprehensive way, and proceeded to sit down quietly on the backbench, with his hands carefully folded in his lap.

I went over to him and verified that he was, indeed, Stanley, my witness. I than asked the good Judge if I could have a moment to confer with my witness. "No!", shouted the Judge..."proceed." Thus, I had to put the poor fellow on the stand without even having a chance to talk to him. But it didn't really matter. Stanley testified in a hesitant, embarrassed way that he had been working at the Hotel for a year when the incident occurred; that the job was very important to him in helping support his widowed mother; and that he would never have done anything to jeopardize his job.

Stanley went on to relate that the two women came onto his elevator from the lounge, talking in a loud and boisterous way, and that as the elevator began to descend, the plaintiff lurched sideways, against the wall. When this occurred, she then began shouting at him, blaming him for operating the elevator badly. Stanley contended that he remained polite to her and did not touch her in any way. When they got to the lobby, he said the two of them left the elevator and made their way, weaving and talking loudly, toward the front entrance and out of the building. Plaintiff's counsel tried to shake Stanley on cross-examination, but in his hesitant, shy way, he stuck with his story.

The evidence was concluded, and counsel presented closing arguments to the jury. Judge Swift then gave brief instructions to the jurors, which I felt did not, exactly, favor the defendant. The jury retired, and I sat fretting as to how my first jury trial would turn out. My guy, Stanley, had done a good job, but they had two witnesses telling a completely different story from his, and one of them looked exactly like Jackie Kennedy, the beloved First Lady.

I was to find out, however, that jurors can often be very perceptive. I don't know if it was because they felt sorry for Stanley, or actually felt sorry for me, the neophyte who was badly abused by a crotchety judge. In any event, the jury came back in favor of the defendant. Thus, I concluded my first jury trial.

HOLDING AN ACE IN THE HOLE.

From 1962 when I first joined Sherburne Powers and Needham, up through the 1970's, one of the more active clients of the firm was a successful businessman, who was an aggressive, self-assured type. Sometimes, he rubbed people the wrong way in his drive for financial success.

The bulk of the legal work the firm provided him related to his business and was handled by attorneys in the corporate department. Toward the latter part of the Seventies, however, he was brought into my office to talk to me about a lawsuit, which had just been filed against him.

The information I obtained from him was that in the early Seventies, he had entered into a partnership agreement with a builder who worked in the community where our client lived. Under the terms of this arrangement, they had agreed that our client would purchase several older properties in the area, and the builder would then renovate the properties, and they would then be marketed and sold, with the proceeds distributed between them.

The builder was to keep track of the labor and materials he used in his work and these amounts would be paid out of the proceeds of the sales. Our client was to recover the amounts he paid to acquire the properties, plus any carrying costs he incurred, such as taxes, utilities, and financing charges. After all these deductions were taken, the two parties would divide up equally whatever profit remained from a sale.

This all sounds good in theory, but when the completion of renovations on the properties was completed, and the properties were put up for sale, the real estate market had slumped badly, and it became difficult to sell the properties at the prices the partners had initially calculated.

When sales were finally made, and it came time to divide up the proceeds, there were disagreements as to who was entitled to pay what amounts. Since our client held title to these properties, however, he received the payments from the sales, which he held pending resolution of the dispute as to who was owed what amounts.

According to our client, the builder had greatly inflated the amounts he was claiming for renovations, and this was the reason he would not pay what the builder was seeking. Of course, in this kind of arrangement, there was great potential for these types of disagreements, particularly when the money received from the sales was much lower than what was expected when the agreement was first made.

The builder was paid certain amounts which our client thought was fair for the work provided, and the builder accepted these payments under protest, and over the next several years, he continued to ask to be paid the balance of what he had set forth in his billings.

This dispute dragged along, but finally the builder contacted an attorney and eventually the attorney filed an action in Superior Court seeking an accounting from our client and payment of the balance of the billings he had submitted for the work he performed. The builder was looking for some $50,000.

We agreed, of course, to represent our long-standing client in defense of this action, and after that I filed an answer on his behalf and the usual discovery requests, seeking information from the plaintiff-builder upon which he relied in claiming additional amounts for his work. Back in those years, there was a big backlog of civil cases and our case lay dormant for a number of years with no activity. Since it was the opposing party who was seeking payment, we had little incentive to push the case along.

Some five years after the case had been filed, the Court finally entered an order that the case be tried before a Master appointed by the Court, for determination of the factual issues involved. This often happened, in those days, in cases involving construction issues and the need for determining the details of accountings.

Approximately 12 ten years had passed since the sales of those properties. The plaintiff did not file his action until some seven years after those events and another five years had elapsed. After the initial meetings with our client, I had had little contact with him thereafter, but I did hear reports that he had suffered some setbacks in his health, which had affected his memory of some past events.

After I had received the notice from the Court of the assignment of the case to the Master, I set up an appointment to meet with the client so that I could explain what was involved with a hearing before the Master, and to review with him again the facts in preparation for the hearing.

As we talked, I soon began to realize, much to my amazement, that, apart from records we had reflecting various costs and charges, he could not remember any of the details of his talks and dealing with the builder. Defending against the type of claims being asserted here, when contemporaneous records the builder had maintained relative to his work supported the amounts he was seeking, was difficult enough, but how, I asked myself, could I possibly mount a defense on the merits of the claims when my client could not recall what had occurred?

The Master who was assigned to hear the case was an older retired District Court Judge. In those days, I had found that district court judges were inclined to favor plaintiffs in their findings, and since the plaintiff here was an ordinary local builder and my client came across as a prosperous and somewhat overbearing businessman, I was not at all optimistic that the Master would be sympathetic to our position.

Moreover, since the defendant's memory was impaired by the health problems he had had, there was little I could offer to counter what the plaintiff would be saying. Indeed, I recognized that I would have to bring out through my client's testimony the reasons why he could not recall those events in the past. Otherwise, the Master would presume that the failure by the defendant to give his version of what had happened meant he agreed with what the plaintiff was claiming.

But I did have one card I could play, an "ace in the hole", as they say in gambling circles. This revolved around the defense that the statute of limitation, which applied to this type action, had expired when the plaintiff filed his action. As is true of all civil claims, there are statutes, which require that the claims be filed in court within certain fixed periods of time. In the type case we had, the statute was six years, and the limitation period begins to run from the time the claimant knew, or should have known, of his claim.

The statute of limitation is an affirmative defense which means that it has to be raised in the answer which a defendant if required to file in response to the plaintiff's complaint. I had included this defense in our answer, along with a number of other affirmative defenses, some of which were simply "window dressing." While not waiving the limitation defense, I did not, on the other hand, want to highlight this as being what I considered to be the key defense to the action.

The hearing before the Master proceeded pretty much as I had expected, with the Master reflecting, almost immediately, his partiality toward the plaintiff. Moreover, when he learned that because of health problems, the defendant could remember little about those past events, it soon became clear that the Master ultimately would be making findings supporting the plaintiff's claims in the report he was required to file with the Court.

Thus, I realized that if we did not prevail on the limitations defense, there would undoubtedly be a judgment in the plaintiff's favor. During my cross-examination of the plaintiff builder, therefore, I asked a myriad of questions, but among the questions were those designed to establish that he had met with my client on a date some seven years before he filed his action, and at that meeting he had protested defendant's refusal to pay the additional amounts he was seeking for his work. He also acknowledged that when our client refused at that meeting to make further payment, he realized this was the basis for his present claims.

At the conclusion of hearings of this type, each side has the right to submit to the Master proposed findings of fact. The attorneys may, if they wish, also submit proposed rulings of law. I submitted various proposed findings of fact, and included among them was the recitation of the plaintiff's testimony about his meeting with the defendant at which he recognized the existence of his present claims. Not wanting to alert the Master to our limitation defense, I did not submit any proposed rulings of law.

Several months later, I received the report of the Master, and as I expected, he found for the plaintiff in the full amount of all his claims, around $50,000. In his subsidiary findings, however, he included all of what I had proposed relative to the meeting of the parties and the plaintiff's state of mind at that time.

The report was then filed with the Court, but when it came time for the Court to act upon the report and to enter an appropriate judgment in accordance with the findings in the report, I finally brought forth the "ace in the hole" I had been quietly holding.

I filed a motion for judgment of dismissal on the grounds that the plaintiff, by his own testimony, had acknowledged that he had knew he had claims some seven years before he filed his action in Court, and thus the action had to be dismissed since it was not filed within the applicable limitation period.

Since the Master specifically included these particular findings in his report, the Court could do nothing but enter judgment of dismissal, based upon the limitation defense, a card we carefully held until the best time to bring it forth.

ALIENATION OF AFFECTION

Trial lawyers have always tended to specialize in particular areas of the law. Some focus upon personal injury cases, either representing plaintiffs who seek recoveries or insurance companies defending claims. Other attorneys, the more cerebral types, handle complex commercial cases or anti trust litigation. Still others specialize, for example, in trademark and copyright cases. Only a few trial attorneys handle a wide variety of cases.

When I started out in trial work in 1962, I vowed to myself that I would, for the diversity and challenge it afforded, handle as broad a range of cases as I could. As it turned out, the senior litigator at my new firm, Tim Donohue, preferred to handle insurance defense work. He was a fine trial attorney, but he simply was more comfortable defending personal injury cases. This meant that I was able to pick up and handle other type cases coming into the firm, which he avoided.

Thus, as it turned out, I handled a broad assortment of cases during my 36 years as a trial attorney, just as I had hoped to do when I started my career. These included products liability cases, contract, commercial and construction cases, trade secret and copyright litigation, anti-trust cases, legal and medical malpractice cases, and litigation involving real estate issues.

There was, however, one type of case I was asked to defend which I suspect few trial attorneys today have ever handled: an alienation of affection suit. Under the common law, a husband or wife is entitled to seek recovery of damages from another person who alienates, or steals, the affection of the claimant's spouse. In practice, after 1950, cases involving claims such as this were hardly ever filed. Around 1970, however, I found myself defending just such a claim on behalf of a client of the firm, who I will call Phil Timmons. Having never before handled such a case, I welcomed the assignment.

Phil was the head of a family-owned successful manufacturing firm. He was estranged from his wife at the time, and although he was a quiet and retiring person, hardly a Casanova type, he developed a flourishing romance with an attractive married Italian woman, who I will call Carla. Although Carla, for financial reasons, still lived with her husband, a hotheaded, overbearing individual, her relationship with him had been dormant for a number of years. Indeed, she could not stand the man.

This did not, however, prevent Carla's husband from becoming suspicious about Carla's activities, and through surreptitious surveillance, he was able to chronicle Carla's meetings with Phil. He consulted with an attorney in Cambridge who was willing to bring an alienation of affection claim for his new client against Phil under a contingency fee arrangement. Phil soon appeared in my office with a copy of the summons and complaint.

When this action was filed, Carla moved into a small apartment and began divorce proceedings against her husband, who continued, however, to press his action, seeking a substantial amount to settle his claim against Phil. After assessing the evidence, as it developed, I concluded that the claim could best be defended at trial based upon the simple proposition that Phil did not alienate Carla's affection for her husband because there was no affection when she first met Phil.

The jury trial of the case began in Middlesex Superior Court in Cambridge before Judge Joseph Mitchell, a wild and unpredictable jurist, often difficult to try before. As it turned out, however, Judge Mitchell had little sympathy for the plaintiff and his claim. Phil and Carla both testified and acknowledged their romance, with Carla describing how her marriage, before she ever met Phil, had fallen apart to a point that she had no relationship or affection for her husband. In my cross-examination of the plaintiff, who was anything but an appealing, sympathetic witness, I hammered on this same theme.

At the close of the evidence, attorneys typically provide the judge with various instructions on issues of law, which they want the judge to include in his charge to the jury. Normally, I would give anywhere from 10 to 30 requests for instructions in the normal case, depending on the complexity of the issues.

This time, I gave Judge Mitchell just one request, taken verbatim from a decision in an alienation of affection case back in the 1930's. This instruction in substance said that damages are measured by the degree of affection the plaintiff lost as a consequence of the defendant's conduct, and the less affection, the less the recovery.

My argument to the jury, on behalf of Phil, dealt primarily on this point. The Judge, as part of his instructions to the jury, concluded by reading the instruction I had requested in its entirety, fitting in nicely with the argument I had given.

The jury then retired, and after about an hour of deliberating, returned with their verdict, which was in the form of answers to special questions. A lawyer may have tried many cases before juries, but he or she always sits there awaiting the reading of a verdict with misgivings and second-guessing.

The first question to the jury was "Is the plaintiff entitled to recover damages from the defendant?", and when the clerk read the jury's answer as "Yes", my heart dropped. The second question was, "What amount is the plaintiff entitled to receive as damages?" As the clerk read the answer, "One dollar," I was tempted to leap from my chair, shouting, "Yes"!

Plaintiff's attorney was not a particularly likeable person, and when the jury left the courtroom, I walked quickly over to him as he sat dejectedly at his table, and handed him a dollar, saying I expected my client would want to pay the judgment forthwith. He was not amused. Phil and Carla were delighted, and went out to celebrate. I begged off joining them and returned to my office to get ready for the "next case." No other case would be like this one which boiled down to "one dollar's worth of affection."

TAKING OFF THE WRONG TOE

One morning, while I was working on a brief in my office, I received a telephone call from a man from Toronto who wanted to set up an appointment with me. He said he wanted to talk to me about a possible claim that he had. Somehow he had been given my name to contact. He was planning to be in Boston three days hence, and so I told him to come by the office the afternoon of the day he was to arrive.

He came into our office, along with his wife, at the appointed hour. As he moved into my office, I noticed that he was walking with a limp. After the usual introductory remarks, he explained to me that he was a dentist in Toronto and had come to Boston some seven months earlier for a medical evaluation by a foot specialist at the Massachusetts General Hospital, who had been recommended to him, about the problems he had with his toes. The dentist had two badly crooked toes, known as "hammer toes", one on each foot, and as time had gone on, these two toes had become increasingly painful.

After examining these two toes, the specialist told the dentist that the hammertoe on his left foot was so bad that he recommended it be amputated. He said the hammertoe on the right foot, on the other hand, could be straightened through surgery. Since even simple walking was painful to him, the dentist decided to undergo the operations, and arrangements were made for him to return to Boston later to undergo the two operations.

Two months later, the dentist, with his wife, returned to the Massachusetts General Hospital for the operations. The dentist was taken to the operating room, placed under general anesthesia, and the foot specialist performed the operations.

The patient regained consciousness and was returned to his room, where his wife was waiting. When the two of them looked at his feet, they were surprised to see that his right foot had a very large bandage on it, whereas the bandage on his left foot, where the toe was to have been amputated, was small.

When the foot doctor arrived later to check his patient, the dentist asked about the large bandage on his right foot, and the doctor, a very self-assured type, explained nonchalantly that this was the foot where the toe had been amputated and therefore had a bigger bandage. Shocked and stunned, the dentist said, "But that was the toe that you said would be straightened, not removed!" The specialist then became very flustered and concerned, saying he would check his medical records and would get back to them.

Shortly thereafter, the foot doctor returned to say that somehow there was a mix-up in the operating room, but that the problem toe on the left foot still ought to be removed and that he could arrange to secure an operating room for the second operation in a few days to remove that toe. Recognizing the pain he had been enduring with that toe, the dentist reluctantly agreed to the second operation. It was performed two days later, and after two additional days of recuperation, the dentist was scheduled to be discharged. Shortly before he left, the foot doctor saw the dentist for a final check-up of the two feet.

The doctor conducted his examination, but before he left, the dentist quietly asked whether he would be charged for the second operation, pointing out that it had been necessitated by the fact that the wrong toe was amputated the first time. The dentist also said he was being charged for two extra days in the hospital and that his wife had had to stay two extra days in her hotel.

The foot specialist, a haughty type, immediately became incensed by what his patient had quietly asked, and told him that if he was thinking of making a claim against him for what had happened, he, the doctor, would say that before the operation, he had asked which toe was to be removed and his patient told him that it was the toe on the right foot.

Often times people, faced with evidence that they had made a mistake, instead of responding in a courteous, sympathetic way, react in an aggressive, overbearing manner, thus enflaming the situation even more. A few concessions by the foot specialist would have satisfied the dentist and his wife, who were not at all litigious, but instead, the doctor reacted defensively, in an arrogant way. Moreover, to exacerbate what had happened, shortly after they had returned to Toronto, they received a hefty bill from the foot doctor for the second operation.

The dentist and his wife became so upset by the reaction of what they thought was a reputable specialist and the fact that he would so readily lie about what happened, that they decided to consult with an attorney, which led to there being seated together with me in my office that day.

Well, it is not often that you are presented with such a well-founded medical malpractice claim. Ordinarily, malpractice claims against doctors require the testimony of another doctor supporting the contention that what the defendant doctor had done, or failed to do, was negligent. This is often difficult because doctors typically do not like to testify against each other. In the situation I had, however, there was case law holding that when a doctor performs an operation on the wrong part (e.g. eye, finger, foot, leg, whatever), this would be considered negligence per se, without the necessity of supportive medical opinion.

I forwarded to the foot specialist a claims letter, and he in turn sent it along to his insurance company. When I discussed the claim with the insurance adjuster, I did not focus upon the costs of the second operation or the two extra days in the hospital and hotel. I talked, instead, about the weeks it took for my client to recuperate from the loss of the toe on his right foot and the fact that he had lost a toe which the doctor said could be straightened so as to function properly.

It was not long thereafter that the insurance company offered an amount, which my dentist client was more than happy to accept. It was far more than what the dentist was thinking about when he first talked to the doctor. The moral of this story is that when you clearly have made a mistake, the best thing to do is to acknowledge it, apologize for what happened, and try to rectify as best you can.

SETTLING FOR A BOGIE

Golf has become very popular lately and today, there are numerous golf courses available on the Cape for the growing legions of whackers and hackers who want to spend their time and money following those bouncing balls. Some of the more affluent of these aspiring golfers, to my amazement, will even pay an enrollment fee of $150,000 simply to become a member at the National Golf Course on Route 39 in Harwich, yet still paying substantial annual fees after attaining their positions.

With charges such as these, simply for the right to play on a course, can you imagine actually owning a nine-hole golf course, located in a beautiful setting, having paid only $9000? Well this was the total amount paid back in the early Forties by ten local golfers to **own** the Brewster Golf Course, which is now part of the prestigious Ocean Edge Golf Course.

Back in those times, there were only a few golf courses in this area, and one of them was the Brewster Golf Course, a nine-hole course off Route 6A overlooking Cape Cod Bay. Ten local golfers in Orleans, including my father, Reuben Hopkins, and well-known businessmen Alton Smith (Smith Boys Hardware) and Lloyd Ellis (Ellis' Market), wanting to be assured of keeping this course operating so that it would be available for them to play upon, bought the course for the grand sum of $9000, working out to $900 per partner.

The course at that time consisted of 125 acres of beautiful rolling hills and several ponds. Thus, the group of golfers paid $72 per acre for this property, not bad by even the standards then existing. In 1948, the partners hired Oren Smith to manage the golf club. After several years, Smith approached members of the group asking if they would sell the golf course to him. He was willing to pay $18,000, which, he pointed out, was twice what they had paid originally to acquire the property.

Our ten local golfers, then in their fifties, had grown up when land values on the Cape were very low and ownership was not a big thing. Some in the group were concerned that, at least according to the books and records maintained by Smith, the club had been making little or no profit. Others felt that owning the course was a nuisance and that as long as they had a place to play and the course remained open to the public, there was little reason to keep the property, especially when Smith was offering twice what they had paid for the course. My Dad was opposed to selling the course, but a majority of the partners favored the sale, and Dad went along with the decision.

In September 1950, the group sold the course to Smith for the $18,000. A provision in the deed, however, required Smith to have the course open for golf at least eight months each year, and if he failed to do so, the grantors could reacquire the property. Each of the grantors also had the right to play, free of charge, for his lifetime. These conditions seemed more valuable to members of the group than the money involved.

The deed also had the following provision: should Smith "desire to sell the above granted premises at any time within the next 25 years,[he] must first offer it to these grantors at a price of $18,000, plus cost of permanent improvements, less four percent depreciation". This provision was later to have great significance in terms of what was to happen later.

Those in the group who remained healthy continued to play golf on the course in the years that followed. While I was in college, during summer breaks in the early 1950's, I often played golf, free of charge, with my Dad at the Brewster Golf Club. He was a decent golfer who typically shot in the low 90's, not long on drives, but accurate around the greens. Based upon my discussions with him, it was clear that he, and other members of his group, were more than satisfied if they were able to shoot bogies.

In 1963, Paul Healy took over the management of the Brewster Golf Club, and in discussions he had with some members of the original group, Healy told them that he had a long term lease with Smith to operate the club. Nobody gave much thought to this or looked into the details of the arrangement.

The years passed. In June of 1973, I received a telephone call at my law office in Boston from Dad informing me that there had been stories in The Cape Codder, the local weekly newspaper, reporting that Oren Smith was selling the golf course to Charles Frazier, a well-known lawyer from Wellfleet, who had a reputation for shrewd dealing in real estate. As far as Dad knew, there had been a restriction in the deed to Smith requiring him to offer the property first to the original owners.

Thereafter, I read articles from The Cape Codder telling about the sale. The stories, as I later was able to verify, were detailed and accurate, revealing facts I was sure Frazier would have preferred to have kept quiet. The stories reported that Smith had agreed in December 1972 to sell the golf course to Frazier and his partner Robert Lessor, for $650,000, and that Frazier and Lessor, in turn, had agreed to sell this property to Martin Rich and Frederick Walters for double that amount, which would have given Frazier and his partner a tidy profit.

Frazier had to have been aware of the restriction in the deed by which Smith had acquired the property. To be sure, he was a seasoned attorney who did know how to wend his way through legal entanglements, but with regard to the golf course, the large quick profit he envisioned may have clouded what otherwise would have been an objective analysis of the legal issues involved. The deed was phrased in terms of when Smith "desired" to sell, for example, and a valid argument could be made that by entering into the agreement in 1972, Smith evidenced his desire to sell within the 25 year period.

As it turned out, however, there was even more involved, which had not been reported in newspaper. In early 1973, I obtained a copy of the so-called lease which Oren Smith and Paul Healy had made in 1963. Provisions in this agreement provided that as long as Healy made annual payments of $22,500, at the end of 10 years (i.e. in 1973, before the 25 year term would have ended), Smith was to "grant, release and quitclaim and does grant release and quitclaim to the lessee [Healy] on the final day of the within lease."

The so-called lease was actually an agreement by Healy to purchase the property, through installment payments, over a period of 10 years. Moreover, the attorney who represented Smith on this transaction and drew up this document was none other than Charlie Frazier, who later was arranging to buy the property himself.

All of this was reported to my Dad with the recommendation from me that he and the surviving members of his group assert their rights to repurchase under the terms of the original deed. They agreed to retain me to assert their rights. When I contacted Smith on behalf of my new clients, I received a letter from Frazier informing me that he was counsel for Smith and that my clients had no rights to repurchase the property. As the reader may realize, it is very irregular for an attorney to represent a seller involving a transaction in which he is the buyer.

Realizing that dealing with Frazier would be fruitless, I filed on behalf of the six surviving grantors a complaint in Barnstable Superior Court seeking an injunction to prevent the sale by Smith and a decision from the Court that the plaintiffs were entitled to repurchase the property. The Court did issue an injunction on August 31 1973 enjoining the sale of the property to Frazier until the issues were finally determined.

As it turned out, the real estate market in late 1973 dropped badly. Rich and Walters were unable to obtain the financing they had lined up initially to complete their purchase from Frazier. Although there were settlement discussions to resolve the pending law suit, without financing, these tentative settlement discussions could not be finalized.

By 1976, moreover, two of the plaintiffs, including my Dad, had died, and because of the age and poor health of the remaining four, there was concern that they, too, might not be with us when the case finally reached trial. Also, the four survivors, as you might expect, had little interest in reacquiring the property for themselves. The real estate market on the Cape, moreover, was still depressed and there was little financing money available for projects such as this.

In reviewing settlement offers which we received, surviving members of the group seemed more interested in being assured that the golf course remained open to the public at large, rather than the money being offered for them to settle their claims. Unfortunately, by not retaining the golf course back in

1950 and managing it carefully thereafter, they lost the power to guarantee that the course would always remain open to the public.

In these days, when so many are chasing the "almighty dollar" and some even proclaim that "greed is good", it is hard to imagine how those early golfers would be more interested in simply assuring themselves a place to play golf than in retaining potentially valuable real estate and riding it into what later could have been a huge payout.

In June 1976, we were able finally to complete a settlement by which the claims of the plaintiffs would be released for a payment of $400,000. Considering the underlying value of the property, this amount should have been more, and if my remaining living clients had been in better health, I would have taken the case to trial.

But for a group of old golfers, in the twilight of life, who were more interested simply in having a place for the average person to play golf, it was acceptable - not a birdie or par, but in their minds at least, surely a bogie.

FREEING THE IMAGES OF SANTA CLAUS

The United States is without doubt the most litigious country in the world. Some people, with the help of their lawyers, are ready to go to court on any perceived grievance and anybody who has handled cases for a period of time will inevitably encounter some outlandish claim. This is the story of one such claim, essentially an assertion by the plaintiff, if you can believe it, that it held a monopoly on Santa Claus. But first, a little background.

Bill Weeks joined our firm in 1983. Bill, a distinguished, soft-spoken and genteel man, worked primarily with trusts and estates, a sedate area of practice. Bill's father was Sinclair Weeks who had served as Secretary of Commerce in the Eisenhower administration. One of his brothers, Sinclair Weeks Jr. (known to his friends as 'Sinny'), had been Chairman of the Board of Reed and Barton for many years.

After Bill came to Sherburne Powers and Needham, the firm began handling legal work for Reed and Barton, and I began representing the well-known, old-line sterling silverware manufacturer in various lawsuits. As a consequence, I came to learn about how sterling silver flatware and other products were crafted. One of the cases I handled, for example, involved a claim by Reed and Barton seeking to recover what it had lost in the market as a result of unlawful advertising practices of one of its competitors, the Towle Company.

Towle had embarked upon a huge advertising campaign in which they listed the price of a sterling silver spoon, for example, at $150, and then offered the spoon at a discounted price of $75, when the actual price was $100, making the prospective buyer think he was getting a 50 percent discount. This type of advertising, known as deep discounting, was in violation of State regulations. As a result of this aggressive campaigning, Reed and Barton's sales dropped and its percentage share of the market decreased while Towle's share increased correspondingly.

Prosecution of the claims on behalf of Reed and Barton required my working closely with Sinny Weeks, as he was known, and others in the management of the Company. I found them all to be courteous, knowledgeable and very helpful in the assistance they provided, and eventually, we were able to work out a settlement with Towle whereby it agreed to pay Reed and Barton some $2 million.

I represented Reed and Barton in several other cases, including an action in the Federal Court in Washington D.C. But for me the most unusual, truly unprecedented case was an action which was filed in October 1986 against one of Reed and Barton's subsidiaries in the Federal Court in Portland, Maine, by a company which manufactured ceramic figurines.

The plaintiff company was making elaborate painted figurines, representing reproductions of the different versions of Santa Claus as he had developed historically in different countries, which they sold at high prices, in the $75 range. They claimed that the Reed and Barton subsidiary, in making brass silhouette replicas of the different versions of Santa Claus as inexpensive tree ornaments, was violating the copyrights which the plaintiff had taken on its figurines.

The plaintiff sought an order from the Court enjoining the production and sale of the tree ornaments by the defendant, as well as recovery of damages which it alleged it lost as a result of the sale of the ornaments. Since the tree ornaments were small brass silhouettes of historical versions of Santa Claus, while the plaintiff was producing larger, more expensive hand-painted statuettes, the plaintiff could not possibly contend that the tree ornaments were copies of the statuettes or that the buying public would be confused by the two products in the market.

The plaintiff's attorney was essentially alleging that the plaintiff had the right to replicate the historical versions of Santa Claus, to the exclusion of everybody else. If that type claim was considered valid, even a small child, in drawing and cutting out a version of Santa Claus, could be accused of violating the plaintiff's copyright. Plaintiff was contending, in effect, that it had a monopoly on Santa Claus, a patently preposterous position.

Except for filing interrogatories to the plaintiff and asking for the production of documents such as sales and marketing records, I did little to develop information and evidence in preparation for trial since I felt there never would be a trial in the case. I made it very clear, moreover, to plaintiff's attorney that when the action was ultimately dismissed, I would file a motion seeking recovery of the costs and legal fees my client had incurred in defending the case based upon the contention that the action was frivolous.

The attorney who originally had filed the case may have had second thoughts as to what he had done because shortly before the pretrial conference with the Trial Judge, he withdrew from the case. A new attorney from Philadelphia, who supposedly specialized in copyright law, filed an appearance for the plaintiff.

As the trial of the case approached, I filed a motion for summary judgment asking the court to dismiss the action on the grounds that since the tree ornaments had no resemblance to the plaintiff's statuettes, there could be no infringement of the plaintiff's copyright. Later, in another conference with the Trial Judge, a crusty, no-nonsense type, he decided to hold the motion in abeyance for resolution when the case came on for trial, which had been set for early May 1987.

I was not really disappointed by what he had decided to do because I felt that trying a case in which I would be attempting to keep Santa Claus from the restrictions of a monopoly would be a unique experience. I concluded, moreover, that the judge recognized the validity of what I had argued and was attempting to apply added pressure, by way of the burden of a trial, upon the plaintiff.

Indeed, approximately three weeks before trial was to begin, plaintiff's new counsel contacted me to ask whether, if they dropped the action, we would agree not to seek recovery of the defendant's costs and legal fees. After conferring with Sinny, since our fees and costs were modest, we agreed not to pursue a motion for recovery and the action was dismissed.

Thus, we were able to free Santa Claus, and his various historical images, from the clutches of a company which was claiming that, through a copyright it had obtained on its statuettes, it had secured rights to use those images to the exclusion of everybody else. A little kid in school may now safely color and cutout a version of Santa without worrying about being the target of an action for infringement.

THE CASE OF THE BENT PEDAL

Although I tried a variety of cases during my career as a trial attorney, the one area, which to me was most interesting and challenging, was products liability litigation. I did handle some cases on behalf of plaintiffs, but the bulk of my work in this area was representing manufacturers in defending cases in which a plaintiff claimed the product was defective, causing him injury.

In order to defend these cases properly, it was necessary for me to learn about the design, function, and safety features of the particular product involved in each case as it came along. One could not go to trial on a products case without a sound understanding of this kind of information. Each case, therefore, could be an interesting learning experience.

Among the manufacturers I represented were Ford, General Motors, Hobart (kitchen appliances), Bombardier LTD (snowmobiles), and Johns Manville (waterpipe, lamps, roofing material, and asbestos products). Working for General Motors and Johns Manville was especially satisfying because the in-house attorneys and technical staff (e.g. engineers and designers) those companies provided to assist local counsel were bright, experienced and helpful.

It was obvious that General Motors, for example, assigned some of their most capable and personable engineers to provide technical support for the defense of products cases. Since these experts often would testify at trial, being courteous, well-groomed, courteous and pleasant were important characteristics.

Another manufacturer I represented in the 1970's, which shall remain nameless, obviously did not give high priority to litigation support. The engineers they furnished to assist in litigation seemed to be "rejects" from the regular engineering staffs. Some were plainly lazy and incompetent, quick to attribute an accident to a cause, which, upon critical analysis, was simply an implausible theory that could easily be destroyed at trial.

When this occurred, I would try to make an "end run" around the company's engineer by recommending we retain a qualified independent engineer to provide me with additional assistance in evaluating and defending against the plaintiff's claim. Since this required approval of in-house counsel, with the company engineer looking on, it necessarily was a sensitive, touchy process.

Engineers at General Motors or Johns Manville, in contrast, were honest, sound and straightforward in their evaluations as to whether a defect really existed to cause an accident. When they found this to be the case, they candidly acknowledged it and efforts were then made to settle the claim for a reasonable amount.

On the other hand, if the experts concluded that there was nothing wrong with the product, in design or otherwise, and that the accident resulted from the neglect or inattention of the plaintiff, there would be no offer of settlement, and unless the case was dropped (which sometimes did happen), the case necessarily went to trial. This policy ("thousands for defense; not a dime for settlement") was followed by most of major manufacturers in order to discourage groundless claims being filed by attorneys who hoped simply to obtain an offer to settle from what they perceived was a deep-pocket defendant.

Such a policy did work in practice. The prosecution of a products case requires the retention of an expert, sometimes more than one, and a great deal of preparation and often-lengthy trials. Plaintiffs' attorneys, handling these cases under contingency fee arrangements whereby they only receive a fee if there is a recovery, soon realized that it did not pay to pursue these products claims unless there was a likelihood of success at trial.

One case I handled for General Motors is a good illustration of the points I am making. This case involved a claim by a man in his late twenties who, while driving his high-powered sports car, ran off Route 128 one night on his way home from a party. The car ran into a solid oak tree at high speed, causing the young man severe head injuries and leaving him paralyzed in the lower part of his body.

An action was brought on his behalf by Edward Ginsberg, an experienced trial attorney who later became a respected judge in Probate Court. Based upon what his client told him, Ed claimed that the accelerator was defective and stuck, causing the accident to occur. Ed was also able to find an engineer who supported the plaintiff's version of the accident.

When I took the deposition of the plaintiff, he acknowledged having several drinks at the party prior to heading home. He testified further that as he was proceeding around a gentle curve on Route 128, heading north at about 60 MPH, the engine began to accelerate; that he placed his foot on the brake pedal, pushing down hard, but that the car continued even faster; and that he lost control of the car, going off the road into the tree.

The GM engineers assigned to this case concluded that the plaintiff's description of the accident was wholly implausible. In order to demonstrate this to me, they arranged for me to be flown out to the GM proving grounds in Detroit so that I could witness an experiment they would conduct with the same type car as the plaintiff was driving. This car was driven by a test driver, with me and the engineers riding as passengers.

The driver accelerated to 60 MPH, then arranged to have the accelerator stuck at that speed, and then firmly applied the brake. Although the engine continued to roar at high RPM, the car nevertheless reduced speed and stopped as a result of the braking action. We then arranged to have this experiment recorded on videotape.

When manufacturers receive notification of a products claim, the first thing they try to do is locate and inspect the product. On claims involving automobiles, the insurer of the car, if it is heavily damaged, usually pays the plaintiff the value of the car, takes possession of it and sells it for parts to a junk dealer. In such instances, the manufacturer against whom a claim is being made will attempt to trace the car, from place to place, and if located, either buys the car or the specific part claimed to be defective.

In the case under discussion, investigators were able to trace the car from a local junk dealer down a facility into New York where it was to be crushed. They arrived at the facility the day before the vehicle was scheduled to go into the crusher, and quickly arranged to acquire the car for a small amount. The car was returned to Massachusetts and carefully inspected by a GM engineer. The inspection revealed that the accelerator pedal was significantly bent inward and that the brake pedal was intact.

A bend in a pedal will occur when the driver's foot is upon the pedal at the moment of impact and the force of the driver, suddenly being thrown forward, is sufficient to actually bend the pedal upon which the foot is resting. The logical conclusion, therefore, was that immediately prior to impact, the plaintiff was pressing down hard on the accelerator, and not the brake, as he thought, which explains, of course, why the car speeded up.

There would not, therefore, be any offer of settlement on this case. Edward Ginsberg, however, had prepared himself well for the trial. He had his own engineer to support the plaintiff and explain how an accelerator can become stuck. Ed, moreover, was capable and experienced, and although he spoke with a pronounced stutter in those days, which would normally be a major impediment for a trial attorney, he had a nice manner and was appealing to jurors who perhaps viewed him sympathetically. You had to be especially careful trying a case with Ed as your opponent.

The trial went forward before Judge Boggle in Middlesex Superior Court and lasted seven days. Ed put in evidence which, if believed, would result in a verdict for his client. The plaintiff, a good looking, polite man, appearing in a wheelchair, could not help but evince a sympathetic reaction from the jury.

I presented evidence through the testimony of my lead engineer, the showing of the video tape, and the photographs of the brake and accelerator pedals in order to demonstrate that the plaintiff's explanation as to how the accident happened simply was not logical and that he actually had his foot on the accelerator, not the brake.

Jurors from Middlesex County tend to be more intelligent and logical than those you might find from other jurisdictions, such as Suffolk County, and are more inclined to be influenced by logic and reason than by emotion and sympathy. The jury in this case was out for about six hours, but finally came back with a verdict for General Motors. The logic of the bent pedal prevailed.

Ed Ginsberg had put in many hours and a great effort into his case. He was a fair and honest advocate, and although he was my opponent, I liked and admired him. After the judge and jury had left the courtroom, I went over to congratulate him on a case well tried and to commiserate with him.

Being the gentleman he is, Ed in turn, although he must have been very disappointed by the verdict, commended me for a fine job in defending and offered to treat me to lunch. Lawyers, as a group, are not popular with the general public, and indeed there are, I know all too well, some obnoxious attorneys. Edward Ginsberg, however, was (and still is) a class act. He simply could not explain how the accelerator pedal was bent and the brake pedal was intact.

SMELLING LIKE A ROSE

As stated in my story, "The Case Of The Bent Pedal", in most of the products liability cases I handled, I represented defendants. Occasionally, however, a client of the firm would consult with me on whether damages he had sustained could be attributed to faulty design or manufacture of a product the client was using at the time of the event. I was willing to take on these cases if evidence developed through investigation was sufficient to show that the product was indeed defective so as to have caused the client monetary damages.

One of these cases involved Johnson Brothers Greenhouses Inc., a family owned business which had been raising and selling high quality roses since 1928. Our firm handled the corporate matters for Johnson Brothers, but one day in April of 1969, the owners of the business appeared in my office to talk about the collapse of one of their greenhouses during a blizzard on February 9 1969. I was not initially enthusiastic about being able to maintain a claim because damages resulting from acts of nature are not legally recoverable.

Our client had a number of greenhouses, but in order to expand its business, it contracted in 1968 to have a new very large greenhouse built on its property. Ickes Braun Greenhouses Inc., a company that specialized in the design and construction of greenhouses, began building the greenhouse in question some six months before the blizzard. This new greenhouse consisted of seven separate sections, each section connected together with a pitched roof. The sections were 400 feet long and 43 feet wide, making the overall size of the total structure 400 feet by 300 feet, more than six times the size of a football field.

After this enormous structure was erected, Johnson Brothers in January 1969 began transferring truckloads of high quality loam into the greenhouse, which was carefully racked out preliminary to the planting of thousands of rose plants. The planting was completed one week before the February storm hit the area.

The amount of snow, which falls, in the New England area can be heavy at times, but greenhouses constructed here are designed so as to avoid roofs from collapsing under the weight of the snow. Basically, so long as the heat inside the greenhouse is maintained, the snow falling on the glass of the roof will melt and the melting snow will slide down the pitched roof into gutters which ring the perimeter of the roof where the water is carried away in the downspouts. Any excess snow will fall over the edges of the gutter onto the ground.

Vertical columns in the side walls of the greenhouse, along the outside of the building, are connected to heavy aluminum trusses which run from the top of the column up at a 45 degree angle to the ridge of each roof, acting as support for the roof itself. Smaller cross pieces are installed, running horizontally at right angles across the trusses, creating spaces into which rectangular pieces of glass are then inserted, thus creating the roof.

The design of the Ickes Braun greenhouse was different from those Johnson Brothers already had in that the older greenhouses had only one roof ridge running down the center of the structure, with sloping roofs on either side of the ridge. The Ickes Braun roof, however, had seven parallel ridges running the length of the building, with gutters both around the perimeter and in the gully created where the seven roofs joined between each of the seven individual sections.

When the February 1969 blizzard hit Massachusetts, Johnson Brother's staff remained in all the greenhouses to make certain the heat was maintained sufficiently to cause the snow to slide safely away. Two workers were present in the Ickes Braun greenhouse to monitor the temperature readings there. As they stood in the new structure around 10:00 P.M., with the storm raging outside, they noticed that one of the roof trusses further down the greenhouse suddenly collapse off the top of the support column. When the weight of the snow shifted to the adjoining trusses, those trusses also collapsed, thus creating a domino effect resulting in all the trusses falling, one by one, along with a shower of sharp, jagged pieces of glass, heading directly toward the two workmen.

Realizing what was happening, the two men immediately began sprinting, literally for their lives, to the door at the end of the greenhouse, and with the roar of the falling trusses and jangled glass moving ever closer, they barely made it out through the door.

The Ickes Braun greenhouse was totally destroyed. The rose plants, cover by snow and glass and exposed to the cold, were all lost. Fortunately, there was not damage to any of the other greenhouses, which raised the question of why they were able to survive the storm, and the brand new Ickes Braun house did not. After reviewing the facts and information furnished by our client, I quickly arranged to retain a structural engineer to review the Ickes Braun design and a metallurgist to analyze the parts which acted as the connection between the columns and the roof trusses which in each instance had torn away, causing the connecting roofs to collapse.

After studying the design and component parts, the engineer concluded that the trusses and columns were properly designed and of adequate weight, but that the connector which held the trusses to the individual columns was improperly designed and could not withstand the prying action which resulted when the weight of the snow caused the trusses to deflect downward.

Moreover, he felt that Ickes Braun should not have installed a greenhouse in the New England area, which in effect had seven roofs, connected together, because this created a valley between each section which prevented the snow from sliding off to the ground. Ickes Braun routinely erected this type greenhouse in the Southwestern areas of the country, without any problems, but there was little heavy snowfall in those areas, in comparison to the New England area.

The metallurgist I retained, using high intensity photography of those portions of the connector between the column and truss, which had split open, found that those parts, cast in aluminum, were excessively porous, with multiple air pockets. As a consequence, each part could more easily split apart when subjected to the increased weight of accumulated snow. Thus, our claim was two-fold: improper design and defective materials, all in breach of the warranties Ickes Braun had given in its contract with Johnson Brothers.

Efforts to settle the claims with Ickes Braun were fruitless. Some companies simply cannot bring themselves to acknowledge that one of their products could be defective or improperly designed. Usually, however, when the evidence is strong, I have found that the defendant, when confronted by a trial before a jury, will view the plaintiff's theory of recovery far more realistically. And so in June of 1969, I filed suit in Middlesex Superior Court on behalf of my client. The usual discovery was undertaken with each side exploring the evidence and positions of the opposition.

Back in those years, there were serious backlogs of civil cases in Superior Court and our case did not reach trial until March of 1975 before Judge Morse in Lowell. Clement McCarthy, a wily, seasoned defense attorney, experienced in products liability cases, represented the defendant at trial. I have found, however, that it is far better to have an experienced attorney on the other side because they will more realistically assess the strength of the evidence, thus creating a better chance of securing a reasonable settlement.

Our evidence was strong and dramatic. The two workmen who ran for their lives to escape the cascade of glass and trusses were present, ready to testify. Our two experts, each of whom had written strong detailed reports setting forth their opinions concerning the design and porous connectors, were on call. Clem had copies of the reports and knew exactly what they said.

Our evidence on damages consisted of the value of the building, the value of the rose plants, and the loss of value of the roses, which would have been harvested and marketed from the plants, which had been destroyed. These amounts totaled about $250,000. Ickes Braun had asserted counterclaims for $50,000, the balance owed on the contract, and $33,000 for cleaning up the site after the collapse.

After I had made my opening to the jury and was ready to call my first witness, Clem McCarthy sidled up to me in the hallway during a recess, as I expected he would, and began a serious discussion about settlement. After going back and forth, and after conferring with his client, Clem finally agreed to agree to pay Johnson Brothers $175,000 while waiving the counterclaims which totaled $83,000. Thus, my clients came away "smelling like a rose."

A FLASH IN THE PAN

Joe Helmund had been a long-time client of our firm. He had consulted regularly over the years with Jack Collins, one of my friends at Sherburne Powers and Needham, about trust and estates matters. Old Joe, as he came to be known, had operated a welding equipment and service business since the 1940's and different corporate lawyers within the firm had also assisted him on questions relating to his business activities.

A couple of times, Jack brought Joe to see me about questions which involved the potential of litigation, thus affording me the chance to meet this interesting, crusty gentleman, very much from the "old school". Short, sturdy and vigorous, with bristly white hair, he was a man of few words who believed in hard work. He reminded me very much of the old Cape Codders I knew growing up.

The questions Joe conferred with me about did not blossom into actual litigation, and it was not until March 1989 that I was called upon to represent Joe and his company in a lawsuit. This was a personal injury claim by a welder who alleged the Helmund Company had furnished defective welding equipment to a construction site in September 1987, causing him to sustain a severe electric shock, which knocked him to the floor resulting in injury to his shoulder.

This incident had happened some two years before the action was filed, and the plaintiff claimed that he was still unable to work as a welder because of the effects of that electrical shock. The plaintiff, who I will call William Baxman, brought an action against the Helmund Company and the manufacturer of the welding machine in question. Joe's company did not have liability insurance for this type claim, and he had to obtain his own counsel.

Shortly after he had been served with the complaint, Joe conferred with me about the incident. As it turned out, he did have some knowledge of the event alleged in the complaint. The Helmund Company had indeed supplied two welding machines as rental equipment to the welding contractor for use in welding steel beams in a skyscraper under construction in downtown Boston.

Joe had sent one of his more experienced servicemen along with the equipment to set the machines up for use on the site. This man, I'll call Henry, was originally from Trinidad where he had trained to be a welding technician. A quiet and dignified man of about 55 years of age, he had moved to Massachusetts and had been working for the Helmund Company for 15 to 20 years. Joe respected his knowledge, dedication and abilities.

At the time this action was filed, Joe was in his late seventies but was still vigorous and very much a part of the everyday operations of his company. He had worked hard over the years to build his company so he could leave a profitable business for his children when he retired. The plaintiff was looking for over $250,000 on his lawsuit and Old Joe was justifiably worried that a large judgment against his firm would bankrupt the company he had worked so hard to develop. He was also concerned about the legal fees he faced in defending the action, and to reassure him, I offered to handle the case at less than my normal hourly rate.

Henry, who had a pleasant, lilting accent, explained to me that he had set up the two welding machines rented to the contractor in a small-enclosed room adjacent to the area where the welding was to take place on exposed steel beams. Henry then ran four long cables, covered by thick insulation, two from each machine, out to the hand-welders which were used by the welders to set beads of molten solder into the cracks where the steel beams came together. These cables had insulated connectors on the end, which were affixed to terminals on the welding machines and when the machine was turned on, current passed along the cables to the hand-welders. When the trigger on the hand-welder was activated, an arc would be created from the

165

merging of the two currents, which melted the welding rod to create the weld.

Henry had set up the machines, uncoiled the cables, connecting them on either end, checked the hand-welders to see if the arcs were proper, and made several adjustments on the dials of the machines to obtain maximum performance. While he was doing this, one of the welders followed Henry around, making remarks that inferred that Henry, a black man, did not know what he was doing. Henry ignored him, concluded his work, and left the building. Later, Joe received a call that one of the welders had received an electrical shock while using the equipment, and Henry returned to the building to check the welding systems again. He could find nothing wrong.

The information Henry received from workmen at the site about the incident was that shortly after Baxman, along with another welder, began welding on the steel beams, he complained about the arc he was getting, muttering "that guy didn't connect the cables correctly." He then went back to the room to check the welding machines. He came back out of the room complaining that he had sustained a shock from one of the cables and after eating lunch, he left work to go home.

According to the story Baxman presented during the deposition I later conducted, he went into the room and without shutting the machines off, grasped one of the cable connectors attached to a machine terminal to remove it. As he removed the connector, there was a bright flash, which caused him to sustain a violent electrical shock, throwing him forcefully to the floor and rendering him unconscious. He said he landed on his shoulder and felt pain in his shoulder when he came to.

Fellow workmen did confirm that Baxman had complained after the incident about receiving a shock and went to the lunchroom to have coffee. After a time, Baxman asked to go home, and later the same day, he went to the local hospital complaining about the shock he said he had sustained.

The hospital record, which we obtained after the suit was filed, stated that Baxman was very agitated and anxious about what had happened, saying his fingers were tingling and that he "felt bad." Tests showed, however, that his blood pressure and electrocardiogram were within normal limits, and that his blood tests did not show the usual changes normally found in a person who has received an electrical shock. He was, however, admitted and kept overnight for observation. There was nothing in the record that Baxman had complained about pain in his shoulder and there was nothing to indicate that he had burned his hand in the incident.

After the incident in September, Baxman contended that he could not work because of the fears and anxiety he had as a result of the shock he had received, and so he began receiving weekly workmen's compensation benefits. The insurance company, which was paying Baxman, arranged for him to consult with a psychologist concerning his anxiety problems, and he saw this therapist several times over the next several months. His condition was diagnosed as post-traumatic stress disorder.

In December, Baxman consulted with an orthopedic surgeon complaining of pain in his right shoulder. At one point, he said he noticed the pain while he was wallpapering, but later he claimed he had had the pain since the electrical shock episode in September. X-rays showed that Baxman had arthritic calcifications in the form of a spur in the shoulder joint, a condition, which builds up over the years from excessive strain. (Baxman had earlier been a pitcher for a number of years.) Because the pain did not respond to normal therapy, the doctor felt that the spur should be surgically removed. This operation was conducted in January and Baxman spent several months thereafter recuperating.

Since Baxman claimed that he had injured his shoulder when he was thrown to the floor by the electrical shock, his doctor agreed that a trauma such as that could aggravate the underlying arthritic condition in the shoulder sufficiently to result in the pain and loss of function Baxman was found to have had when he was seen in December. Now, in addition to disability supposedly resulting from post-traumatic stress disorder, he now claimed disability from the shoulder problem, which prevented him from working as a welder. He continued, therefore, to receive workmen's compensation benefits.

Under the Workmen's Compensation Act, a person injured while working may not sue his employer in a law action but is entitled to receive workmen's compensation benefits. If he can show, however, that his injury was caused by the negligence of a third party, other than the employer, the injured person may sue that third party in court to recover all damages available under the common law.

When Baxman brought his action against Helmund Company and the manufacturer approximately two years after the so-called electrical shock incident, he was still contending that he was suffering from fears and anxiety, and that he still had problems in his shoulder, both of which prevented him from working as a welder. The insurance company continued paying him benefits. Indeed, the workmen's compensation carrier had even arranged for Baxman to take courses, which would qualify him for work in another area. Yet, he still did not return to full-time employment. (After the action was filed, we did develop information that Baxman was playing golf on a regular basis.)

I had had some experience with electrical systems while working as an electrician's helper several summers as a teenager. My knowledge of the nature and characteristics of electricity was sketchy, however, and I knew next to nothing about how welding equipment worked. As is so often true in products liability cases, I had to be educated quickly about welding machines and how they functioned, sufficiently to defend this action. Old Joe and Henry tutored me on how the machines operated.

Basically, a welding machine works on low voltage and high amperage. The high amperage provides the bright hot arc in the hand-welder created by the two currents travelling through the cords coming together when the trigger on the hand-welder is activated. This arc melts the solder contained in the welding rods so as to create a weld, which will harden as it cools.

Joe explained that electrical shock you receive off a wire is the result of voltage, not amperage, and that the voltage emitted from the welding machines is less than what you normally would find in an outlet in your home. The amperage, however, can cause a burn if your hand comes in contact with the arc (Baxman did not have a burn). He and Henry explained that when Baxman pulled the cable connector off the terminal with the welding machine still turned on, it would have created a flash, caused by the high amperage, but that there would not have been an electrical shock associated with it because the voltage is so low and the connector held by Baxman was so heavily insulated.

He and Henry demonstrated this for me several times on a welding machine similar to the one in question by reenacting what Baxman said he did at the time of his alleged "shock". In each instance, all that happened was that there was a bright flash from the connector coming off the terminal, but no shock to the person who was removing the connector or burns to the hand.

Joe went on to tell me that he could actually hold the bare terminal while the machine was on without receiving a shock. Now Old Joe had worked with welding equipment for more than 50 years, but being leery myself of the nature of electricity, I was a little skeptical of what he was saying. He ended my skepticism very quickly, however, by going to the machine, turning it on and setting the dial to the same amperage as it was at the time of the incident in question, and then holding the bare terminal with one hand, turning to smile back at me while he was doing this. Joe did point out that if you were barefoot, wore leather shoes, or was standing in water, you could feel a mild shock, still less than what you would receive from touching an open wire on a house light, for example.

As part of our investigation into this claim, we talked to those men who had been near or at the scene of the incident, and as it turned out, one of them had actually witnessed what happened when Baxman went into the room. Watching from the outside, this witness said that Baxman walked up to the welding machine on the right, that he grasped the connector on the cable and pulled it off the terminal creating a bright flash; that Baxman dropped the connector and backed away; and that he then came out of the room making accusatory statements about "that stupid technician".

The case proceeded along with the usual discovery. I took the deposition of Baxman, and he came across as evasive and quibbled about the wording of questions posed to him. He had trouble explaining a number of inconsistencies, including the fact that the hospital record had no entry stating that he had complained about his shoulder. Baxman acknowledged playing golf, but said he was told to do so in order to relax and overcome his anxieties.

Joe was deposed and did well under questioning by plaintiff's counsel. He was straight-forward, convincing and direct in his answers. When he described how the welding machines had such low voltage that you could hold the terminal while it was live, the plaintiff's attorney could not hide his puzzlement.

Baxman's counsel also arranged to take the videotaped deposition of the orthopedic surgeon who had performed the operation on Baxman's shoulder in order to present it to the jury at trial. Videotaped depositions of attending physicians have become routine in personal injury cases such as this. After preliminary type questions to bring out a description of the plaintiff's medical problem, the treatment provided, the extent of his disability, and the prognosis, the plaintiff's attorney will always conclude with a hypothetical question to establish a causal relationship between the accident or incident and whatever medical problem the plaintiff has, one of the legal requirements in this type case.

In this case, the question went like this: "Now doctor, I ask you to assume that Mr. Baxman, your patient, had the underlying arthritic condition involving a spur in his shoulder, as you found; that prior to the accident in September, he had had no pain in his shoulder; that while working as a welder, he grasped the connector of a welding cable attached to the terminal of a welding machine turned on; that in removing the connector he received a severe electrical shock which threw him to the concrete floor where he landed on his shoulder; and that he had pain in the shoulder after that up to the time you saw him in December. Now assuming those facts to be true, do you have an opinion as to whether there was a causal relationship between the incident in September and the shoulder problem you found he had when you first saw him in December which required surgical removal of the arthritic spur?"

When the doctor answered "Yes", he was then asked to give his opinion, which as anticipated, was that there was a causal relationship in that the underlying condition which Baxman had, symptom-free before the accident, was aggravated by the trauma of the fall resulting in pain and loss of function.

The doctor's opinion, of course, was based entirely upon the facts he was asked to assume, namely, Baxman's version of what happened. During my cross examination of the doctor, after posing questions aimed at bringing out various points we relied upon, such as Baxman's failure for several months to complain of pain in his shoulder, I asked the doctor to assume a set of facts which were based upon the evidence we had, focussing particularly on the contention that he was not thrown to the floor as he was contending.

At first the doctor tried to duck the question by saying that those were not the facts presented to him by his patient, but I countered by saying "Yes, I realize that, doctor, but I ask you simply to assume the set of facts I have given you, and ask again that assuming those facts, would there have been a causal relationship between the incident in September and the shoulder condition you found in December?" Grudgingly, the doctor quietly answered "No, on those facts, no." I had the answer I was looking for.

We were getting close to trial. Plaintiff's attorney was looking for a settlement and had made a demand of $130,000. The manufacturer had offered $35,000 and I had offered nothing, pointing out that Helmund Company was small, with little assets and had no insurance and that, in any event, there was no basis for the claim against it.

As the trial approached, I conferred with the attorney for the manufacturer about how to best demonstrate to the jury what Joe and Henry had shown me earlier at their shop. One thing I had learned was never to conduct a live demonstration in a courtroom before the jury because if anything can go wrong, it will do so. I have seen this happen on several occasions and the effect upon the jury can be devastating.

So long as you can convince the trial judge that the conditions of the demonstration are the same as what transpired at the time of the incident, videotapes of demonstrations are routinely accepted into evidence. Unlike a live demonstration in front of the jury, you know precisely what the videotape will be showing, but even better, in asking the trial judge in advance of trial for permission to use the videotape, as you must, you are also showing opposing counsel the key weapon you will have at trial, in this instance one that is hard to refute.

So we arranged to have what Joe had earlier shown me recorded on videotape and we presented copies of this to the judge and opposing counsel. The latter, after having viewed the videotaped demonstration did an effective job of covering his dismay over what he saw, but I could tell that he was stunned by these developments.

As shown on the video, there was only a flash, but no shock when the connector was pulled off the terminal. Moreover, when Joe held the live terminals, he received no shock. When these events were being filmed, the dial on the welding machine, visible in the pictures, showed that the current was at the same level as it was when Baxman had his incident.

Plaintiff's attorney had retained an electrical engineer to support the plaintiff's claim, a man I had concluded had had no experience with welding equipment, and apparently, this self-styled expert could not explain why Baxman had received such a severe jolt sufficient to knock him to the ground from merely holding the connector when Joe Helmund was able to hold the live terminal with his hand without any adverse effect.

The complexion of the case for the plaintiff had changed completely, and being an experienced trial attorney, plaintiff's counsel realized the problems he faced. He knew, from having deposed Joe Helmund, that Joe, with his vast experience with welding equipment, would be a very convincing witness for the defendants at trial, particularly in contrast to the plaintiff. And the videotape, which the judge was going to allow to be shown to the jury, was compelling evidence supporting our position that although there was a big flash when Baxman removed the connector, an electrical shock would not have been associated with the flash.

The manufacturer was willing to pay the $35,000, which had been previously offered, and plaintiff's attorney was willing to drop the case against Helmund Company for a nominal sum far less than what it would have cost for me to try the case for the estimated seven days of trial. Having in mind that an adverse judgment could have crippled the business Old Joe had worked so hard to develop, the result we had obtained was very satisfying.

But in truth, I felt that this favorable result was primarily attributable more to Joe, what he had done, what he stood for, and the type of convincing person he was, rather than to anything I had done on the case. Old Joe died several years after this case was resolved, but he died knowing that his little company, still active and profitable, was a tangible asset in his estate.

FENDING OFF A $60 MILLION CLAIM

Johns Manville had manufactured asbestos cement water pipes for many years. These pipes, varying in size from eight to 15 inches in diameter, were composed of hard cement mixed with a small percentage of asbestos fibers, which served as a bonding agent. In earlier years, before the development of hardened plastic pipes commonly used today, the cement pipes were used throughout the United States.

In the New England states, however, it was soon discovered that the hardness of the water in some locales would, over time, eat away on the interior of the cement pipes. Initially, the pipes were coated inside with a tar mixture to protect the interior from this corrosion, but this eventually could affect the taste of the water. JM technicians then came up with the idea of coating the inside of the pipes with a vinyl coating which was cleaner and would not alter the taste of the water, while still protecting the interior from the corroding effects of the hard water.

In order to spray the vinyl coating onto the interior of the pipes, the vinyl materials had to be reduced to liquid form. To do this, JM used trichloethelyn (TCE) as a solvent with the vinyl material so that it could, with the use of a long nozzle, inserted into a pipe, spray the interior. TCE for many years was a standard chemical used as a solvent in many commercial applications, including dry cleaning. Because TCE, when exposed to the air, dried very quickly releasing its chemical properties, it was considered to be the most effective liquefier for the spraying process.

Large subdivisions of single family homes were sprouting up in various communities in Eastern Massachusetts during the 1970's. The new roads and homes in these subdivisions required the extensions of water systems into the various subdivisions to service the new houses. In almost every instance, JM asbestos cement pipes, with the vinyl coating, were installed in these new water lines. Personnel in the water departments in these towns found the new lining of the JM pipe was far better, in terms of the taste and quality of the water, than the tar coated pipe used before.

Water quality technicians from the State routinely tested the quality of water in the towns, and in the latter part of the seventies, they began testing for the presence of chemicals such as TCE. This was at a time when concerns were developing about the possible relationship between industrial chemicals and certain types of cancers. Tests had been conducted by exposing rats to TCE, for example, and the rats over time, were found to develop cancerous tumors. As a result of these tests, water quality people on the national level established a maximum safety level on TCE in drinking water of 20 parts per billion (PPB) Any water found to be over that count was considered to be unsafe for drinking.

It was never clear how these health technicians had extrapolated the results of the testing on rats to the use of water by much larger humans. Rats, of course, are small creatures, and the dosages of TCE to which they were exposed in these tests were highly concentrated and were administered repeatedly over a long period of time. Moreover, those conducting the tests used a breed of rat determined to be especially susceptible to the development of cancerous tumors.

This was at a time when there was a lot of publicity about relationships between cancer and industrial chemicals of various types and different chemical compositions. This raised public concerns about the health risks involved, and in Massachusetts, the Public Health Department, wanting to be doubly safe, set a standard of 10 PPB on TCE in drinking water.

As a consequence, when a technician from the State went to an individual town to check the water quality, they also conducted tests to determine whether TCE was present in the water, and if so, at what levels. These tests revealed levels of TCE ranging form 5 PPB to 70 PPB in water taken from water lines in a number of towns.

The higher concentrations were found to be in the water of JM asbestos cement pipe recently installed in new subdivisions, particularly those lines which terminated in dead-ends. For example, the highest readings were from lines in new subdivisions where only a few house had been sold. The water lines in these lines had had little use or flow, and indeed, the water was lying stagnant in some of those lines. Water taken from lines consisting of the same type pipe, which had been in regular service for several years were found to have little or no TCE.

State health officials contacted JM about their findings, and the company immediately sent qualified personnel to review the test results and to investigate the situation. They concluded that after the spraying process, when the vinyl was drying, not all TCE used as a solvent evaporated into the air, and that, as a consequence, there were still small amount of TCE in the lining of some of the pipes. They found, however, that the residues of TCE would be removed if water were flushed through the lines and released through the regular flushing valves (e.g. fire hydrants).

This information was passed along to the individual towns which in turn set up programs to flush water through those lines, which showed higher levels of TCE in the water. With publicity about the presence of TCE in these water systems, increased concerns, and even fear and panic, about the health risks became overwhelming in some communities. Some people felt that flushing might not remove all TCE and that, to have 100 percent safety, all JM supplied pipe should be removed and replaced, an extremely costly proposition. JM was willing to recognize financial responsibility for the extra testing and the costs of flushing, but would not recognize the need for the very costly removal and replacement proposals.

In August of 1982, JM, faced with liabilities of many thousands of personal injury cases, in which plaintiffs claimed they had developed lung diseases from exposure to asbestos in insulation materials, filed against it and its associated companies across the country, commenced Chapter 11 proceedings seeking protection in the Bankruptcy Court in New York City. Following the filing of this application, the Bankruptcy Court issued an order staying all law actions against JM and if affiliates until an acceptable reorganization plan was worked out. Anyone having any claim against JM was required to file the claim in the bankruptcy proceeding for resolution.

The office of the Massachusetts Attorney General, acting on behalf of some 40 towns, had been in negotiations with JM's counsel concerning the claims of the towns to recover the costs associated with the presence of TCE in some of the water systems. Some of those towns, however, were seeking recovery of the costs estimated for the removal and replacement of the JM pipe, which represented huge costs. When JM refused to recognize those estimated amounts, the Attorney General filed a claim in the Bankruptcy Court in New York in the JM proceeding. The claim was for approximately $60 million, and JM, of course, denied the validity of the claims.

The claim filed by the Attorney General in bankruptcy remained dormant up until June of 1986 when the Bankruptcy Judge, Leonard Lifland, set the matter down for a trial so that he could determine what, if any amount, the claim should be. The attorneys representing JM in the bankruptcy proceeding pointed out to the Court that the claims were extensive and complicated, involving some 40 towns in Massachusetts, and they requested that JM be allowed some time to conduct discovery in order to determine the nature of the claims, what evidence existed concerning them, and allow the parties time to prepare for the trial.

Although there were 40 towns which had records requiring review in preparation for trial, Judge Lifland allowed just two months for discovery and preparation. At this point, JM contacted me to conduct the all-important discovery and to prepare and conduct the trial in New York, scheduled to begin in mid-September.

JM had always been a good client. I accepted the assignment and asked Paul Killeen, a bright and energetic attorney who had worked with me on a number of complicated cases, to assist me with this assignment. In order to accomplish the necessary discovery and prepare for trial in such a short time, however, I had to enlist the services of almost all the attorneys in our Trial Department.

Some were sent off to review water department records and depose town officials of the various towns. Others were assigned to research the studies and tests which related to TCE, consider the validity of the argument of the Attorney General that the presence of TCE in drinking water, even in very low levels, was a serious health danger, and line up expert witnesses on our side of the case. Still others were assigned the job of researching the law relating to the various, different types of claims the AG was making and prepare a comprehensive brief contesting the legality of these claims for filing with the court.

When discovery was completed, we also planned to prepare a comprehensive analysis, for submission to the Court, of what each town was claiming, compared to what was actually found in the records of the towns and through the depositions of the town officials we were conducting. Many towns, we were finding, were relying on TCE test results which were conducted several years before, showing levels of TCE at 15 PPB, for example, when recent testing taken from the same locations showed little or no TCE. The levels of TCE, as had been predicted, had gone down through flushing or the normal flow of water through the lines, which was the position JM had taken from the beginning.

On the scientific side, we found experts who questioned the validity of using results of testings on rats to establish standards for TCE at 20 PPB in drinking water, and were particularly critical of the Massachusetts standard of 10 PPB. One of them calculated that cancer could only develop in humans by drinking two to three gallons of water with TCE at levels around 200 every day for some 25 years. As an interesting side note, it was discovered in our research that TCE in diluted form was given to persons in South America in the 1920's as a type of medicine to eliminate pinworms.

As we approached the trial date, Paul and I were ready to defend the claims of the towns. We had evidence lined up, both as to the science and technology, and also to show how the claims for the costs of new water systems were bogus. But there turned out to be one major glitch. Paul and I discovered less than two days before we were required to file our brief with the Court that the attorney assigned to oversee the research and write the brief, who shall remain nameless, had not done so. The legal issues in the case were extensive and complicated, and a great deal of work was required to brief all those issues properly.

The younger attorneys designated to do the legal research had done their job, but the more senior attorney who was actually supposed to pull together the arguments and write the brief had not written anything. Paul and I took over this task, and working all day and into the night, we pulled together a brief containing our arguments for filing within the time allowed. Needless to say, we were not at all pleased with the lack of performance by our partner. I never gave him another assignment after that.

Trial before Judge Lifland began on September 22 1986 in the Federal Courthouse in New York City. Paul and I traveled down to New York the day before the trial to confer with JM's bankruptcy counsel and to organize the mass of evidence we had and prepare generally for the trial. The

Attorney General's office sent a team of attorneys, headed by John Cratsley, who later became a well-respected Superior Court judge. John did not have a great deal of trial experience, but he was a dogged, hard-working advocate, with high ethical standards.

Since they had the burden of going forward with the evidence, they had come down several days earlier to line up their witnesses and organize the documents they planned to use. Although I had handled cases in the Federal Courts of other states, I had never conducted a trial in New York City. Moreover, I had never defended a case in which the opposition was seeking to recover $60 million. Although I was confident that we could defend these claims, nevertheless, with all of JM's New York counsel and its own in-house attorneys looking on, I was concerned and nervous as we began the trial.

After we presented opening arguments to the Court, John Cratsly began the presentation of evidence through the testimony of health and water department officials from several of the towns. They attempted to establish that the TCE in the water lines was sufficiently high that the JM piping should be replaced in the interest of health safety.

They were relying, however, mostly upon test results obtained several years earlier, and on cross-examination, I was able to bring out that recent testings showed either no TCE or levels below 10 PPB. Under my questioning, they also had to acknowledge that traces of TCE in the water were eliminated through flushing of water or the passage of water through the lines through normal operations.

If the trial continued, it undoubtedly would have taken at least four weeks to be completed. After three days of trial, however, and with the encouragement of Judge Lifland, attorneys for JM, along with their bankruptcy counsel, conducted intensive settlement discussions with the lawyers from the Attorney General's office.

Paul and I did not participate in these discussions because JM's bankruptcy counsel said it was important for us to focus on the trial while they worked on a possible settlement. (New York City attorneys have a reputation for their aggressiveness, and I felt that, since they had been sitting in at the trial, they wanted to play some role to justify their presence and share in the benefits of the results.)

Finally, after hours of haggling back and forth, it was agreed that the claim of the towns would be fixed at $4.5 million, which was approximately what it had cost the towns to conduct periodic testings for TCE and to flush certain lines which showed levels of TCE. The case our office worked so hard to prepare in a very limited time, was over. Our long-time client was very pleased with the result: as a result of effective discovery and trial preparation, $60 million claim had been reduced to $4.5 million.

MY LAST TRIAL

When I started my law career in 1962, it was not unusual to see attorneys in their seventies still active in practicing law. "Age, wisdom and experience" were recognized virtues in those earlier times, and those senior attorneys were greatly respected within the profession. Caught up in the excitement and challenge of trial work in those early years, I had visions of continuing my law work beyond age 70, and I could not envision leaving my career while still in good health.

In the early eighties, however, my law firm set up a mandatory retirement age of 70. (You also had the option to retire at age 65, with limited retirement pay.) As I approached age 65, after 35 years of a very active trial practice, my views on retirement shifted and I began to look forward toward the day when I would be able to retire with some financial security, namely after I turned age 65. My plan was to retire effective on April 1 1998.

Over the three month period before the retirement date, I notified my clients of my decision to retire, while trying to substitute other attorneys within the firm as contacts with those clients. I also took steps to pass along to others in the Trial Department the active cases I was handling, wrapping up by trial or settlement as many of these cases as I could. One of these cases I had taken over just three months earlier.

Back in October 1997, I had been asked by Paul Troy, the new Chairman of the Trial Department, to take over a case which had been pending in the office for four years, involving a complicated lease dispute between our client, Enos Marine, a small company involved in repairing and servicing marine engines, and the landlord, a wealthy owner of a marina where Enos was located.

Enos had a very favorable rent under the terms of its long-term lease, far less than normal market value, and the landlord was attempting to terminate the lease based upon various alleged grounds. We had filed a preemptive action seeking to enforce Enos' right to remain on the property.

The attorney in the firm, who had been handling the case, had spent many hours on discovery and pretrial motions, generating large billings which the financially strapped client, after a time, could not pay. Since Enos had not paid its bills, our attorney asked the Court to be allowed to withdraw as counsel for Enos, a significant rupture of the attorney-client relationship. The Court did not, however, allow the request to withdraw.

The firm management wanted me to take over and try to move the case along toward resolution. The attorney-client relationship between the firm and Enos Marine had soured and I could see that the firm wanted substitute a seasoned trial lawyer to placate the client and to avoid any criticisms from Enos later concerning how the case was handled. After reviewing the file briefly, and realizing the role I would be playing, I agreed to handle the case. I did so, recognizing that I might never be paid for my work. (And indeed, although we did eventually receive a fee, as it turned out, I did not receive compensation myself for my work on the case.)

In reviewing the voluminous files on the case, it was obvious that the only way the dispute could be resolved was to press for a prompt trial which would either result in (1) a decision upholding our client's right to remain on the property, or (2) a settlement by which Enos would give up its claims under the lease in exchange for a payment by the lessor.

The attorney on the other side was Colin Smith, a seasoned attorney from Gloucester. After sparring with him for two months on pretrial matters, the case finally went forward for trial in Essex Superior Court in mid-January 1998. Prior to trial, I had submitted a settlement proposal to the lessor-defendant, pointing out that if the Court held that the long-term lease was still valid, the lessor, over a 15 year period, would lose approximately $350,000, representing the difference between what my client was paying in rent, compared to the rent the owner could obtain in the current open market. I proposed that if the lessor paid Enos $220,000, my client would end the lease and vacate the premises, allowing him to rent at standard rates.

The defendant lessor was unwilling to pay anything close to the demand figure, and so the trial began. Over the first three days, I presented background evidence through four witnesses and various exhibits. Some of this evidence contradicted key allegations the defendant was relying upon in seeking to terminate the lease.

Each time such evidence was presented, I stared meaningfully over at the defendant, as he sat on the side bench, listening to the testimony. Since the defendant was vulnerable on these key points, I was looking forward to calling him as a witness and cross-examining him. I informed Colin Smith that I intended to use the defendant as my first witness on the fourth day.

When I arrived at Court the next day, Mr. Smith approached me to discuss settlement. I think the defendant had come to recognize that his stint on the stand would be anything but comfortable. After going back and forth, it was finally agreed that, in exchange for my client giving up all rights under the lease and vacating the property, the defendant would pay $130,000 cash, give a note for an additional $50,000, and waive all claims for past rent. The landlord had been harassing our client in various ways for several years, and Enos was more than happy to take the money and move its business to another location.

This settlement required the preparation of various documents, which were not completed and signed until some six weeks later. I made certain, however, that the settlement would be completed and the payment made before my April 1 1998 departure date.

The morning of my last day with the firm, I met Colin Smith to conclude the settlement on the Enos Marine case. We exchanged executed settlement documents and I received the promissory note running to Enos and a bank check for $130,000. The check was endorsed over to our firm with the understanding that our unpaid fees and outstanding disbursements, would be deducted from the amount, with the balance paid to our client. I thanked Colin for his cooperation and wished him well.

My last official act as a member of the firm was to present the check to the firm's Managing Partner, explaining how this difficult case had been settled, the fact that we had recovered all our fees, and how the settlement check was to be handled. Even though I was not offered any part of the fee we received, I left the firm with considerable personal satisfaction, having settled a difficult case in a positive way. Yes, there is something to be said for "age, wisdom and experience."

CALM, COOL AND COLLECTED

When I was serving in the Army in Germany in 1956, I bought a print of the professional soldier depicted in Rembrandt's "Man in the Golden Helmet". This rolled-up print, carried back by me from Germany, languished among the paraphernalia I had collected until I began working as a trial attorney in 1962. Seeing a relationship between what I was doing and what the painting signified, I dug out the print, had it framed, and placed it on one of the walls of my office at Sherburne Powers and Needham.

The soldier in the painting appeared self-contained, battle-hardened, and quietly confident. Reflected in his face there appeared a readiness for warfare regardless of what the odds might be. Except for the overly grim expression on his face, his countenance, for me, represented what a trial lawyer should be when he or she was confronted with the realities of an adversarial court contest. Namely, they had to display at all times the appearance of being calm, cool and collected.

There are many reasons why a trial attorney must appear to be self-assured, confident and unruffled while participating in trials or other court proceedings. First of all, the clients he represents and the witnesses he will be using are usually very nervous and tense about participating in a trial, and in order to provide them with reassurance, confidence and morale support, the lawyer must come across as being calm, composed and confident.

Moreover, even if you have concerns about your case, as trial attorney, you must still reflect a sense of self-assurance in dealing with opposing counsel because if you display hesitancy, nervousness, or anxieties, they will immediately interpret this as a sign that your case has weaknesses. This is also true of his dealings with judges. When you present arguments to a judge about legal points, you must do so forcefully and with confidence.

Not all attorneys are able to hide the anxieties and concerns they have in taking a case to trial. Described here is the example of a lawyer who, when faced with the pressures of a difficult trial, clearly lost his confidence and composure. He was defending an action I had brought on behalf of a young woman who was injured while riding as a passenger in a rental car. The car was being driven along a major highway when it drifted slightly to the right, and then when the driver steered back to the left, the car abruptly turned to the left, crossing three lanes and smashing head-on into the center barrier. The driver said she could not control the steering as it veered to the left.

An engineer I had retained to check the wrecked car found the front tires to be significantly under-inflated, and expressed the view that the soft front tires would have contributed to the uncontrollable swerving of the rental car. My plaintiff had sustained injuries to her knee, which left her with a permanent disability even after surgery.

Our case reached trial before a jury in Superior Court. I had made a demand to settle the claim, which I thought, was fair. The attorney for the rental agency, in his late thirties, was from a defense firm in Boston (i.e. a firm that typically represents insurance companies). I had never run across him before, but I sensed that this case, involving complicated products liability issues, was beyond his trial experience. Several days before trial was scheduled to begin, he offered, as I expected, about a third of what my demand was. I replied that that would not do and we should be ready to go forward with the trial.

When we got to court and were waiting for the case to be called, opposing counsel approached me to inquire again about settling, and I replied that they would have to come up with an amount much closer to our demand figure in order to settle the case. I was calm in what I told him, but he became visibly agitated. Although the corridor we were in was cool, sweat began to run down his forehead as we talked. I liked my opponent and tried to make him feel better by saying, "Fine, I can understand if you can't get additional funds, and we'll simply try the case". This seemed to make him even more nervous. After some delay, we empanelled a jury and then the trial judge recessed the case to resume the next morning.

When I arrived at court the next morning, defense counsel, still in an agitated state, came up to me to ask if we would come down a little on our demand. I could see he was caving into the pressures he was feeling, and in a way, I felt sorry for him. I conferred with my client, and after several back-and-forths on figures, with frantic calls by the distressed defense counsel to the insurance carrier, he finally came up with a figure close to our demand.

When we accepted this figure, he breathed an audible sigh of relief, and we reported to the judge that the case was settled. Defense counsel was unable to maintain the appearance of being calm, cool and collected, and when I saw that he was palpably fearful of trying the case, I held tight on our demand, ending up with a settlement, which was more than what I otherwise would have expected.

When you are trying a case in front of a jury, you are always mindful of the eyes of the jurors, who are sitting silently within the jury box, watching and assessing your performance, not only when you are questioning a witness, but also when you are simply sitting at your table taking notes while opposing counsel is asking the questions. Recognizing that you are always "on stage", you must not show any visible adverse sign the jurors may pick up from the expressions on your face.

There are often times when your witness will unthinkingly give an answer, which is very damaging to your case. When this occurs, your stomach may turn over, but you must grit your teeth and not show any discernible reaction, proceeding along routinely, with self-assurance, as if nothing unfavorable had occurred.

Later, if you have a chance to talk to your witness during recess or lunch while he is still on the stand, you can point out to him what he had said. Often, he has no recollection of having given such a dumb answer or is nonplussed as to how he could have given such a damaging response. Later, if he is still on the stand, you can ask questions seeking to clarify what he had said earlier.

In the situation outlined above, it is necessary to maintain a "poker face" which does not reflect any reaction to the adverse answer. There are other times, however, when your facial expressions can be used to silently convey signals to the jury. For example, when you are cross-examining an adverse witness and he gives far-fetched or exaggerated testimony, a mild expression of disbelief can have the effect of causing jurors to consider the testimony more critically.

Facial expressions such as arched eyebrows, looks of puzzlement or frowns, can be used even as you sit at your table listening to the answers of a witness to the questions of opposing counsel. An expressive face can do a lot. If you have already conveyed to the jury an attitude of calm and self-assurance, an occasional facial expression reflecting disdain or skepticism, at an appropriate time, can be even more effective.

Some judges are known to bully lawyers through veiled threats and comments in front of the jury. When this occurs and has gone too far, you must stand up to the judge to protect the rights of your client. But you must do so in a calm yet forceful way to be most effective with the judge.

During one trial I had in the Federal Court, actually my longest trial, the presiding judge kept pressing me to speed up the presentation of my evidence for the plaintiff, warning that I would have only so many more days to present my case. I knew this judge fairly well and had considered him generally to be fair-minded, but for some reason, he had "a bug" about facing a long civil trial. (On the other hand, judges never seem to be concerned about how long a criminal trial may take.)

In this case, I was representing a computer company in a complicated anti-trust case in which we claimed that the defendants had engaged in a conspiracy to restrain trade. I had to present evidence on specific points in order to make out a claim, which would be legally sufficient. In attempting to conclude the case within the fixed period of time he had set up in his mind, the trial judge was in effect precluding me from presenting all the evidence I would need to support the claim legally.

When he began making these "hurry up" comments in the presence of the jury, implying that I was wasting time, I finally had had enough. I asked to approach the bench, and with the stenographer present to record what I was about to say, I calmly told the judge that I objected to the prejudicial remarks he was making in front of the jury which would make them think I was wasting their time; that I should be allowed to present my evidence without obstruction, particularly having in mind that opposing counsel had made no objection; and that if he continued to obstruct me in what I had to do as plaintiff's counsel and made any further prejudicial comments with the jury present, I would move for a mistrial.

The judge was no fool, and as noted above, usually he was fair in dealing with counsel. He recognized, I am sure, that he had gone too far, and at this stage of the trial, he did not want a motion from me for mistrial. After that, he said not one word about "hurrying up" with the evidence, and the trial proceeded along smoothly toward a conclusion.

Almost all the seasoned trial attorneys in Boston handled themselves as the professional soldier depicted in Rembrandt's painting, confident, unflappable and self-assured. Several of them, however, stand out in my mind. Tom Burns, for example, for many years and into his seventies, acted as defense counsel in some of the most serious liability cases. As one of the "lions" of the Boston trial bar, he was highly respected by judges and fellow attorneys. I was involved in several trials with Tom, representing co-defendants in those cases, and so I had a chance first hand to observe him in action.

In his later years, Tom usually had associate attorneys in his office prepare his cases for trial and lining up the evidence and legal arguments Tom would be presenting. He approached even the most serious case with a tremendous sense of self-assurance and good humor. Nothing rattled him. Oh, to be sure, Tom could, at an appropriate time and for special dramatic effect, show disdain, disbelief or anger to make a point with the judge or jury, but other than that, he was wholly controlled and composed.

Tom and I participated in a hard-fought two-week trial in which I represented Ford Motor Company and Tom was defending the auto dealership on a very serious personal injury claim involving a small boy. In this case, there was definitely a defect in the car which did contribute to the injury, and instead of being allied in defense, each of us was actually attempting to place the responsibility for the defect and the accident on the other defendant, careful to do so in a calm, civil way.

The one thing which stands out in my memory of Tom from this difficult trial was that during each recess or the lunch hour, while I was busy preparing for the next witness or whatever, Tom, a real history buff, would take out one of Winston Churchill's book, and sit calmly reading it at his defense table. The guy was amazing. The jury ultimately returned a verdict finding both defendants liable, but awarding damages much lower than anyone expected.

Another trial attorney who, for me, personified the calm composure of the professional soldier was Jim Meehan. Jim handled both the defense of liability actions but also represented plaintiffs in cases of that type. Some of the cases Jim was assigned to handle were gruesome in their details, and yet Jim handled them calmly and with good humor. Indeed, perhaps to be able to deal mentally with those type cases, Jim displayed almost a macabre humor in discussing them outside the courtroom.

Nothing and no one could intimidate Jim. One time when he was still relatively young, Jim was trying a case before an ill-tempered, impatient judge in his late seventies (this was before the rule was adopted that all judges had to retire at age 70). The judge had taken a dislike to Jim and the party he represented, and was sustaining every objection raised by Jim's opposing counsel, thus encouraging even more objections.

Back in those years in order to preserve the right of appeal from adverse rulings of the trial judge, it was necessary for the attorney against whom the ruling was made, to verbally state on the record "my exception to your Honor's ruling". In each instance the judge sustained an objection and disallowed Jim's question, Jim carefully noted his exception.

Finally, the trial judge got so irritated with Jim's taking exceptions to his rulings, he bellowed at Jim, "The next time you take an exception to my ruling, counselor, I will hold you in contempt of court." Jim calmly walked up to the bench, looked the judge in the eye, and with a small smile, said, "I take exception to the statement your Honor has just made."

The judge's face reddened and he was about to respond when his trial clerk, who had worked with the judge for many years, turned and spoke to the judge in a whisper. Realizing at last that his bad temper was taking him over the bounds of judicial propriety, the old judge, still visibly fuming, sat back in his chair and the trial proceeded in more orderly fashion.

Many trial attorneys routinely display the characteristics of the professional soldier. Al Zabin, Leo Boyle, John Cannarton, Bill Dailey, and Allen David come to mind, to mention a few. And one of the more important features of the professionalism these attorneys display is how, even in the most hard-fought contests, they always treated their fellow attorneys, their adversaries in court, with civility and respect. This, too, is an important component of being calm, cool and collected in courtroom battles.

The man in the golden helmet

COURTROOM TACTICS

In some of the stories I have written about cases I have tried, there were descriptions of strategies used in the trials, namely, how the evidence was marshaled and presented either to advance the claim or raise the defense. This article will focus not upon strategies, but rather upon trial tactics, techniques used during the trial to facilitate or enhance the presentation of your evidence, while hindering or diminishing the evidence of you adversary.

In planning for a trial, the trial attorney must decide what evidence can best advance the case he wants to make. This usually is in the form of testimony or something tangible, such as a document. Some evidence, upon objection of opposing counsel, may be excluded under the Rules of Evidence by the trial judge.

If such evidence seems important, the attorney seeking to have it admitted should consider alternative ways of getting it before the jury, and this may involve inducing opposing counsel into making a misstep. There are also instances when you have a perfectly valid objection to certain evidence the opposition will be offering, but for tactical reasons, you choose not to assert the objection. Let's look at an example of what I'm saying.

There was a dispute between a window supplier, who wanted payment for windows it had supplied, and the contractor who had ordered the windows. The supplier had forwarded an order form, which contained contractual terms, to the contractor. The form set forth a fixed price for 340 "window assemblies" which were to be delivered to a construction site by a certain date. Before signing and returning the form, the purchasing officer for the contractor called the manager at the supply house to verify that the term "window assemblies" included frames for the windows, and once he was assured of that, he signed and returned the form.

Several months later, the windows were delivered at the job site, but they did not include frames. When the purchasing officer called the manager to question this, he was told that this order was only for windows and did not include frames. The contractor had to obtain framing from another source, at increased cost, resulting in serious delays in the completion of the project. The parties were soon involved in litigation over the dispute, and I ended up representing the contractor. The case could not be settled and eventually went to trial before a jury.

The supplier's attorney relied upon the completed order form and the testimony of the manager that they supplied 340 "window assemblies" as required by the written agreement. The manager was also asked by his counsel whether he had a discussion with the defendant's purchasing officer about how payment would be made following delivery. Now, since there was a written contract, this type conversation, upon objection, would usually be excluded (i.e. the so-called parol evidence rule). For tactical reasons, however, I did not object, and the manager testified that the purchasing officer told him they would pay within two weeks of delivery.

When it came time for the presentation of our evidence, I called as our principle witness the purchasing officer and had him describe what he did when he first received the order form. He recited how he saw the term "window assemblies" and called the supply house manager to ask what the term included. When I asked what the manager said, opposing counsel immediately was on his feet, loudly objecting to any oral discussion seeking to vary the terms of the written contract.

All I had to do was remind the judge that the conversation which occurred between the two men was already opened up through questions by "my learned brother" during the direct examination of his own witness. (In the courtroom, we often referred to our adversary as "brother", or in the case of a woman, "my sister", which I came to realize caused a great deal of puzzlement among the jurors who were not familiar with courtroom etiquette). The average judge usually enjoys catching a lawyer in a tactical mistake, and as I expected, he ruled "Yes, counselor, you already opened this up; your objection is overruled." The crucial discussion about what the term "window assemblies" meant came into evidence, and later, the jury returned a verdict in favor of my client.

There was also another instance when you know that the witness you are about to cross-examine, for example, had sent a written report to a third party setting forth a description of critical events which are contradictory to the story he has just given during his direct examination. And yet, you were unable to obtain a copy of that document because the third party had not retained it. The witness, however, does not know this, and when you question him, you play upon concerns and insecurities he has as to how much you know and what you may have.

After asking some innocuous preliminary questions, you begin moving on to more accusatory type questions, aimed at challenging his credibility. As the witness becomes increasingly uneasy, you move deliberately over to your table, search through a file, and extract a one-page document, which you then study carefully. Standing some distance from the witness, holding the document before you, you ask, "Now, isn't it a fact, Mr. Jones, that you wrote a report letter in March of last year to Mr. Johnson at XYZ Corporation about this very incident?" The witness, seeing you holding what to him looks like a letter, slowly acknowledges that he did write such a letter.

Looking again at the document you hold, you ask, "And in that letter, Mr. Jones, you said [thus and so], isn't that a fact?" As his attorney, who knows nothing about the letter, looks on with a perplexed expression, Mr. Jones reluctantly admits that he may have said that in the letter. You follow with "And that is contrary to what you testified earlier as to what had happened, isn't that so?" Looking abashed, the witness concedes it could be viewed as being a different version.

You then look pointedly at the jury, and say, with a trace of disdain in your voice, "No further questions of this witness, your Honor." Returning to your table, you slip back into your correspondence file the document you have been holding, a letter from the court scheduling the case for trial. Never once during this interrogation have you said anything to suggest that the document you held was the letter in question, but ah yes, the power of suggestion.

A few trial attorneys utilize not so much tactics, but rather subtle tricks, to gain an advantage, for example, by distracting the jury during a high point in the opposition's evidence. Various ruses are employed to do this, but the most popular is the "falling book" trick. The trickster lawyer would bring to court every day a very large book, which he would place on the edge of his table toward the jury box. A juror, seeing it sitting there, would assume that it contained important law relating to the case at hand, but actually, it was for an entirely different purpose.

Just when opposing counsel has asked the key question of his most important witness, and as the witness is concluding his crucial answer, the trickster would nudge the book over the edge of the table to crash loudly on the floor. Then appearing perplexed, he would apologetically move to retrieve the book, smiling at the jury in an embarrassed way, hoping, of course, that jurors have been thoroughly distracted from the crucial evidence they have just heard. The good old "falling book" trick.

One time, in the midst of a complicated case I was handling in the Federal Court, and while opposing counsel had one of his key witnesses on direct examination, I dropped a large book on the floor, and truly embarrassed, I, too, went through the apologetic routine. This was not, however, calculated on my part and had truly been inadvertent.

Several minutes later, we had a conference with the trial judge at the bench about some point of evidence. The judge was John McNaught, who had, for many years, been an accomplished trial attorney, representing plaintiffs in personal injury cases. When we concluded our discussion at the bench, Judge McNaught turned to me and said very sincerely, "Steve I commend you for what was one of the most convincing falling book performances I've ever seen." At that point, I was not inclined to tell the judge that I did not believe in using tricks such as these in trials and that it was simply an accident, and so I mumbled "Thanks, judge", and walked away.

Indeed, I always felt that ruses such as these went over the line, and in my experience, only a few attorneys used them. There were, however, other types of tricks trial attorneys would sometimes employ in their desperation to win a particular case. And when they were your adversaries, you had to be especially vigilant. There was a case in which I represented Johns Manville in defense of a claim by the owner of a large warehouse that the roofing materials JM had furnished were defective, and that as a result the roof had begun to leak after 10 years of service. The owner was represented by an experienced trial attorney, I shall call Michael Norris.

Michael practiced law by himself, working out of a modest walkup office in downtown Boston. He was a short, muscular man, then about 55 years of age, with a flattened nose and cauliflower ears, but he could be ingratiating and did have a certain charm and affability, which he used effectively before, juries. It was easy to like Michael, but I had learned from having had other cases with him that he had plenty of "street-smarts" and was a dogged and dangerous adversary. You had to be on "your guard" with Michael at all times.

On the claim against Johns Manville, Michael not only claimed the cost of a new roof but also had claims for damaged goods and merchandise stored in the warehouse, which supposedly had been damaged from rain leaking into the building. The plaintiff was seeking $175,000, a large sum in those days. Michael, I know, was handling the case on a contingency fee basis, whereby he would receive one-third of the amount recovered.

One of our defenses was that the defects in the roof (blisters in the membrane) were the result of poor installation. In addition, we contended that JM had issued a 20-year roofing bond in the amount of $25,000 to cover any and all defects and that the owner accepted the bond in lieu of any other warranties. Michael, however, claimed that his client did not have the bond and had no record of receiving it. Fortunately, JM's bond office kept a copy of this bond and had a record of having mailed it to the owner 10 years earlier when the roof and been completed and inspected.

The trial began jury-waived in Suffolk Superior Court. Michael presented evidence for a day and a half, resting just before lunch break at 1:00 p.m. the second day. Before going to lunch, Michael sidled up to me and asked to see the bond I was planning to introduce through my principle witness in the afternoon. He earnestly studied the bond, with little comment, and I than returned it to my file. In those days, the courtroom doors were locked for lunch, and it was customary for attorneys to leave their files on counsel tables during the lunch break.

When I returned from lunch, Michael was already in the courtroom checking through his papers. I chatted with my witness, and then went to obtain the bond from my file to show him. The bond was gone. The document was very easy to recognize because it was rather fancy, slightly oversized, with a fancy green filigree border around its edges. Thinking I may have placed it in another file, I frantically went through all my papers, but could find nothing.

I asked Michael if he had seen the bond, and he stated with all innocence that he had not. Then, from a short distance, I saw at the bottom of a pile of pleadings on Michael's table, the telltale green edging of the bond sticking out slightly. I asked Michael, "Isn't that the bond there?" Michael, without batting an eye, lifted up the papers on top, revealing the bond, and said, "Oh, I must have picked it up by mistake."

I thought for a moment that I would bring this to the attention of the Judge, but I knew that Michael, in his ingratiating way, would simply say he had picked the bond up by mistake and that would be the end of it. Instead, I proceeded with the presentation of my evidence, introducing the bond as an exhibit.

Months later, we received the Court's decision in which it was held that the plaintiff was controlled by the terms of the roofing bond and could only recover the $25,000 which the bond provided. Plaintiff fell far short of the

$175,000 they hoped to recover. Yes, Michael was a likeable guy, but you did have to be careful in dealing with him.

Steve Hopkins and Paul Killeen preparing for trial, circa 1982

LOOKING BACK

My goal, upon graduating from law school, was to become a trial attorney. I viewed trial work as an honored profession, which would allow me to provide unique services to clients through protection of their legal rights, while competing with my adversaries within the framework of the ethical rules.

Everything worked out as I had hoped, and I spent the next 36 years handling and trying cases in and around Boston, and as far away as Providence, Rhode Island; Portland, Maine; Hartford, Connecticut; New York City; and Washington DC.

You really cannot enjoy trial work unless you are willing and ready, at all times, to be "on stage" prepared to play the central role in the drama of a trial. While going to school, I had lead roles in several plays and also was assigned to give speeches in public. I did not feel uncomfortable in these activities, and indeed, often enjoyed them.

Later, being center stage in a trial never bothered me. Trials, in many respects, are like a stage play, with the attorney acting as both director and lead actor in presenting the story of your client's case. He must organize the cast and direct their performances, while knowing fully each player's script. He is always in a lead role himself, but while performing, he must at all times study his audience (the judge and the jury) to assess how the performance is playing out.

Yes, I did love trial work. One of the younger lawyers in our Trial Department, a woman, told me, as I was about to retire that she viewed me as "the model for a trial attorney". "God must have known", she said, "what your future avocation would be when you were made." I am not sure God thinks of those things, but she was right in that I cannot imagine that I could have been as in any other occupation or profession.

Yet, as I look back on my career, I would be less than candid if I did not acknowledge that there were developments toward the end of my career that diminished the satisfaction I had in my work and adversely affected the profession. Without intending to tarnish the positive aspects of being a trial attorney, I do want to share with you some of my thoughts and concerns about those recent developments.

When the courts first implemented discovery procedures, the purpose behind those procedures was to allow each side in a case to develop and assess all the evidence before trial. Discovery involved the questioning in advance of trial, by way of depositions, of parties and witnesses; the production of documents through discovery requests; and written interrogatories requiring answers from opposing parties.

When used for the purposes intended, namely the development of evidence to enable the attorneys and their clients to better assess the merits of their cases, the discovery procedures were very beneficial. With the aid of discovery, trial preparation was more thorough and there were not as many "ambushes" during the trial when you suddenly were faced with an unexpected bombshell. This also encouraged settlements.

In the earlier years, there were fewer trial attorneys in Boston, and within this group, we came to know and respect each other. Opposing attorneys in the bigger cases I began to handle, on the whole, were capable, reasonable, and ethical practitioners. Judges, too, were generally better versed in the law by this time, in contrast to when I first began my practice. Also, it became mandatory that judges retire at age 70, and you no longer had to face old, crotchety judges (although there still were a few young crotchety judges.) As a consequence, trial moved along more smoothly.

Since discovery did increase the work of the party to whom it was directed, however, some lawyers, unfortunately, began to use discovery, not so much as a way to find the truth, but rather as a method to overburden an opponent. Some large corporations promote such tactics in the hope their opposing parties could not financially sustain further litigation.

There are lawyers, I am sure, who sincerely believed that discovery, rather than the trial itself, was what litigation is all about. (I referred to them as "litigators", not trial attorneys.) But all too often, particularly later in my career, I found discovery was sometimes being used as a method to harass the other side, while, let's face it, creating increased billable hours for the offending lawyer, resulting in higher fees from his client.

The success of discovery in developing evidence and narrowing factual issues in a case necessarily depended upon the honesty and ethics of each trial attorney and the parties he or she represented, to respond fully and truthfully to discovery requests from the opposition. Cases involving claims of corporate wrongdoing are more easily proven through discovery of a so-called "smoking gun" memorandum, which reflects unlawful conduct by officers within the corporation charged. I found instances in the later years, however, where it seemed clear that documents such as these did indeed exist, but were either destroyed or withheld from production.

Some attorneys became more interested in winning at any cost than they were in "playing the game" by the rules of ethics. It is one thing for a party to be willing to do anything to win, but attorneys are governed by the Canon of Ethics which set forth strict guidelines on what is acceptable in adversarial situations, and it is up to the attorney to channel his client in the proper direction.

Apart from these developments, there were also notable changes in how attorneys dealt with one another. In earlier years, members of the Boston trial bar, even when they were opposing each other in hotly contested cases, treated one another with courtesy and civility. Unfortunately, in recent years, some attorneys who have been coming along have the attitude that, to be successful, they must adopt an aggressive "pitbull" approach in dealing with opposing counsel, attacking and obstructing them as much as possible.

When I was about to retire, I wrote to various attorneys I had respected, with whom I had trials over the years, telling them of my plans and saying how much I valued them as adversaries. A number of them were nice enough to respond. Included at the end of this particular section are excerpts from some of those letters which reflect how much they, too, value courtesy and civility in the difficult, contentious work in which we engaged.

You tend to move along in your career without giving much thought as to how you are perceived by your peers, and as you move into retirement, it is especially gratifying to know that those, in the best position to evaluate your work, namely your adversaries, had generous views of you, particularly in the areas of courtesy and civility, which seems to have been slipping away.

Another factor that has developed which, in my mind, resulted in negative changes in the nature of trial practice had to do with the commercial emphasis placed upon the practice of law. Law became less of a profession focussed upon skillful service to clients, and more upon practice as a business, with the prime goal of increasing firm profits.

As with any law firm, each lawyer was required to maintain a certain quota of billable hours, all aimed at maximizing the firm's fee income. They were also assigned hourly rates which, over time, went higher and higher. Hourly rates of $400 were not uncommon. The billable hour requirement sometimes resulted in the "padding" of hours so an attorney could meet the quota assigned to him.

Based upon what I heard and observed, our firm, when I was there, was not as caught up in the money-making push as were some of the other firms in Boston and elsewhere. We did, nevertheless, have a few attorneys whose primary focus, it was clear, was to make lots of money. Moreover, those with high levels of fee income, regardless of how it was derived, were often treated within the firm with a respect bordering on reverence. "Money was king." This kind of attitude, unfortunately, is not limited to law firms, but is prevalent throughout the country in various areas of enterprise.

In the trial practice, the push to increase billable hours and make money encouraged some litigators to take depositions, for example, of witnesses who clearly had little or no knowledge of facts bearing on the issues in the case. Or they would spend three days asking repetitious or needless questions of a witness (with one or more associates sitting in attendance) when the deposition could have easily and effectively been concluded in one day, with one attorney present. There was an obvious increase in useless discovery, and I attributed it in part to the emphasis to increase billable hours and firm profits.

The commercialization of the law and the emphasis on profits have added greatly, in my mind, to the cynical attitude, which the general public has developed toward lawyers. Lawyer jokes are not funny; they reflect the scorn many people now have toward the law profession which now ranks along with used car salesmen in opinion polls. Many see lawyers as motivated by self-promotion and greed.

I am not alone in having concerns about present day law practices. Other trial attorneys, with whom I have been friendly over the years, often discussed with me these very same problems. Too many students, I fear, are now selecting law as their careers, not to join an honored profession which would afford them the chance to provide valuable services, but rather as the golden opportunity to earn high levels of income.

The larger law firms, moreover, have consistently encouraged this attitude by paying graduates, fresh out of law school, ever increasing salaries, recently going as high as $150,000 per year. Such salaries for untrained graduates, in my mind, are ludicrous, particularly when you consider that skilled, veteran teachers receive half that amount.

Compare this starting salary with what is paid to experienced lawyers who work in the public service areas, such as in the Bar Advocate Programs, performing the important function of representing indigent defendants in criminal cases. They often earn around $40,000. And how are these ever increasing levels of salaries in these big firms to be covered? Why through increased fees to clients, by way of more hours and higher billing rates, of course.

You may ask, "Why, if you love the law as you say, do you write disparagingly about it?" It is because I do love the law profession, and what it should be, namely an honored profession, that I am writing about these things. Other than writing, I am not in a position now to do anything about it.

Hopefully, this essay may be read by a student in law school, or one who is considering law school, and maybe it will influence them to approach the practice of law as a respected profession, and not simply as a business geared to make money. Maybe a law firm leader will read this and recognize that what I say is true and try to do something about it within his own firm. An executive in a company, reading this and facing ever-increasing legal fees, may scrutinize more carefully the bills he receives and ask critical questions about the need for some of the work described in the bill.

These comments will not make me popular with the "beancounters" who will continue to emphasize the need to increase hourly rates and billable hours, but I do believe there are many active attorneys who, reading this, would agree with me. Maybe they, too, will step forward and assert themselves more by resisting and reversing these recent trends. For the sake of what I have always considered an honorable profession, I surely hope so.

LETTERS UPON RETIREMENT

Russell Conn, Boston.
"Your work epitomized the happy balance, now frequently missing, of thorough and aggressive advocacy on behalf of a client, without sacrificing a professional and courteous respect for one's opponents."

Leo Boyle, Boston.
"The combination of intelligence, wisdom and gentlemanliness which you brought to the litigation world is indeed a rare thing. I fear that those qualities may be becoming rarer as the years go by."

Albert Zabin, Boston.
"I have always thought of you as one of my outstanding colleagues and adversaries. There are very few trial attorneys these days who mange to combine intellectual power, trial skills, and dedication to the cause of the client and civility and honor."

John Connarton, Boston.
"You have always been a perfect example of what it meant to be a true trial lawyer with knowledge and capacity to be a gentleman and worthy adversary."

Allen David, Boston.
"Somewhere along the line, there developed the unfortunate notion that disagreement between counsel involved in litigation had to translate into personal disagreements. Neither of us ever subscribed to that notion. It has been a pleasure to be involved in cases with you over the years, and a privilege to have been able to observe someone who always conducted litigation according to the highest personal and professional standards."

CHAPTER IX. MOVING INTO RETIREMENT

During the first half of my 36-years of service to my law firm, in Boston, the firm did not have a mandatory retirement age, and some lawyers stayed on as partners into their early eighties. In the latter part of the 1970's, the firm, then larger in size, adopted a mandatory retirement age of 70, and if someone wanted to retire earlier, they could do so at age 65.

It soon became apparent that some members of the firm, whose lives and self-image apparently revolved totally around "being a lawyer", found it very difficult to retire under this new policy. Some attempted to work out special arrangements so that they could stay on in a reduced capacity. Others, who did retire, feeling the pull of their life-long routines, frequently came back to the office and wandered longingly through the halls or sat alone reading in the library. It seemed that, sadly, they had no other interests or pursuits to occupy the time they had in their "sunset" years.

As noted above, I thoroughly enjoyed my career as a trial attorney, and yet, as I approached retirement age of 65, I concluded that it was time for me to move on, and indeed, I began looking forward to retirement. But then, I knew that there would be various activities and interests I would want to pursue, including writing stories.

When it came time for me to retire in April 1998, I was able to walk away from the work I had been performing for 36 years easily and without any pangs or backward glances, anxious to begin my new role in life. To be sure, after I left, I have maintained contacts with my friends at the law firm, but for me there is no prowling the halls of the firm, seeking to recapture myself in the role of attorney. The door to that chapter in my life was firmly closed, and I am in a new phase, which has been most satisfying.

I am frequently asked what I do with my time. The fact is that I am very busy with trips we take and my various other pursuits, and I often find I cannot do all I would like to do. Two of the stories in this chapter discuss several travel incidents, which I now can view with humor. The others focus upon the time we spend in Anguilla in the Caribbean, where we built a home and now reside half the year, looking forward, of course, to our return each year to my birthplace, Cape Cod, for the summer months, where I am able to prowl the woods, beaches and coves, just as I did as a country boy.

WHY WE CHOSE ANGUILLA

Since Sylvia and I have always been attracted to beaches and warm sunshine, when we were looking for places to go for our winter vacations, we began looking to the Caribbean. We had tried Florida in the winter, the Sanibel Island area, but found it to be crowded and overly commercial, with the weather often "iffy".

There were certain islands in the Caribbean we would never consider for vacations because of the stories of armed robberies and other violent crimes, including murder, committed against tourists. We had not heard of these type reports about Barbados, and so decided to find out what that island had to offer.

The first year we were there, we stayed in a nice second floor unit of a small resort on the west side of the island where there were lovely beaches and the quiet waters of the Caribbean were located. Although the island seemed somewhat crowded and driving to Bridgeport, the commercial center of the Island, could be hazardous, we enjoyed swimming in the clear warm waters and relaxing by sunning on the sandy beaches.

The next year, we returned to Barbados and rented a house on the beach on the west side, along with our friends from Kittery, Maine, Frank and Susan Crotty. As before, we enjoyed the beaches and swimming, this time, sharing the experiences with good friends.

Besides having the space and openness of the house, which had a large porch on the seaside, we also had the benefit of a housekeeper who cleaned up after us, doing dishes and such. Sylvia insisted on cooking since otherwise our handy handmaiden would have handled those tasks as well.

There were, however, two incidents, which affected my attitude toward the island. The first one took place when I was swimming in the water in front of our house and noticed a young local cruising down the beach, peering here and there. I had pulled a chaise lounge down onto the beach and had left my towel on it, taking off my watch and placing it on the towel.

As the young man approached the chaise lounge, I could see his head turn toward it, and sure enough, in a flash, he ran up, grabbed the watch, and sprinted quickly down the beach. I yelled loudly at him, knowing that it would merely spur on his running, which of course it did.

The thief, I am sure, thought he had secured a prize, but fortunately for me, the watch was a $20 Timex (always kept perfect time though), which was hardly a valuable possession. But this was not so much the loss of an object, but rather the realization that there were brazen thieves on the island. To be sure, he did not come up to me brandishing a gun in order to rob me, as could happen on some islands, but it was a crime nonetheless which affects your sense of security and trust.

The second episode is actually quite humorous, although it did reinforce the concerns we now had about the level of honesty of some of the local inhabitants. Frank and I were sitting on our porch as the sun was setting in front of us, having our evening beverages, in my case my old standby, Mt Gay rum and soda water with a lime. The girls were off somewhere in the rental car.

As we sat savoring our drinks and the view, a young local entered through the gate in the wall in front of the house, and approached us. He said he was related to our housekeeper and had learned from her that we were looking for lobsters and that he could get some for us from friends he had down the beach.

Indeed, we had, that morning, asked our maid where we could get some lobsters, and so this story sounded completely plausible. Our new entrepreneur friend explained that we would have to pay a deposit and that we could pay the balance when he came back with the lobsters. He wanted

$20, but being cautious, after some haggling, we agreed to give him $10. Off he went down the beach.

We resumed our sipping, wondering aloud about the reliability of our agent and whether we had just lost $10. Well, within 20 minutes, he was back holding a large burlap bag. It was now dusk, and instead of coming up to the porch, he remained at the opening in the wall, which seemed odd. Frank and I walked out, and our friend reported he had four lobsters and that we owed him another $30.

Following my father's advice never to buy a "pig in a poke", I asked to see the lobsters, and when he seemed reluctant to do so, asking for the money first, I went on "high alert", refusing to give him anything until we saw the lobsters. As I reached for the bag, the guy let it go and ran off down the beach. I lifted the bag, which felt very light, and looking inside, found a collection of lobster shells, apparently our helpful friend's version of the "shell game".

To be sure, he got away with our $10, but how did he possibly think he could fool us to obtain an additional $30? Did he perceive us as such easy targets that he could get away with this ridiculous ruse? You become totally disillusioned when a person passes himself off as friendly and helpful when in fact his goal is really aimed at ripping you off. You begin to wonder who you can trust.

We related this misadventure to the wives when they came back home, and they got a good laugh out of it, at our expense of course. Yes, it can be viewed as comical, but nevertheless, these petty acts of thievery lead to misapprehensions and a basic lack of trust, feelings which are not compatible with vacations. This, at least in part, resulted in our deciding not to return to Barbados. We began, instead, looking elsewhere in the Caribbean for our winter vacations.

The summer after the trip to Barbados, we were at the Land Ho in Orleans, a popular bar and eatery, and began chatting with the owner, John Murphy, about our interest in the Caribbean. John, it turned out, had been taking his family, including two young boys, and vacationing in Anguilla in the British West Indies.

John extolled the virtues of Anguilla, telling about the great beaches and clear waters; the lack of crowds and the low amount of crime; the stability of the government, which was affiliated with the United Kingdom; and the honesty and friendliness of the local people.

Based upon John's glowing reports, Sylvia and I scheduled our next winter vacation for a stay in what was then a small resort right on Shoal Bay, one of the island's best beaches. (At the time, the resort, now known as Shoal Bay Resort, had two buildings with 13 units; it now has five buildings, with 31 units.)

The beach at that time was quiet, with few people there and the main action was at Uncle Ernie's, which was next door. Our unit, which was right next to Uncle Ernie's on the third floor, was large, with a balcony looking to the west from which we usually watched the sun set over the water. It was wonderful.

It did not take us long to recognize that everything John had told us about Anguilla was true. The second day we were there, for example, we were driving up the hill from Shoal Bay, heading for the Valley to pick up groceries, when we spotted an older local man trudging up the hill carrying a heavy burlap bag. We stopped and offered him a ride, which he gladly accepted. As it turned out, he had about two miles to go to his house.

We chatted with him as we moved along. We told him we were staying at Shoal Bay. And we learned that he was a fisherman with a small boat, which he used to fish off Shoal Bay. He was carrying in his bag the catch of the day, consisting of lobster and crayfish. When we asked if he would sell us four crayfish, he immediately agreed.

When we reached his home, he took four lively crayfish out of the bag, weighed them, and gave us a price of about $25 US, as I recall. It turned out, however, that apart from Travelers checks, which he could not take, we had only $10 US with us. "No problem", our new friend said, "take the crayfish, keep the $10 and pay me the $25 tomorrow at the beach." Certainly, a far cry from the lobster transaction we had in Barbados. Naturally enough, the next day, Sylvia immediately went searching for our trusting friend on the beach to be sure to pay him what we owed.

Dishonesty and betrayals lead to mistrust and alienation. Honesty and fidelity, on the other hand, create a sense of trust, which, in turn, promotes honesty and fidelity, so important in human interaction. It operates like a growing circle of trust.

This initial episode turned out to be just a series of similar pleasant contacts we had with Anguillians during that first visit. After that first trip, we returned each winter for our vacations in the sun, each time enjoying the natural beauty of the island, its waters and beaches, and finding the people always good natured, friendly and honest to deal with.

Indeed, we had become so impressed with the island and its people that, when I retired from law practice in 1998, we built a house there where we now stay for six months each year when the weather in New England turns cold. We have been coming to Anguilla now for 14 years, the last four of those years staying at our home.

In that time, we have developed close friendships with many ex-pats who either vacation here or have homes on the island. But in additional, through Sylvia's work with the Soroptimist and my singing with the St. Augustine choir and chorale, plus other contacts, we have also developed warm friendships with many local Anguillians, relationships we greatly value.

Yes, we made a very good choice in selecting Anguilla for our winter home.

Steve and Sylvia at Shoal Bay in Anguilla

HURRICANE LENNIE, A STORM TO REMEMBER

After I retired in 1998 from my law practice, now, when November descends upon us, along with day-light savings time, and the cold winds begin to blow out of the north, my wife, Sylvia, and I retreat from our home in Orleans, and head down to our house in Anguilla. It is not that Cape Cod has harsh winters, but rather, that we both prefer to spend our latter years in sunshine, on beaches and swimming in warmer waters, the Cape in the summer, Anguilla in winter.

There are several reasons we selected Anguilla for our winter home. The island, first of all, has great weather and what are reputed to be the best beaches not only in the Caribbean, but also in the world. But more important than the weather and the island's natural assets, we have found, in the years we have been going to Anguilla, that the local people are extremely honest, hardworking, kind, and good natured. The government of the island, affiliated with Great Britain, has been basically sound and the crime rate is low.

Our house in Orleans is nestled in tall trees, a combination of locust, oaks, pines and birch. You can barely see our house from the road. During northeast storms or an occasional hurricane which is able to make its way up into the cool waters of New England, we sit comfortably in our house, surrounded by swaying trees which I am sure reduce the force of the winds.

Our house in Anguilla, on the other hand, is perched high on the point of a cliff, facing southeast, with an unobstructed 280 degree view of St. Martin, St. Barts, and on a very clear day, St. Kitts. There are no trees to deflect storm winds, but only low bushes, which are able to survive the sun and exposure to the sea. On a typical day in the Caribbean, this location is idyllic. But as we soon learned after coming down here on November 3 1999, in a major hurricane, this location is particularly vulnerable to storm winds.

Indeed, when our house was being built, I knew from what was said indirectly that local people, who lived nearby, but away from the coast, had concerns about the nearness of our house to the sea. In the 1920's and earlier, Cape Codders had the same concerns about having their homes near the water. In terms of safety and maintaining a warm house snug from the winter winds, you simply did not build near the coast. But our Anguilla house, built mostly of cement, was 50 feet above the sea, on a rugged coral cliff, and we felt that, unlike a wooden house built on a sand dune, we would be safe.

To be sure, we were mindful of the fact that hurricanes originate or move through the Caribbean frequently during hurricane season. Up until Hurricane Luis in 1995, however, Anguilla had not had a serious hurricane since 1960. Still, one must be concerned about them. Fortunately, the buildings of our house were designed by Iain Smith, well-known local architect who knew first-hand the force of the winds of a hurricane, having survived Luis which had sustained winds of 180 MPH.

The buildings were very sturdily constructed of cement block walls and cement framing, with the large rafter beams embedded deeply at the top of the walls in 18 inches of solid cement. Indeed, the buildings had already gone through two hurricanes, one in September 1998 while partially constructed, the other after completion of construction in September 1999 while we were still back in Orleans enjoying the fall season there.

The hurricane season, as everyone knows, begins in July, peaks in August and September, and ends in late October when the ocean waters cool. With this in mind, our program has been to come down here in early November, after day light savings sets in and the chill winds begin to blow, thus free of the threat of any hurricane. Yeah, right!

So to prove us entirely wrong, along comes Hurricane Lennie, first spawned near Jamaica around November 8th, and instead of moving westerly or northerly as tropical storms typically do, it began heading in an easterly direction. At first, we viewed this as an interesting phenomena, but as the days passed, and Dr. Steve Lyons on the Weather Channel (never forget to call him Doctor) upgraded Lennie to a category four hurricane and projected its path toward Anguilla, then we began to pay more attention.

Still, Dr. Lyons consistently reported that the track of Lennie would pass to our north, passing us Wednesday night, November 17th, moving along out to open ocean Thursday morning. Nevertheless, on Wednesday, we began "buttoning up" the buildings, bolting preformed panels over the doors and sliding shutters across over the many windows.

Wednesday night, we holed up with our two Great Danes and one Siamese cat in our main house, with a microwave oven for cooking and TV to stay updated on the progress of the hurricane. We still had power and the Weather Channel provided constant reports for us this first night. Dr. Steve, who we thought was infallible (what with his doctorate degree and all), continued to predict that the storm would be gone by Thursday morning.

But if Hurricane Lennie violated established norms by (1) generating itself into a hurricane in November, and (2) moving easterly rather than westerly, it would also contradict the predictions of our hurricane experts as to direction and timing. We went through heavy winds and rains Wednesday night, but although they were strong, perhaps 100 MPH and directly hitting our buildings off the sea, it was entirely bearable.

On Thursday morning, however, while we still had telephone service (electricity was lost during the night), a friend called us to say that Lennie had stalled over St. Martin, 12 miles away, and it was not clear when or where it was going. So much for Dr. Steve's learned forecasts.

Having already gone through a night of heavy weather, which was still continuing, we became increasingly concerned. And rightly so. The center of Lennie, as it turned out, began moving slowly in our direction during the daylight hours of Thursday, and by nightfall, it was on top of us, still moving along slowly. Rains and winds increased sharply, and around 2:00 a.m., as I lay in bed with Sylvia and our two dogs, everything damp and wet, the storm abated. I was not sure whether the storm had passed or whether we were in the eye of the hurricane, or a portion of it.

Later, in talking to others who lived on the westerly end of the island, some 12 miles away, they told me they had experienced this temporary "lull" earlier around 9:00 p.m. After 30 minutes, it was soon clear that the storm had not passed and that we were now getting the stronger back-winds of the hurricane reported to be up to 150 mph, coming in on us off the ocean. The fact that it took so long for the eye of the storm to move 12 miles indicates how slowly it crept along.

From about 3:00 a.m. to 6:30 a.m. the winds were horrendous, lashing our buildings with driving rain and sea blast from the huge waves on the cliffs below. The noise from all this was so loud, you could barely think. Water pushed its way in around the shutters and door panels, but fortunately, drains built into the floors of each of the rooms carried this excess water away. Others on the island, as noted below, were not as fortunate.

As I lay in bed listening to the roar of the wind on our buildings and roof, I could not help but wonder why a storm should form this late in the year, grow to such strength, and head directly to our island where it decided to stall. Why did it come here? And there is a tendency to personalize it by wondering whether I had offended God to be subjected to this ordeal.

Finally, after what seemed and interminable time, Lennie moved away from us, heading southeasterly toward St. Barts and other islands down the Leeward chain, and we were able to emerge from our bunker into the open. The three buildings had withstood the impact of the storm, firm and solid, with only minor damage to some of the protective door panels. Trees and bushes were shredded by the wind, rain and sea blast, and our pool was full of vast amounts of dirt, leaves and even bushes torn up by the power of the winds. Still, we were lucky.

Others on the island were not as fortunate as we. An earlier hurricane in September, Jose, had dumped much rain on the island, flooding several low-lying areas and leaving the ground in a saturated condition. With the heavy rains of Lennie, calculated to be 24 inches, there was even more severe flooding in low areas.

People were forced to flee their homes as floodwaters rose during the hurricane. Some were not aware there was water in their houses until it reached them as they lay in bed. One woman stepped into knee-deep water, and when she opened her front door, found herself up to her neck as the water rushed in. There is also the story of a woman who spent the night holding the head of her blind, diabetic mother up above the water in their home until rescuers were able to take them out by boat the next morning.

Friday afternoon, we drove out to the East End, near our home, which had been previously flooded, and climbed to a high hill overlooking the flooded area. Many homes were under water up to the eaves of their roofs. As Sylvia and I looked upon the scene, Phoenix Fleming, from whom I had bought loads of crushed stone for our yard, came along and greeted us in his usual pleasant, smiling way. He seemed perfectly relaxed. As he passed along, a friend of his told us quietly that Phoenix' house was almost totally underwater and that Phoenix spent the night during the height of the storm, clinging to the roof of his house.

Like Phoenix, most Anguillians were philosophical and cheerful about the dangers they encountered in the storm. Each was thankful that nobody was killed as a result of the ravages of Lennie and everybody seemed prepared to begin the work necessary to return the island to normalcy. Phoenix, and his fellow Anguillians, it was clear, with their good-natured, indomitable spirit, would rise again, not from fire, but rather from the floodwaters. And indeed, that is exactly what they have done.

Within a week, we had our electricity restored at our home. Within three weeks, power was restored to the whole island. Having in mind the damage to the poles and wires, this was a remarkable achievement. New, hard-packed roads were constructed in a few days, up and over hills, to afford access around the flooded areas. People who were forced from their home by the floodwaters moved in with others, as extended families reached out to help. Within two weeks, except in the badly flooded areas, where water was still receding, the island had pretty much returned to normal. Sylvia and I had not misjudged the resilient people of Anguilla.

But one thing we learned was that nothing could be taken for granted. Hurricanes can develop in November. They can move easterly, rather than to the north or west. And you can, indeed, experience a taste of the fury of nature in your island paradise retreat. But you accept this and carry on.

TRAVELLING WITH PEACHY

Since my retirement in April 1998, my wife Sylvia and I have been taking innumerable trips out of the country. Many of these involved our going and coming from our winter home in Anguilla, but there have been other trips to Europe. Sylvia (when I feel a special fondness for her, I call her "Peachy") handles the logistics for these trips and does a remarkable job in lining up inexpensive flights, and when necessary, car rentals, reservations at hotels, and on two occasions, rentals of canal barges.

Most times, these trips have been accomplished without a hitch, but other times, there have been major or minor calamities of one sort or another. I will describe here two of those misadventures, one involving a trip to Anguilla, the other, a trip to Europe.

Sylvia (a.k.a. Peachy) and I, along with our two Great Danes and her two cats, were scheduled to fly down to Anguilla in early November 1999 to stay for the winter. These trips require the use of two dog containers, the largest allowed, and because of the size of these containers, plus the other things we normally take down, we necessarily have to rent a small trailer to accommodate those items for the trip to Logan, with the dogs confined in the back of our Explorer.

For this particular trip, our friend Michael Pare had generously offered to travel with us to Boston in order to bring our car and the trailer back here to Orleans. Michael seldom ever drives into Boston, and he demonstrated extreme valor (or maybe ignorance) in offering to handle the chore. Little did he know what he was getting into.

For several months before our trips to Anguilla, Sylvia stocks up on various household things she feels she needs to have down there. These items pile up over time and then, just prior to departure, Sylvia packs them into an enormous trunk, with wheels, which she had obtained on sale from Walmarts. In addition to this, we also have normal luggage for clothes and other sundry things.

Each time we are getting ready for the trip, I tell Peachy that she's "taking too much stuff," but even though I use terms of endearment, she pays little heed to my concerns. This time, I pointed out that the trunk seemed particularly heavy, but Sylvia assured Michael (he was staying over night at our house) and me that it would pass through as baggage without any problem.

The flight to San Juan from Boston, the first leg of our journey, was at 7:00 A.M., which meant that we had to get up at 2:30, leaving the house at 3:30, for the drive from Orleans to Boston. The weather forecast was for the morning was rain. The trailer was already packed, and bleary-eyed, the three of us and our pets, with me driving, left the house exactly at the time appointed.

When I was about a mile down the road, Sylvia asked if I had the tickets, and I automatically felt into the jacket pocket where I always keep them, only to realize that I had, in the rush of getting out of the house, left them on the kitchen counter. With the trailer behind, I did not want to stop and turn around, and so I did a loop around on Main Street, to Meetinghouse Road, and back along Hopkins Lane to the house, grabbing the tickets to resume our trip. Not the best way to start.

We did not have just rain that morning. It was a real northeaster with heavy rain being driven hard by strong winds, gusting up to 60 MPH. With the wind whipping against the car and the trailer, causing them to veer to the left, the two-hour trip to Boston was tense and arduous. For me, as I gripped the steering wheel, it was the proverbial "white knuckle" trip.

Finally, we arrived the departure area for American Airlines, secured the services of a luggage attendant, placed the dogs readily in their giant containers, and, with the assistance of porter, began moving the containers, luggage and trunk on dollies inside to the ticket counter. Michael was left to attend the car at the curb until we had been cleared for the flight.

All went well with the dogs, but when the overloaded trunk was placed on the scale, the weight registered 140 pounds. "Sorry", said the clerk, "this will have to go as air freight." I said "fine, please designate it as freight," but she said that this could only be done at the American freight office, which was in another part of the airport, about a mile away.

Naturally, with the flight taking off in less than an hour, I could not carry the trunk to the freight office. Out to the curb we went to tell Michael about our predicament and what he would have to do before returning to the Cape. He did not, of course, have any idea where the freight facility was. Moreover, he was hauling a trailer and the storm was still raging.

But Michael stoically said he would take care of the 140 pound trunk, although he looked anything but happy about the prospects. After getting directions, off he went on his mission, and Sylvia and I went down to the gate to await our flight.

We learned later from Michael that, after a number of missed turns, all difficult to handle because of the trailer, he finally found the American freight office. After a lengthy wait, he was able to talk to an attendant who wanted to know specifically what was in the trunk, and of course, Michael could not say. They then required that he open it for their inspection, but since the two end-handles were locked with a chain and Michael did not have keys to the locks, they had to cut through the chain to gain access (making the trunk, of course, now vulnerable for theft).

Finally, around 11:00 A.M. the freight office completed the necessary papers, the trunk was closed and sealed with shipping tape and it was accepted for air shipment delivery to Anguilla. Michael, who thought he would be back to Orleans by 9:00 A.M., did not get back to return the trailer to Brownie's until 2:00 in the afternoon.

To be sure, the first leg of that trip was, for me, especially harrowing because of the drive to Boston in the roaring storm. But the trip for Michael, the good Samaritan, was even more difficult. Since that time, Michael has not offered to assist us again on this part of our journey, and I can't say as I blame him.

The second trip problem I will tell you about related to a trip Sylvia and I had planned to Europe in late September 2000. This was a two-week trip we were looking forward to eagerly. We were scheduled to land in Paris, take the TGV fast train to Avignon where we would stay overnight, pick up a rental car and then travel through Southern France, on to Nervi in Italy for a night, up to Merano in the Italian alps to stay with friends for three days, on to Munich for two days, over to Strasbourg, and then back to Paris where we would stay with my cousin, Carol Denis, for three days, in the condo she and her husband, Gonzague, owned.

Peachy handles all of the logistics for our trips, often using the Internet. As noted above, she obtains airline tickets (usually at the lowest possible prices), secures reservations for rental cars and hotels, and determines what clothes to pack. And other than over-packing, she does a fine job.

All these plans had been made for our trip to Europe, and on the appointed day for departure, we were all ready to go. Our friend, Bob Munson drove us to the bus stop in Barnstable for the bus ride to Logan where we were scheduled to fly out on the American Airlines flight to Paris at 9:00 P.M.

The day was clear and sunny. We arrived at Barnstable some 15 minutes before the bus arrived. The bus trip moved right along and we arrived at Logan around 7:30 with plenty of time to check in. Now our trips usually have one hitch or another, but everything was moving along perfectly, indeed so perfectly that I should have known something would go wrong.

As we waited in line to check in at the American counter, two old friends from Manchester-by-the Sea where Sylvia and I lived before returning to the Cape, entered the line behind us. We greeted them and learned that they, too, were flying to Paris and would be staying in a town in Southern France close to where would be on one of our nights. As we moved along in the line, we made plans to get together on that particular day.

Full of excitement and contentment, we moved up to the counter to present our tickets and passports and check our bags. When the clerk opened my passport, however, she pointed out that it had expired and that we would not be able to fly out to Paris with an expired passport. Sylvia and I looked at each other completely non-plussed. Peachy had grabbed our passports from my desk, and instead of taking my active passport, she had taken the expired one by mistake. Neither of us had checked the passports after she had picked them out.

Ordinarily, you can get a replacement passport from Immigration Services in Boston fairly quickly, but it was nighttime and getting a substitute passport was not an option. After the circumstances of our predicament had finally sunken in and we realized that we would not be flying out that night, we concluded that the only thing we could do was to return to Orleans in a rental car, pick up the active passport, return to Boston the next day for the same 9:00 flight.

With great embarrassment, we went to our friends from the North Shore who were still waiting in line, and explained what had happened. They thought the whole thing hilarious, pointing out that once, when they had arrived at the airport for a flight to Greece, they discovered that they had forgotten to bring along Dick's passport.

This did make us feel somewhat better, but the prospect of returning home and then going through the same two hour trip back to Logan the next day was not appealing. (Since that time, we have been told five different stories about people forgetting their passports, losing them, or putting them in their luggage which had already been checked.)

Well, we asked for a compact car at the rental agency, and had the good fortune of being given a roomy, comfortable Buick for the ride to the Cape. We rode along home in style but the mood was very subdued. We said little to one another. I could not muster up the word "Peachy". But, of course, what's done is done.

We spent a quiet day at home, retrieved the active passport, and embarked again on the trip to Logan. Somehow it was not as exciting as our trip the day before. Everything went along smoothly after that, and except for the fact that we had to cancel our stay at one of the French hotels, we had a wonderful tour through France, Italy and Germany.

There have been other problems, which have cropped up on the trips we have taken, especially with the trips Sylvia has taken by herself. For example, one time when she arrived at the airport in Anguilla for the 1:40 American Eagle flight to San Juan, her usual 15 minutes before the flight time, the clerk, who had had prior experiences with Sylvia, told her she was actually booked for the morning flight that day. As it turned out, there was space for her on the afternoon flight, and they arranged to get her on, although just before the doors of the plane were shut.

There is a story her friends (including Michael) tell about taking a trip with her years ago, before I knew her, back from Florida. She had purchased and was carrying back a large bag of grapefruit. After the plane had landed and as they were getting up to move off, the bag burst, and grapefruit began rolling up and down the aisle causing complete confusion among the other passengers seeking to disembark as they sought to avoid the rolling fruit. Sylvia was only able to retrieve half of the grapefruit that had wandered off.

On my trips with Sylvia, even when everything is going along nicely, until I'm on the plane and actually flying out, I have the disquieting misgivings that something will surely go wrong. Yes, travelling with Peachy can, at times, be hazardous. Just ask Michael.

MAD COW'S DISEASE

Whenever we travel down to Anguilla, we carry along a large cooler of food items Sylvia has pulled together. This container, weighed down heavily with its bulky contents, fortunately has wheels, but it still requires me to muscle it around through the airports.

Although there are far more quality food stuffs available now on our small island than there were when we first started going there, Sylvia still cannot resist taking down such items as cheeses, steak tips, boneless legs of lamb, bags of shrimp, cans of tuna and dog food, and for me, more important, shellfish, which we cannot get down there. She claims they are less expensive here than what you can get in Anguilla. I never priced these times to compare with the costs in Anguilla, but I often wondered if all the work of packing the cooler and hauling it down there is worth what modest savings are realized.

Anyway, that is not the point of this story. When we arrive at our island home, we immediately unload the contents of the cooler into our freezer, ready to use at dinner parties or our routine meals. Of course, as our stay continues, new items are purchased and the freezer becomes replenished, and the amount in the freezer never seems to go down.

As we approach the time when we are to return to the Cape, the freezer still contains a quantity of food items. We keep the refrigerator going when we leave since it is better, with the salty moisture that exists, that it continues to operating since otherwise, it can corrode quickly.

Sometimes, however, Sylvia decides that we should take back to the Cape some of the choice items we brought down, which we never got to use. Thankfully, a smaller cooler is used for this type thing. Several years ago, when we returned from Anguilla, we carried back a package of about five pounds of boneless lamb, which Sylvia had arranged for me to purchase earlier from a market in Cambridge, which specialized in that sort of thing. We had taken several packages of the lamb down with us, but did not get to use this one packet, and so, decided to take it back with us.

The first leg of our journey home was on an American Eagle flight from Anguilla to San Juan, where we picked up a jet for the direct flight to Boston. Passengers arriving in San Juan, with connecting flights to the United States, must go through United States Customs at the San Juan airport. Ordinarily, we have always found that dealing with the customs agents, at least for us, is a routine event. After all, we don't exactly look the part of shady, shifty-eyed drug dealers.

On this occasion, however, when Sylvia was asked what was in the cooler, she said some meat we had originally bought in Massachusetts, which we were taking back home. Hearing this, the custom agent went into "high alert", and directed that go into a side room. There we encountered two rather large Hispanic women, who, in their crisp uniforms, projected an overblown air of official importance. The way they looked at us made me feel that, in their eyes, I did indeed look like a nefarious drug dealer. (Surely Sylvia didn't.)

"Open up the cooler", the obvious leader of the two brusquely ordered. Inside was our packet of lamb, still in the same wrapper as when I had purchased it, which showed the place it was bought in Massachusetts. Pulling out the package and handling it as if it was a kilo of cocaine, the imposing customs official demanded, "What's this?" We replied that it was lamb we had bought in Massachusetts, as the label showed, which we had taken to Anguilla, but since we did not eat it, we were taking it back home. "Oh no, you cannot take this to the States", the leader said, "we gonna have to confus-cate this." "Why?" Sylvia and I exclaimed in unison. "Mad cow's disease", replied the woman disdainfully, as if speaking to first grade students.

"But it's lamb, not beef," we explained, and moreover, "It was bought in the United States which is not under quarantine." All this meant nothing. "It don't matter cuz of mad cow's disease", she repeated like a mantra. So what can you do? I began to think that if we continued protesting, seeing how the woman was reacting, we might very well be escorted away to a holding cell in handcuffs.

"Can we leave?", I asked, and when she nodded in a dismissive way, we headed for the door, with me muttering to myself "how stupid can you get?" Sylvia, however, had a different slant on what had happened, and when we got outside, she turned and said to me, "Well, somebody is going to have nice barbecued lamb tonight".

Sylvia arriving at Anguilla airport with her cats, November 1998

FELLOW TRAVELLERS TO CARIBBEAN

It is now March of the year 2002, and Sylvia and I are on the terrace of our house in Anguilla, looking out to sea toward St. Barts. In the distance, we notice first a water spout rising 10 to 15 feet out of the water, perhaps 200 yards off shores, and then the black fin and humped back of a whale as breaks the surface, moving slowly toward the north. As we watch, we see other whales moving in similar fashion, some large, others obviously small newborns. These are humpback whales returning back to New England after spending the winter here in the Caribbean.

Back in September of 2000, as part of my 50th High School Reunion celebration, Sylvia and I went with a number of my classmates on a whale-watch cruise out of Provincetown on Cape Cod. Along with several other whale-watch boats, our vessel was going out to the Stellwagen Banks area where humpback whales collected to feed. I had been on a whale-watch cruise perhaps 20 years before out of Gloucester, Massachusetts, and although we did see a few whales, I did not find that earlier trip to have been particularly exciting or memorable. The September trip turned out to be entirely different.

First of all, as we traveled out to Stellwagen, some 30 miles off the tip of the Cape, the naturalist who was acting as our guide gave a lecture about the whales, explaining how they congregated at Stellwagen Banks during the warm months, then travelled south to the Caribbean for the winter where they mated and gave birth. Stellwagen Banks was a raised plateau composed of sandy materials, ideal as a habitat for sand eels. Throughout this area, there was a plentiful supply of these eels, the humpback whale's favorite food. The whales gouged themselves on these eels in preparation for their journeys to the warmer waters in late October.

There are, of course, a variety of fish in Caribbean waters, but they are not the type which humpbacks feed upon, and moreover, the ocean bottom in the Caribbean, unlike the flat sandy surface of Stellwagen Banks, is mostly hard coral, typically sharp and irregular, good for small fish to hide in but dangerous for a whale to feed around. In the same fashion as bears eat heavily in preparation for hibernation in the winter, the humpback whale build themselves up by excessive feeding for the trip and stay in the Caribbean where they have little or nothing to eat.

As we cruised to the Banks on the September trip, learning as we went about how the humpback traveled from their summer home off Cape Cod to their winter domicile in the Caribbean, I assumed that, as before, we would see at a distance a few whales moving through the water. But when we arrived over the Banks area, we found our boat surrounded by humpbacks on all sides.

Some merely showing their telltale hump as they glided along the surface, blowing out spray. Others could be seen breaching as they leaped headfirst out of the water, crashing back down with huge splash. This was a dramatic spectacle. As we cruised around the broad area for over an hour, there seemed to be at least twenty whales visible from our boat during the entire time.

Our naturalist was able to recognize particular whales by the shape and markings of their tails, each assigned a different name, and over the address system, he pointed out certain ones, explaining a little about the background of each one he identified. One of those he identified had been wrapped in a fishing net for many months, with the net around its mouth hindering feeding. The netting was finally removed by Stormy Mayo and his rescue crew who worked from a Zodiac to approach the weakened whale and cut away the netting. Mayo had become an acknowledged specialist in this type of hazardous activity.

Now my wife and I feel a special kinship with the whales we see every March, moving slowly in front our island house. They come down to the Caribbean, just as we do in early November. And like us, they return to the Cape area for the warm months, enjoying what is offered here. To be sure we do not gouge ourselves before our trip to the Caribbean, but we follow the same travel schedule.

We cannot see the tails of our partners clearly, as we watch their return to the North, and even if we could, I wouldn't be able to tell one from another. Yet, I am confident that some of the whales we saw back in September, on our whale-watching cruise, are now passing slowly and sedately before us, as we sit and watch from our terrace.

THE RAINBOW ISLAND

Since home owners on Anguilla rely upon their cisterns for their water needs, it was very important that rains come along periodically so that they have enough water for personal use.

In New England, when rain comes, it covers a broad area, sometimes from Maine to Connecticut, and ominous gray clouds, which carry this rain often hang around for several days. In the Caribbean, however, rain comes through rapidly in small, isolated clouds, often accompanied by a squall with heavy winds, and if this rain front passes over your home, you might be fortunate enough to have a torrential downpour for 20 or 30 minutes, enough to put 300 to 500 gallons into your cistern.

As you sit through such a downpour, often times, you can look over to the horizon and actually see the sun shining in the distance. At any given time, it is possible to have two or more isolated rain clouds, with sunshine between them, passing over the island at different locations.

When this occurs, rainbows usually appear, sometimes as many as four scattered across the sky, some complete from end to end, others, simply half of a rainbow. Indeed, rainbows are so common in Anguilla that the island is often referred to as "The Rainbow Island".

Those rain showers can be so localized that as they approach you, you can see a definite edge between the curtain of rain coming down and the dry area. It appears as a wall of rain as it approaches. A friend told me recently that he and his wife were sitting on one end of their veranda, dry and comfortable, while rain poured down at the other end of the veranda. That is how localized the rain can be.

When the rain ends and you travel downtown, for example, you often come to a point, not far from your home, where the road and ground is totally dry. The wall of rain passed close by but did not go over that portion of the island. And whether rain comes and where it goes is totally unpredictable.

Sylvia and I had gone down to Anguilla in April of 1998, after I had retired to stay for a month. Work on our house was in progress at that point, and we were able to follow the progress of the construction of the three buildings. At that point, the buildings had been erected but were still unfinished.

On the day before we were to leave to return to Cape Cod, a Sunday when there would be no workmen at the site, we took a picnic lunch, with appropriate beverages, to our home in progress and set up on the large veranda facing the ocean to enjoy our last day.

The weather, up until then, had been totally sunny, but as we drove to our home-to-be, I noticed a large blackening cloud toward the East (weather almost always moves from East to West). Sure enough, as we set up for our little party, a distinct curtain of rain was heading from the sea in our direction. After days of sunshine, how could the cloud come now and "rain on our parade?"

Amazingly, however, as we watched with apprehension, the curtain of rain stopped moving toward us about 100 yards off shore, and then a beautiful rainbow appeared in front of us, where it remained for some five minutes. The rain curtain then passed off to our right and moved along down the channel toward the west end of the island. Rainbows are supposed to be good omens, and we saw this event as representing good fortune for our future home.

The house was finished in December of 1998, at which time we moved into it with our two cats and two Great Danes. Our male Great Dane was Spocky, a large and handsome animal, but he had been diagnosed as having bone cancer the previous September and given six-month to live. By May of 1999, his condition had deteriorated to the point that we concluded he should be "put down", and we arranged for the local veterinarian, Pat Vanterpool, to come to our house for that purpose.

In one of the most difficult things I had to do, as Spocky lay on the dog pillow on his favorite spot, the gazebo, with his head in my lap, he was administered the necessary shots. Afterwards, Pat and I placed him in a box, nailed on a top to the box, carried the heavy box to a large hole, which had been dug in our yard facing the water, and lowered the box into the hole.

We were in the midst of filling in the hole, when, as if on cue, a large and beautiful rainbow appeared off shore next to a bank of rain clouds where it remained for some five minutes, clearly representing for us another omen.

That was my poignant rainbow story. Now for a funny story, which Iain Smith told me about one of his rain experiences. Iain, who designed our house, has lived on the island with his wife, Aileen, for many years. Some years back, they were living in a small house with a correspondingly small cistern, which held perhaps 5000 gallons (our cistern holds 15,000 gallons). It had been especially dry at one point, and because the level of the water in their cistern was very low, they were planning to have the local water company bring them a truck-full of water.

There were some clouds on the horizon, however, and so they held off ordering the water to see if those clouds came their way. Sure enough, the next morning, a cloud formed in the East, blackened in color, and began heading in the direction of their house showing the typical curtain of heavy rain. Over the house the clouds moved and the rain came down in torrents.

Unfortunately, however, although the rain poured buckets into their backyard, flooding their gardens, not one drop landed on their roof where it would have gone into their cistern. The cloud passed along down the island, leaving no water in Iain's cistern.

So Iain and his wife, Aileen, concluded that they would have to obtain that truckload of water after all, and before the end of the day, the truck arrived and pumped enough water into the cistern to practically fill it up.

The next day, shortly after they had finished breakfast, they saw another isolated black cloud heading their way, pouring down rain as it moved along. Sure enough, it came over their house, but this time, instead of raining in the backyard, it hammered down on the roof of the house for 30 minutes.

Every cistern has an overflow pipe, through which water may escape when the level of the water reaches the top of the cistern. As the water from the downpour went into Iain's cistern, which was already full, this extra water passed through the overflow pipe into the rear yard where excess water had already collected from the rain two days earlier, raising the water in the yard by several inches.

Thus, by getting the truck of water, they in effect added more water to the already flooded backyard. Ah yes, the vagaries of rain in Anguilla.

Stephen A. Hopkins

THE CHALLENGE OF SCOTTISH DANCING

During my teenage years, square dance events were very popular on Cape Cod and well attended by both older couples and teenagers, such as myself, along with whomever we were dating at the time. Square dances were held regularly at the Eastham Town Hall in those years. Over time, those participating in the dances became quite proficient, with our partners, in following the dance calls and the live music with smooth coordination. Certainly, everybody enjoyed those dances, and I am surprised that square dancing has not remained a popular activity.

During the past several years, while we have been living in Anguilla in the winter months, Sylvia and I have become part of a group, which meets regularly for Scottish country dancing. The group is composed of people from Canada, the United States and Great Britain, and has included both the Governor and Deputy Governor of Anguilla. The dancing is held in the living room of a couple who built the wooden floor of this very large room especially for dancing.

Most in the group have been involved in this form of dancing for some time and are able to perform well. Scottish dancing has similarities to square dancing in that you dance with a partner, but instead of dancing in a square, with your partner beside you, you dance in two opposite rows, with partners facing each other. There is nobody calling out the dance movements, only the typical Scottish music from the tape player. Also, unlike square dancing in which there are a limited number of basic movements, there are unlimited variations of movements in Scottish dancing, I was told over one thousand.

When you go through the various steps, you dance on your toes, hopping along, putting great strain on the muscles of your lower legs. Until you get to know the movements, it is all a complete mystery. To be sure, as novices in the group, we are told what to do by others, but I often found myself hopping along gingerly on my toes, heading off in an entirely wrong direction, until somebody redirects me.

Fortunately, everybody is very good about our blunders, really humorous in a way. And when I would lament on my errors, the veteran dancers would always reassure me that I was doing "very well" (yeah, sure, I think). After several sessions, Sylvia and I began to improve. Indeed, we even could go through several of the simpler dances without any direction and free of errors.

In April 2001, the dance group had agreed to perform in a talent show being sponsored by local women's group in Anguilla. They need eight dancers to perform, but several of the veterans were "off island", as they say, and not available the night of the show. The then Deputy Governor, Roger Cousins, a good friend of ours, entreated us to complete the group, assuring both of us that "we'd do fine". Not wanting to disappoint the group or Roger, we reluctantly agreed, not without trepidation.

The first two dances our group performed were ones Sylvia and I had done before, and I hopped along through the movements accurately, although not especially gracefully. I guess the leaders of the group wanted to finish with a flourish for the audience, because the third dance was very complicated and different from anything I had done before. Sylvia and I had no idea of where to go or what to do.

It soon became a comedy of miscues, and I concluded that the best thing to do was to let the crowd know and maybe enjoy my predicament. So when I went tripping off unknowingly in the wrong direction, I'd turn to the audience, rolling my eyes, and showing mock bewilderment.

There were about 100 people in the audience, many of whom Sylvia and I knew. Anguillians enjoy a good joke, and when they saw that Sylvia and I, the two novices, had no idea of what we were doing, they all laughed with good humor, and when the dance was mercifully over, they gave us all a sound applause for our efforts.

Yes, Scottish dancing is far different than the square dancing I was used to when I was a teenager. Perhaps this is even more reason why I look back so fondly to those nights when I traveled down to the Eastham Town Hall, with my date for the evening, to participate in what I now realize were the simple movements which are part of square dancing.

Stephen A. Hopkins

BECOMING A BELONGER IN ANGUILLA

My wife Sylvia and I first traveled to Anguilla in 1988 for our winter vacation. We were both working then as trial lawyers, Sylvia in Salem and me in Boston, and after our first stay on the island, we recognized what a treat it was to leave the cold of New England and the rigors of our jobs to spend time relaxing in the sunshine on the pristine beaches of Anguilla. At first, we came for 10 days, but soon our vacations on the island became two weeks, and by 1997, three-weeks.

During those visits, we came to know and appreciate Anguilla and became friends with both local people and so-called "ex-Pats" we met. Anguilla, which is affiliated with the United Kingdom, has a sound government and little crime. The majority of its people are friendly, God-fearing, good-natured, generous and hardworking. We were impressed by these positive qualities.

As I was approaching retirement, scheduled to be in 1998, Sylvia and I began thinking about building a house in Anguilla and spending our winter months there, returning to our home on Cape Cod for the months of May through October. After looking at various properties, we finally found a nice lot, owned by Osbourne Fleming (now Chief Minister of Anguilla), high on a cliff overlooking the sea, with views of St. Barts and St. Martin.

People who come to the island from other countries are referred to as "non-belongers" or "aliens", less than flattering names. Before such a person is allowed to purchase a property on Anguilla, he or she must submit an application for an alien landholding license to purchase for approval from the office of the Chief Minister.

This application must include affidavits by a police chief and judge attesting to the applicant's good character, and the applicant must also present a listing of assets and bank accounts. The government is justifiably concerned about the character and substance of persons they allow to buy property on the island. Since we were purchasing the lot from one of the leading political leaders of the island, our application moved along, and by July of 1997, we had our "Alien Land Holder's License."

Our good friend, Iain Smith, an architect on Anguilla who had been trained in Scotland but had lived for many years in the Caribbean, developed detailed plans for our house. Actually the "house" consisted of three distinct buildings, separated by a courtyard and a pool. Iain also lined up a contractor for us, Oliver Brooks, whose company had built the Courthouse and the Police Station in the center of town, and work began in October of 1997, with a completion date a year later. (I expected to retire in April 1998.)

As it turned out, work on the house was completed so that we were able to move in on December 24 1998, not bad having in mind all the work that had to be done and the fact that there were three separate buildings which had to be connected together with wiring, plumbing, etc. We spent the next five months enjoying our new home while performing all the landscaping and plantings, which was necessary in the courtyard and surrounding areas.

We soon learned that there is a vast difference in your outlook between when you are on Anguilla for vacations and when you have a home and spend six months on the island. For example, when we were on vacation, as beach-lovers and sun worshippers, we had to be on the beach every day and would be very disappointed if clouds carrying rain passed by to block out the sunshine.

Now that we have a home, we are dependent upon rain to maintain the water in our cistern, our only source of water. Rain falls on the roofs of our three buildings, flows from the gutters into downspouts and large pipes underground leading to the cistern below the kitchen. During dry spells, which can last for two months, the level of the water in the cistern can go down significantly.

Thus, unlike before when, as vacationers, we lamented whenever a rain cloud appeared, now, we rejoice when we see large dark clouds, full of rain, approaching. And the longer it rains, the happier we are because we know water is pouring into our cistern and the level of the water (and the pool as well) will rise accordingly. After all, what's one day of rain when the rest of the week is bright sunshine. Although we still may have been "aliens", we slowly were beginning to develop attitudes more similar to those of the local people.

In addition, as vacationers, we felt compelled to be at the beach everyday. Now, we will travel over to Shoal Bay, one of the best beaches in the entire Caribbean, perhaps twice a week. Of course, having a pool does make a difference, and if I cannot swim at the beach 100 yards, as I usually do, I will swim laps in the pool instead.

Sylvia and I have now spent five winters in Anguilla, and during this time, we have become more and more part of the social fabric of the island and its people. Apart from hosting or attending dinners and cocktail parties by others, as we did before, Sylvia was invited to join the Soroptimists, a group of predominately local businesswomen, who are very much involved in various charitable activities. Sylvia was one of only several ex-Pats invited to join this organization.

Although she was never keen in the past to join and spend time with clubs and women's groups, she has faithfully worked to support the worthwhile events the Soroptimists put on, and she clearly enjoys the interaction and camaraderie with the local distaff leaders.

On Monday nights, we attend Scottish country dancing sessions, which are held regularly at the home of a nearby neighbor. The leader of these sessions, who now provides instructions for the complicated, sometimes baffling, moves of the various dances, is Peter Johnstone, the Governor of Anguilla. The Deputy Governor, Roger Cousins, had acted as the leader before he retired back to the UK in October 2002. Sylvia and I tend to stumble around, but it is fun and, since you dance mostly on your toes, it is good exercise as well.

But the really worthwhile, rewarding activity for me was my participation these past two years in the choir of The St. Augustine Anglican Church, located near our house. This choir sings at each Sunday service, but in addition it presents cantatas twice a year, at Christmas and later at Easter time.

I had attended one of the Easter performances in 2001, and later, the Christmas performance that year. I was totally enthralled and moved by the splendid singing of the chorale group, and noticing that there were only two basses in the chorale, I decided, after the Christmas performance, that I had to join. I can cover a range of two octaves, but my normal singing voice is deep, low bass.

I talked to several members of the local choir I knew about becoming a member, and they strongly encouraged me to do so. I joined the choir by attending a practice in early January 2002, and was warmly greeted and accepted by the other members. The congregation of St Augustine, I soon found out, was also warm and friendly, both to me as well as Sylvia, who began to attend church. We both had a distinct feeling of community and fellowship during church services.

While living in Marblehead and raising our children there, we regularly attended St. Andrews Episcopal Church. The Episcopal Church is America's version of the Anglican Church of England, and the prayer services of these two churches are almost identical. After moving from Marblehead, I had attended church only occasionally, but upon joining the choir at St. Augustine, apart from enjoying the singing, I soon found my return to the familiarity of the prayer services to be a reassuring comfort.

It was a novel experience for me to join the choir, but since I was, in that time frame at least, the only white person on the choir, it also had to have been a novelty for the local people who were members of the choir. Shortly after I began singing with the group, however, friends of ours from Canada, who had been told about my being in the choir, also joined our group in late January.

These members, William and Sheila Allan, had been singing with chorale groups for many years (Will had also taken piano lessons for many years when he was younger), and they welcomed the opportunity to participate with the choir in the regular church services and the Easter cantata, which was being planned. Will is a bass, and so now, we had four basses in our choir, a big boost for our low-voiced group.

Unlike Will, my musical experience was limited to taking piano lessons for two years when I was a boy and singing a few times with the chorale of my fraternity while attending the University of Massachusetts, pretty limited experience to be sure. But I always liked to sing and could, to a certain extent, read the notes the basses were to follow in any particular composition. I soon found myself able to stay in tune, listening to and following along with my fellow basses, Will, Kenneth Harrigan and Evans Harrigan.

Harrigans have a major presence in the St. Augustine choir, and they all display musical talents. In addition to Ken and Evans, there is Calvin Harrigan, a tenor, who is Evans' son, and Ambrose Harrigan, also a tenor. Margaret Augustus, an alto who leads us when Lennox Vanterpool, our choirmaster, is not available, was also a Harrigan before she married.

For the Easter cantata in 2002, our choir combined with the women's choir from St. Mary's, another Anglican church on the island, and our combined chorale group, consisting of 40 singers, was to present two performances, the first on Easter Sunday at 5:00 p.m., and the other the following Sunday.

The cantata, entitled "He Shall Arise", consisted of eight separate pieces, which described the arrival of Jesus in Jerusalem, the Last Supper, the trial and crucifixion, and the Resurrection of Christ.

As with the earlier cantatas, in terms of the singing involved, the pieces are beautiful, but with four separate parts, sopranos, altos, tenors and basses, these pieces are complicated and required a great deal of practice. As Easter approached, the chorale group met with Lennox, our capable conductor, three evenings a week over the last three weeks, to learn, synchronize and perfect our singing.

The two performances, before packed audiences, went well, and after singing our final piece, Handel's Hallelujah Chorus from the Messiah, we received standing ovations after each performance. The cantata was so popular that we were asked to sing two pieces from the cantata at a concert, which was presented one week later by another civic group.

I did not simply enjoy singing in the cantata; I found the whole experience moving and inspirational. But perhaps more importantly, I came to feel a tangible sense of fellowship and friendship with the local Anguillians who are both part of the choir and in the congregation of St. Augustine.

The Government of Anguilla may view me as an alien or non-belonger, but I now feel very much like I have been accepted by and belong with my friends at St. Augustine. And I'm sure Sylvia feels the same sense of belonging through her affiliation with the Soroptimists and the wonderful friends she has made with members of that group.

I was so touched by the way I had been accepted as a part of the choir and congregation that I wrote a story in late April 2002 similar in content to this story, and sent it to the local weekly, The Anguillian. It was printed in that paper in June, after I had left to return to the Cape.

My participation in the St. Augustine choir ended, of course, when I returned to Cape Cod in mid-May to spend my summer and fall months here, but as I enjoyed those summer months at our home on beautiful Cape Cod, and visiting with most of my children and grandchildren, I paused and thought back to singing with my friends at the St. Augustine Church, looking forward to rejoining the choir when we returned to Anguilla in November.

Upon our return on Thursday, October 31 2002, Sylvia and I attended church the following Sunday. As we sat in the pew, members of the choir, having seen us come in, waved to us with big smiles. Later, when it was time for the exchange of peace between members of the congregation, as a regular part of the service, several of those in the choir, which was singing a hymn at the time, waved me over to their section and members of the choir shook my hand and gave me hugs.

When the announcements were made, Ingrid Lake, a member of the vestry, identified Sylvia and myself, welcoming us back. As we stood up to acknowledge her warm greeting, the congregation burst into applause. A very warm and gratifying reception!

Later in early December, a friend of ours from New England, who comes down with her husband to Anguilla twice a year for vacations, told me she had seen my story in the June issue of "The Anguillian", which she subscribed to, and she wondered whether the way in which Sylvia and I had been received earlier was simply a form of courtesy by local people.

In reply, I told her about how we were received, with hugs and applause, when we first reappeared at the church shortly after we had returned in early November, and she realized then that the manner in which we were accepted was, indeed, genuine. Yes, it is nice to feel like you belong and are accepted in a community.

CHAPTER X. POTPOURI

Here are seven stories which do not fall under any of the categories of the preceding chapters, and since they represent a miscellany or mixture of stories, I have included them together in this Chapter entitled simply "Potpouri".

THE GERMAN SUBMARINE ATTACK

Looking back over the major events during the past century, some of the developments were significantly newsworthy because they involved changes, which would have far-reaching effect upon the future of a particular area (e.g. for Cape Cod, the creation of the Cape Cod National Seashore). Other events occurring on the Cape, however, did not have long range implications, but are especially notable because they were unusual, dramatic and historically unprecedented.

Falling into the second category is the appearance of a German submarine off the coast of Orleans on July 21 1918 and the bombardment it launched over the next 35 minutes upon nearby American targets. The historical significance of what happened on this day was that the shelling represented the only time since the War of 1812 that a foreign enemy fired upon a target on the United States mainland. This is a description of those events, based upon the account of an eyewitness who saw what transpired from a special vantage position.

It was warm and sultry the morning of Sunday, July 21 1918, a typical summer day on Cape Cod. The sea off Nauset Beach was calm and although there was a haze over the water, the haze was lifting and visibility off the coast was relatively good.

One or two miles off-shore, the tug boat, Perth Amboy, with four barges attached by cables towing behind, moved slowly through the water in a southerly direction. There were approximately 30 people on the five vessels, including Captain Joseph Perry of New Bedford, with his wife, daughter, and nephew, on the second barge in line.

The war in Europe was then in full swing, but the United States and its allies had scored victories by crossing the Marne and the final defeat of Germany seemed close at hand. Now 85 years later, it would be unusual to see a tugboat towing barges, moving so close to the shores of Nauset Beach, but in those days, it was a common sight. Because of reports during this period that German submarines were prowling off the East Coast to the United States, ocean-going commercial vessels stayed close to the shore for protection.

On this particular morning, however, with bathers visible off the starboard side on the beach, Captain Perry was unconcerned about possible enemy submarines. According to reports in an article in the New Bedford Standard

Times, he assured his worried wife, as they proceeded along, that "We're absolutely safe here, so close to the shore."

All was quiet also at the Orleans Coast Guard Station, located approximately one mile south of what is now Nauset Beach, now the most popular beach in Orleans (the station has long since disappeared). Personnel at the station on this day consisted of Captain Robert Pierce and a crew of eight men, including my father, Reuben S. B. Hopkins of Orleans.

Surfman William Moore, brother of Charles Moore Sr., who was a well-known local character in Orleans known as "the Mayor of Tonset", was on watch that morning. Reuben, who had earlier been on watch in the tower, went to his bunk on the floor below around 10:30 a.m. "to catch forty winks." Suddenly the tranquility of the quiet summer morning was shattered by the firing of a heavy gun offshore. Reuben immediately jumped up and joined Bill Moore in the tower. In his own words, this is what Rueben observed:

"I observed before me a tug and tow of four barges. A little further offshore, and perhaps a quarter mile from the tug, I could discern a submarine lying low and broadside to the beach in the water. She was difficult to see because of the haze, which cleared somewhat later. I had barely taken all this in when I saw the flash of a gun on the submarine. The shell landed in the water aft of the tug which by now had come to a dead stop.

"The tug took a direct hit on the pilot house and a short time later the tug's lifeboat loaded with her crew and a white flag showing was seen rounding her stern and pulling to the shore. The submarine was shelling first the tug then one of the other of the four barges. The crews of the different barges had all left in their small boats and were rowing for Nauset Inlet. The first barge, loaded with granite, sank almost at once. Two others sank slowly after that, and the fourth sank by the bow, leaving the stern in the air, remaining in that position for a week or more. The tug, an iron vessel, never did sink although it was gutted by fire."

When these events were first unfolding, Captain Pierce had ordered his crew to launch a surfboat to assist those on the tugboat. Because he was adept at signaling and knew the Coast Guard communication systems, Reuben had been directed to stay in the tower where, with the help of high-powered binoculars, he had a "ring-side seat" to the proceedings.

When he realized this was a sub-attack, Reuben immediately notified the Naval Air Station in Chatham about the attack. The Naval Station was undermanned that morning because many of the personnel were in Provincetown for a baseball game. First they managed to get a flying boat airborne, and it circled the submarine and returned to Chatham. Next, a pontoon plane took off and flew low in a straight line toward the submarine, passed over it, and returned to circle again.

Reuben did not see any explosions near the submarine as the plane passed over. According to reports later, the plane did drop bombs normally used in target practice, often found to be unreliable, and again on this occasion, they failed to explode. There were also stories that after dropping the useless bombs on the first run, the pilot, in his frustration, while making his second pass over the submarine, threw a monkey wrench at the enemy vessel.

Dr. Daniel Taylor, who was an eyewitness to the sub-attack from his Nauset Bluff's home, later met by chance a steward on a German transatlantic steamer. The German told him that he was a member of the crew of U-156 and confirmed that the pilot did, indeed, throw something at the submarine, and the U-boat crew members, in return, thumbed their noses at the plane as it passed over.

Back in the tower, after the pontoon plane had made its final swoop over the submarine, Reuben observed the crew of the U-boat entering and closing the hatches. The submarine quickly submerged. He breathed a sigh of relief, which was short-lived, because after five minutes, the submarine surfaced again. Now, instead of being broadside to the beach, it was facing directly at the station and began to head toward the beach. Reuben described what happened next:

"The crew of the submarine started to elevate their gun and I realized I was looking down its muzzle, which gave me mixed feelings. However, I reflected it had taken three shots to hit the tug— I would give them one, than decide what to do next. I saw a flash and heard the shot scream past, just east of my tower window. I heard later it landed in the tidal estuary called "The River" by local people.

No additional shells were fired, however, and the sub-crew was seen "buttoning up" to submerge again. This time the submarine disappeared into the depths and was gone for good. The U-boat had been on the surface, firing some 150 shells from its two heavy guns, for approximately 35 minutes. The shelling from the submarine caused four barges to sink and inflicted substantial damage to the Perth Amboy. Fortunately, nobody on these vessels was killed, and only one man sustained serious injuries. Most escaped without any injuries.

Startled by the sudden appearance of the submarine, Captain Perry on the second barge in line of tow, for example, quickly directed his family and crew into a lifeboat as soon as the shelling began, and they were able to pull away from the barge before the submarine began hitting it with shells. When the lifeboat reached shore, summer residents, living on Nauset Bluffs, greeted then and took them to their homes.

The tugboat sustained heavy damage, but remained afloat. The crew of the tug had crowded into the one lifeboat and had begun heading for shore when the Coast Guard surfboat met them. Because the lifeboat was overcrowded, some of the tugboat crew were transferred to the surfboat for the journey to he shore.

The helmsman who had been in the pilothouse when the shelling began, identified later as John Bogavich, was badly injured by a shell fragment passing through his left arm near the shoulder and was bleeding heavily. Bill Moore quickly applied a tourniquet and administered first aid to Mr. Bogavich as the boat was pulled toward the beach. (See photograph.) This was credited with saving his life.

As the boats were moving slowly toward shore, Reuben watched as a person stood up in the surfboat, and using wigwag, signaled that a doctor should be called. Later, it was discovered that the signaler was Gilbert Payson, a 17-year-old summer resident, who was allowed by Captain Pierce to assist "the coasties" in their life saving efforts.

Reuben immediately called Dr. Robert McCue to treat the injured man and after the party landed on the beach, Dr. McCue arrived to provide medical treatment. When the boat had arrived to the shore, Reuben, who by then had been relieved of tower duty, was there to hold Mr. Bogavich's struggling body as Dr. McCue poured iodine into the open wound, a common but very painful method of treating wounds in those days. The arm, however, was too badly damaged and later had to be amputated.

The Perth Amboy was still floating off the coast, and that afternoon, two members of the tugboat joined personnal of the Coast Guard Station, including Reuben, to row out and check the condition of the tug. It was still smoking and had many puncture holes from the shelling, but otherwise was in reasonably good shape. Reuben noted that "the only unusual thing we saw during the trip out and back was a bedraggled hen, floating freely in a coop, evidently from the deck of one of the barges."

The Perth Amboy was salvaged and restored to operate again under the name, Nancy Moran. She later ferried goods and materials among ports in England under the Lend Lease Agreement during World War II, assisting in the second war effort against Germany. On May 31 1946, the Nancy Moran sank in the English Channel after colliding with a tanker.

It was never clear why the German submarine undertook what in hindsight seems a somewhat futile gesture. Some theorized that U-boat 156 had been assigned the job of cutting the transatlantic cable linking Orleans to Brest, France, and spotting the tugboat and barges, could not resist attacking them. Others believe that with Germany facing impending defeat, the Kaiser had ordered German submarines to attack American shipping near our shore, hoping to discourage us from continuing to participate in the war against Germany.

Whatever the reasons, the submarine bombardment generated a mixture of great excitement, high drama, a bit of comedy, and determined acts of courage here on Cape Cod. Certainly, it was a brave act for service for the crew of the surfboat, seeing that the U-boat was continuing to shell the tug and barges, to row resolutely out to the area of the bombardment in order to assist those who were under fire. And in doing so, they probably saved the life of one member of the tugboat crew.

Crew of the Perth Amboy tug arrive in surf boat after shelling.

235

BUILDING FENCES

Robert Frost once wrote an essay about the value of fences, saying that "fences good neighbors make." There is some truth to this, but having been involved for almost all of my adult life in building fences, fences of every type and description, and in various locales, I have found that they do serve other important functions as well.

Most of the fences on Cape Cod in the earlier years were stone walls which divided properties and acted as barriers for farm animals. This type of fence was very common on the Cape because the soil was rocky, and farmers, in readying their land for farming, necessarily had to remove the boulders and rocks. Further, wood was scarce in earlier times, and fences made of wood were rare.

Since the forties, however, fences on the Cape, as in other areas, have taken various forms. And over the years, I have found myself involved in every conceivable type of fence. First, there was a tall stockade fence in front of the modest house my first wife, Hattie, and I bought in 1958 on South Main Street in Cohasset.

The house, an old carriage house that was part of the Logan Estate, was in need of considerable repair. It was close to a street, which served as a main road into the Town's center, and this fence created a sense of privacy, while cushioning the traffic noise of cars commuting in and out of town. Thus, the fence had a utility unrelated to our having neighbors.

After renovating the Cohasset house, we sold it in 1960 and moved to an old house in the center of the Olde Town of Marblehead. This house was high on a rocky hill, with a sharp drop-off in front. By this time, we had two small, adventurous sons, Christopher and Joshua, and a frisky Dalmatian dog, and it was necessary, therefore, to erect a fence around the perimeter of the property for confinement and security. The fence was made up of pickets in the back, wire along the rocky side, and pickets again in the front, with a gate.

This was also the spot where, under the influence of my early years in "tending the farm" I raised mallard ducks. This required the construction of a wire pen and small shed to confine my pets while keeping predators out. As you can see, all of the fences I built thus far have had utilitarian value.

In 1970, we purchased a lot of land on Ocean Avenue on Marblehead Neck, with an unobstructed view of Boston. By this stage, our family had grown to six children, our two sons, two daughters born to us, Jessica and Bethany, and two adopted daughters, Victoria and Juliana. We were in need, therefore, of a bigger house with more bedrooms, and commenced construction of our new house.

When the house was completed, a great deal of landscaping had to be done, and I ended up doing it, both because I enjoyed the work and for financial reasons. This required the grading and seeding of lawns around the building and the plantings of shrubs and trees around the foundations and in various other locations. And in addition, came the fences.

Initially, I installed a picket fence along the front line, with splitrail fences down each side and in the rear. I also built a small house and pen for my mallard ducks. I did not, however, clip their wings, and eventually, attracted by the open sea across the street, they all flew away, coming back occasionally for brief visits and handouts of corn.

Within a short time, our oldest daughter, Jessica, was "into horses". Starting off by riding at a stable in Danvers, she moved up to acquire eventually her own horse, a beautiful five year-old Saddlebred filly, which was boarded at the stable. This was not sufficiently close, however, and we soon had a stable out back, where the horse was housed. Naturally this led to the construction of a paddock next to the stable and a fenced-in area for lunging the horse. More postholes, more posts, more railings.

Events moved along, and by 1979, our family had grown by the addition of two more adopted children from Vietnam, Joscelyn and Minh. My wife and I concluded that, for our large and diversified family, it would be better to be in a more rural area. We ultimately located a large lot on the marsh of Ipswich River in Ipswich. Another house was designed for the even larger family we had, and we made the big move to Ipswich.

We had a stable built at the new site for Jessica's filly and because we had so much room, I arranged to have a large, sturdy paddock constructed next to the stable. This was the first time I had arranged to have a fence built for me. We did have a huge lawn area around the new house, about the size of a football field, and again, I seeded the lawn and planted numerous bushes and shrubs as part of the landscaping. Although we now had a Great Dane named Velvet, our new home was so isolated, we did not have the need for a fence around the perimeter of the large lot.

The children grew up and the older ones had gone off to college. My oldest son, Christopher, was married to Sharon Gilmore, a "wee lass" he had met in Scotland during his junior year abroad, while attending Trinity College. Jessica was now in Mt. Holyoke and Bethany had entered school at Umass-Amherst. Unfortunately, at this point, my marriage had fallen apart, and by mutual agreement, my wife and I separated in 1984 and later divorced.

Eventually, in 1990, I married Sylvia McMeen, a lawyer from Salem, originally from my hometown, Orleans on Cape Cod. Sylvia owned a house in Manchester-by-the-Sea. The house was located in a residential area, and when we acquired two Great Danes, Isak and Spocky, in 1993, we soon realized that a fence to confine the dogs while we were at work was necessary, and so I was back into fence-building.

Sylvia also owned a house on Captain Curtis Way in Orleans, which she had built in 1972 on a lot of land she had purchased, coincidentally, from my Dad. In 1994, we decided to sell the Manchester house and move to the Cape house. After we had moved into our new home, we discovered that our two dogs, young and inquisitive, tended to run off through the woods near our house (the very same woods where my cow had roamed through 50 years before (see Daisy and The Peach Tree in Chapter I). So again, I installed a wire fence around the perimeter of the property to confine our dogs.

But my landscaping and fence-building activities did not end. After retiring from my law practice in 1998, Sylvia and I built a house in Anguilla, an island in the Caribbean we had been going to for vacations for some 12 years. Our new house consisted of three separate buildings, with a courtyard and pool in between, and when the buildings were completed in December 1998, I again undertook the work of landscaping and tree planting.

We still had our two dogs which necessitated a fence around the property, but in addition, herds of goats roam freely in surrounding fields (indeed, they move freely over the whole island), and if they gain access to your property, they would quickly destroy your trees and shrubs. Although a high concrete wall surrounded the courtyard within the complex, we needed fencing around the remainder of the lot. A local man, Maxwell, and I cemented 38 wooden posts into the hard coral rock, and then strung heavy wire, approximately 350 feet long, between the posts. Three wooden gates were installed at appropriate locations.

In addition, I discovered in grading the land around the buildings that the earth was full of rocks in varying sizes. Now I understood what my forebears encountered when they attempted many years ago to clear fields on the Cape for farming. The rocks were so numerous that I simply placed them along the outskirts of the cleared area until they soon became a small stonewall, another Hopkins stonewall, this one in a foreign land, where I expect it will remain for many generations to come.

In the summer of 1999, I also installed a long white picket fence between the family cottage, Red Shutters, and a new house constructed by the Mitchells on what had been the site of the second cottage my Dad built,

Blue Shutters (torn down for the new building). This was a fence built more for "good neighbor" reasons, in accordance Robert Frost's suggestion.

This, then, was the eighth property upon which I had erected a fence of some type. In addition, I had done major landscaping in connection with the construction of three separate houses. And although I have long since departed from five of those properties, some of the fences, I know, are still in place, serving the same purposes, which necessitated them in the first place. Strangely enough, this gives me a sense of satisfaction.

MAN'S BEST FRIEND

As I sit in the gazebo at our home in Anguilla, looking out over the sea, with my two Great Danes at my feet, my thoughts turn to how dogs have played such an integral role in my life. Some people, to be sure, view dogs as a nuisance and I suspect some would like to see them banned from any human interaction. Others, such as myself, develop bonds of kinship with our pet dogs, sometimes deeper than those we have with all but our closest friends and relatives. A dog can, indeed, be "man's best friend."

The first dog I really became attached to was a female harlequin Great Dane we bought in 1972. My then wife, Hattie, and I named her Velvet. She grew to be large and rangy, weighing about 140 pounds, but she was exceedingly gentle, especially with the small children we had at that time. They petted and played with her constantly, but she always was very patient with them as they crowded over her. It is for good reason that they call the Great Dane "the gentle giant."

Dogs, particularly large dogs, need exercise, and I regularly walked Velvet down to the nearby beach which was adjacent to the causeway to Marblehead Neck in Massachusetts where we were then living, to let her run on the long stretch of sand, down and back. In the few contacts she had had with other dogs, Velvet seemed shy and reticent. I did not know how she would be if confronted by a large aggressive dog, but on one of our beach-runs, I soon found out.

On this particular day, as Velvet and I were approaching the parking lot at the western end of the causeway, a man got out of a car with a very large German Shepherd on leash. Upon seeing Velvet moving along near the water, the Shepherd immediately assumed a menacing crouch, at which point, the owner released the leash, and his dog sprang forward toward us. I am still convinced that the man was looking for a fight as much as his dog.

Before describing what happened next, let me point out that the Great Dane was originally bred in Germany to hunt the wild boar. Because of the danger posed by the boar's method of ripping low with his tusks, the Great Dane over time developed powerful shoulders and strong forelegs which were used to ward off the boar when he charged. And indeed, when Great Danes play with each other, they still leap up, using their shoulders and forelegs in efforts to fend off or topple one another.

I was aware of all this as the German Shepherd was racing across the sands directly toward Velvet, growling and snarling, but I was still concerned because my dog, a female and basically very gentle, had never encountered this kind of situation. I yelled loudly at the Shepherd, but he kept coming, low and ready to attack.

When Velvet saw the dog coming, instead of retreating, she charged the Shepherd herself, barreling into him like a linebacker in football, and knocked him head over heels with her powerful shoulders. Before he could get up, she battered him with her forefeet and muscled him with her shoulders, knocking him down each time he tried to rise. Amazingly, she never once tried to bite him. After being pummeled for a time, the Shepherd finally got up and ran back to his master.

After that, I was never again concerned about whether Velvet could handle a large, aggressive dog. Indeed, Velvet had two other similar encounters, one with a large Doberman on the beach during a run, with the same result as the first encounter. Another time, our neighbor's German Shepherd jumped over our back fence and attacked Velvet in our back yard. Again, the Shepherd, after being knocked about, quickly jumped back over the fence to hurry home. Great Danes are gentle, but they can be tough, too, when the need arises.

Later, we moved with our family in 1979 from Marblehead to a new house we had built in Ipswich on five acres of upland near the Ipswich River. Great Danes, as with most large dogs, live an average age of 10 years. After being in Ipswich for several years, Velvet had slowed down and suffered from hip displacia. Nevertheless, Velvet remained close to members of the family, was still quiet and gentle, and never complained.

One cold night, as was our routine, we let Velvet out before retiring for the night, but this time, instead of rushing back in from the cold, she had disappeared. My second son, Josh, and I went looking for her, and Josh found her standing quietly, deep in nearby woods. When we urged her to come home, she dutifully followed us, entered the house, and lay down on the rug in front of the wood stove, her favorite spot.

The next morning, I came downstairs, into the kitchen early because I had a trial in court that day. Ordinarily, Velvet would get up and greet me, but this morning, she did not move. When I checked her, I found that she had died during the night. As often happens, dogs know they are about to die and wish to be away, by themselves, to do so, in this case, even in the bitter cold.

After Velvet, I did not have another dog until 1992, a ten year hiatus. By this time, I had gone through a divorce, and later, in August 1990, I married Sylvia McMeen, a lawyer I had met in Salem. We made our home in Manchester-By-The-Sea on the North Shore of Massachusetts.

When I first met Sylvia, she had an Irish Setter named Guinness. Guinness died soon after we had met, leaving her with three Siamese cats. In 1992, shortly after her older cat died, Sylvia, emotionally in need of a replacement pet, saw two harlequin Great Danes in a parking lot downtown in Manchester, where we were then living. We petted and admired the dogs, and Sylvia was so greatly impressed with their gentleness, dignity and beauty, as well as my description of what a great dog Velvet had been, she soon became insistent that we get a harlequin Great Dane for ourselves.

As it turned out, one of the dogs we saw downtown had been bred through a Great Dane breeder in Biddeford, Maine, Lillian Reps. When we heard about this, we arranged in June 1992 to buy one of the puppies in the litter, a harlequin female. Sylvia's favorite book (and movie) is "Out Of Africa", written by the Danish writer, Isak Dennison. Our little puppy, then so small I could hold her in one arm, was named Isak. (Later, after Isak had become fully grown, she still attempts to climb into my lap just as she did as a puppy; she succeeds only in sitting her rear down.)

Approximately two months later, Lillian called Sylvia to say she had just acquired a male harlequin, sired by a champion Great Dane, which she planned to use for breeding; that Isak, being alone all day while Sylvia and I worked, would necessarily be lonely; and that we could have the dog so long as it was available to her for stud. The male, the same age as Isak, had perfectly pointed ears, as it turned out, and therefore, was named Spocky after the character in Star Trek. I was somewhat dubious about getting a second dog, but agreed to consider it.

We took Isak up to Maine so she could meet Spocky. Lillian let the two dogs out together into a large fenced area, and Spocky, who was much the bigger dog, immediately began chasing Isak around the yard, knocking her down repeatedly. Little did I know, as I watched Isak being battered around by this big bully, that I would eventually develop a close bond with Spocky and that he was to become my all-time favorite dog.

When I expressed concern to Lillian as to what was happening, she assured me it was simply play, and that Isak, basically an Alpha dog, would soon take control. Indeed Lillian's prediction was proven correct: within ten minutes, Spocky was played out and began following Isak around the yard in a dutiful fashion.

Eventually, we loaded the two dogs into our car and headed back home. Spocky, we soon discovered, had a habit of drooling when he was excited, and overcome by the thrill of traveling with the three of us, he dribbled drool from the corners of his mouth most of the way back to Massachusetts.

Several months later, we took Spocky for a checkup to our veterinarian, who noticed a cataract on his eye. He was then seen by an opthamologist who said he had a congenital eye condition and would go blind in six months. With a condition such as this, Spocky could not be used for breeding. Lillian offered to take Spocky back, but we had become so close to him by this time that we could not imagine being without him, even if he did become blind.

When we noticed him having trouble seeing, we put a bell on Isak's collar so he could follow her around by the sound of the bell. Spocky and Isak became inseparable. They played together, ran together, ate together, and slept together. As time went on, either Spocky had accommodated himself to his loss of vision or he did not lose as much of his vision as predicted, because he was able to get around fine, easily running around trees and other obstacles.

Several times, they skipped off into the woods around our home in Manchester for exploratory runs, requiring me to wander through the woods looking for them. I finally built a pen and arranged for the construction of a large doghouse to keep them outside and confined during the day. After two years, they got over their "puppy ways", grew to full size, and settled down (sort of). Isak was then about 125 pounds and Spocky, a solid handsome dog, weighed about 160 pounds.

In 1994, Sylvia and I sold the Manchester house and moved with our pets to the house she had built many years before in Orleans on Cape Cod. This house was surrounded by heavy woods owned by the Orleans Conservation Society, and the dogs, now over two years old, had vast new territories to explore, as we soon found out. A large dog pen was built, along with another roomy dog-house, and we also installed an Invisible Fence (electric) which supposedly were serve to keep them confined within the large front yard.

The Invisible Fence simply did not work in keeping our two large and rambunctious dogs within the yard. After several incidents in which they left the yard, willingly enduring the shock from their collars, to challenge other dogs passing by on the road out front, the decision was made to install a regular fence around the perimeter of the lot, a job which I assumed. A large, white double, wooden-gate was installed across the driveway, completely closing the yard.

Both Isak and Spocky were friendly and gentle with guests visiting our home, as well as the ever-increasing number of grandchildren who were also now coming along. Spocky was particularly solicitous of the small ones who wanted to pet him. And yet, as he grew older, he became aggressive toward other dogs, particularly larger dogs. Isak was keen on hunting down squirrels and rabbits, but was disdainful toward other dogs. Spocky, on the other hand, ignored the wild creatures, but had a thing about other dogs. It may have been a form of protection for Isak. Fortunately, the fence and our care in assuring that the gate remained closed at all times precluded any further incidents.

I retired from my law practice in April 1998 and had more time to spend with Isak and Spocky. The three of us took long walks every day together either through the conservation land or along the shores of the Mill Pond, a nearby salt-water cove. My walks with them became a ritual, and the dogs each morning sat patiently waiting for me to finish breakfast so that I could take them out.

Sylvia and I also took the dogs for long runs on the sand flats near Rock Harbor, on the bayside of the Cape, when the tide was out to expose a vast open area. It was a joy to see Isak and Spock gallop, side by side, across the flats, running like two race-horses.

In September 1998, Isak developed a neurological condition which prevented her from chewing or swallowing. We were very concerned, but our veterinarian, Dr. Watts, told us the problem would run its course in about six weeks and that we should feed Isak liquid food through a syringe in the meantime. Indeed, as it turned out, after about five weeks, during which time she lost 15 pounds, she slowly began to chew and swallow regular food again and eventually regained her weight.

In the middle of Isak's recovery, however, I noticed that Spocky was limping slightly on his left front leg. I assumed he had sprained his leg during one of his runs, but decided to have him checked by Dr. Watts. An Xray was taken, and the diagnosis Dr. Watts came up with could not have been grimmer: Spocky had virulent bone cancer in the form of a tumor on his left front leg, and even with treatment, would only live six months or so.

During October, we arranged to have Spocky treated with radiation and chemotherapy at the Angell Memorial Hospital in Boston. The chemotherapy supposedly would slow the cancer spread and the radiation would alleviate future pain.

Earlier, in October 1997, Sylvia and I had already begun construction of a house in Anguilla, an island in the Caribbean where we had been going for winter vacations for some 10 years. The house was to be ready in a year's time, and we planned to spend that winter in our new house in Anguilla, returning to the Cape in May of 1999. And it had been our intention to take our two Great Danes down with us. We continued with our plans even though we realized that Spocky, undoubtedly, would not be returning home with us in May. We felt he deserved to spend his last months with us in the warm Caribbean sun.

We had traveled with the dogs, without any problems, on several long trips in the car, one as far away as New York. They were very contented to be in the back of the car. But we had never taken them on an airplane, and we were both concerned as to how they would handle such a trip.

As it turned out, they did remarkably well. Given a slight tranquilizer when we reached JFK Airport in New York, they were placed in their crates, the biggest ones you can buy, transferred into the terminal on a large dolly, and then carried up the conveyer belt into the hold of the plane, for the four-hour flight to St. Martin. The American Airline pilot was nice enough to assure us that the dogs were safely on the plane before taking off. (Sylvia also carried her two Siamese cats by our seats in small carry-ons.)

Landing in St Martin, which is five miles from Anguilla, the dogs in their crates were transferred over to a small plane we had hired for the 10 minute flight to Anguilla. The dog crates barely fit into the plane, and with all the luggage we had, Sylvia and I had the smallest of space within which to sit, jammed up against the crates and each other. The dogs, particularly Spocky, remained calm and quiet throughout the various moves, and we arrived safe and sound.

The house, of course, was not ready for occupancy, and we stayed for six weeks until the house was finished at Spindrift, a resort managed by a good friend of ours, Aileen Smith, where we had stayed on previous occasions. Our builder worked feverishly to finish the house, and the day before Christmas, we were able to move into our home, along with our dogs and cats, and my daughter, Torie, who had just arrived for a five-day holiday from Brown Medical School.

The new home had a fenced-in yard, and the dogs could, therefore, move around freely. Spocky always wanted to be with me while I worked in the yard, grading the terrain, moving rocks, and planting bushes, and he often came to wherever I was working, contented to lay in the shade near me. The dogs also looked for their customary walk each morning, and Sylvia and I walked them regularly on leashes in the nearby fields. There were always goats grazing in these fields, but the dogs generally ignored them.

Spocky did not seem to be in pain, but as time went on, he had increased difficulty walking. Several times he could not return from his walk, and I had to drive our Suzuki Sidekick into the field to pick him up. This did not deter him, however, from looking to take his walk each day.

Part of our house included a large gazebo, supported by four concrete posts, over our pool. The gazebo was raised and shaded, and the view from the gazebo out to sea is spectacular. We placed two large pillows on the gazebo for the dogs, and it soon became Spocky's favorite place to stay. I often sat with him reading, with his big head resting on my foot. As the tumor on his leg grew, Spocky became weaker, but you always could find him lying on his pillow on the gazebo, head held high, ears pointed, in his noble way. He was amazingly dignified and stoic in those final months.

By early April, we felt that Spocky had reached a point where he had maybe another month of time. We did not want him to suffer and if his quality of life was bad, we were prepared to "put him down." Looking toward the inevitable, we arranged to have a large hole dug in our front yard and a wooden box built big enough to accommodate him. We wanted to be ready when the time came.

During this same period, Sylvia had heard that a Great Dane on the island had given birth to 11 puppies. She visited the litter several times, and as I anticipated when she began her visits, she soon was keen on having another Dane before Spocky passed along. We thereupon acquired a three month old male puppy, half Harlequin, half Boston. After trying various names, we finally named him Tango.

Spocky and Tango got on amazingly well. Spocky was particularly kind and solicitous to his new little friend. They often napped, side by side, on Spocky's pillow on the gazebo. I think the puppy gave Spocky a focus and diversion which was good for him in his last weeks.

In early May, Sylvia and I realized it was time for Spocky to be put to rest. We arranged for our veterinarian, Pat Vanderpool, come to our house to administer the necessary shots, first a sedative to put Spocky to sleep, and a shot to stop his heart. Pat, his assistant Amy, Sylvia and I sat in the gazebo with Spocky as he lay on his pillow in his quiet, dignified way, and after the first shot, he went to sleep with his head in my lap, as I stroked his ears.

Sylvia and I left before the second shot was to be administered. Afterwards, Pat and I then carefully placed Spocky in his box, carried the heavy box to his hole in the yard, lowered the box into the hole, and covered it with earth from the nearby pile. Spocky and I had developed a close bond, particularly in those last weeks, and this final event was an emotionally trauma for me; my favorite dog was gone.

As we were working to cover Spocky's box, a rain cloud appeared off shore, and with the sun's rays passing through the isolated rain shower, there appeared a beautiful rainbow directly in front of us. It lasted five minutes and disappeared. Because there are frequently small rain clouds moving around the island, rainbows are common, but we felt it was provident that one should appear in such a timely way. Amazingly, a year later, on the anniversary of Spocky's death, another rainbow appeared in the same spot, at about the same time.

Looking back, Sylvia and I were so glad we were able to take Spocky to Anguilla where he could spend his final six months in the warmth and sunshine of the island. You could tell that he especially enjoyed, even in his last weeks, being on his pillow on the gazebo, with his nose lifted, sniffing the cool winds off the ocean or the smells riding on the warm breezes from the nearby fields. This is how I shall remember him.

Tango, a very active and affectionate dog, is now bigger and taller than Isak. He will continue to grow, and although he is tall and rangy, I expect he will eventually weigh as much as Spocky did. Having a young dog as a companion, Isak, even at age ten, has never looked better, nicely muscled and trim. The two dogs enjoy taking long walks and running together on the isolated beaches nearby. Sylvia's idea of getting the young dog has proven to be correct.

It is now May of the year 2002, and as I sit in our gazebo on Anguilla, with Isak and Tango resting on their pillows beside me, I can look over to the spot where Spocky is buried. It is covered now with grass and next to the grave there is a little palm tree, which I planted to mark the site. He was a great dog, and although I do have Isak and Tango, I still miss Spocky greatly. To me, he is the best illustration for why a dog is referred to as "man's best friend."

Spocky with little Tango on gazebo, 4-27-99

Stephen A. Hopkins

THE JOYS OF BOATING

In earlier stories, I described boating mishaps, which had befallen two of my uncles, Alfred on my father's side, and Abbott Knowles on my mother's side. Alfred (a.k.a. Captain Dick) lost his battery when he unwittingly carried it off the wrong side of the boat in Rock Harbor. Abbott ran out of gas as his boat was cruising close to the breakers at Coast Guard beach and the boat came close to being caught in the surf.

These two were both experienced boatsmen, but the operation of a boat, even by seasoned skippers, seems to go hand in hand with potential problems and various types of mishaps, and even the most skilled helmsman, at one time or another, is confronted with some kind of boating calamity.

Now, if an old salt cannot avoid boating mishaps, you can multiply that tenfold when you consider those people who begin operating a boat with no prior experience. As boating has become more popular and owning a powerboat seems to have become a type of status symbol in some circles, the number of novice boatsmen who are plying our waters has increased greatly in recent years.

Unlike a car, you cannot apply the brakes to suddenly stop your boat from moving forward. Winds and tidal currents will greatly alter the direction you want your boat to go. Misfortunes of all types lie hidden on every boat, lurking, ready to surprise the hapless neophyte boater. And in the waters around the Cove in Orleans, the Inlet and the Mill Pond, where the tide goes up and down quickly, leaving little water clearance over rocks and sand bars, the potential of mishaps is even greater.

Stories of boating problems abound, but one of the funniest mishaps I can think of occurred in the channel below the cliffs of Nauset Heights, easterly of Pricilla's Landing, back when there was enough water through this channel to travel out to the Inlet. Fortunately, nobody was hurt in this misadventure, and we can, therefore, view it as the comedy it turned out to be.

Our group of friends were sitting on the inside of the beach, facing westerly toward Pricilla's Landing, when one of the group pointed to several people, in sitting positions, very low in the water, moving along from the Landing toward the beach. It appeared as if they were sitting on the surface of the water. As they came closer, passing toward the channel, which moves to the Inlet, you could see that there were a total of six people in a Whaler, perhaps 14 feet long. Most of the passengers were large and heavy, and as a consequence, there was only about three inches of freeboard around the boat, explaining why they appeared so low on the surface.

Fortunately, it was a calm day with only a few ripples in the water. As the boat moved slowly toward the right, however, you could see a large motorboat heading along at a good clip from the direction of the Inlet toward the overloaded Whaler. As this larger boat passed, the waves of its wake hit and carried over the side of the Whaler. With several of the larger passengers sitting in front, the bow of the Whaler, pushed along by the motor, planed downward at an angle into the water, causing all of the passengers, except the man who was manning the controls, to tumble forward, creating even more weight in the bow.

Everybody but the helmsman fell in disarray into the water, which fortunately was only about four feet deep. By this time, the stern of the Whaler was up out of the water, and the propeller of the motor was whirling loudly in the open air. The helmsman apparently thought he could bring the boat back to level by accelerating the engine. Finally, he realized that the better choice would be to shut the motor off, tilt the engine up, and see if the boat could be righted by hand. There were a number of buckets in the boat (maybe there had been similar mishaps in the past), and everybody began bailing water out of the boat.

When the water had been removed and the Whaler was floating again, they all clamored back into the boat, and still maintaining a sense of aplomb, even though soaked, they resumed their journey to the Inlet. The helmsman started the motor, put it in forward gear, and accelerated, only to realize that he had not lowered the engine back down into the water, resulting in more roaring from the over-revving engine.

There are many other similar type stories, such as the guy who took off from his mooring at high speed, having forgotten to disconnect his mooring line, resulting in his boat whipping around in a very sharp circle.

One time, I launched my boat from the ramp on the Mill Pond and son Josh was to take it over to our mooring while I returned home with the car. As the boat moved away into the open water, the rear slowly sank as water came in through the transom because nobody had remembered to put the plug back into the drain hole. Fortunately, I yelled to Josh and he realized what was happening and put in the plug before the boat sank. Others, I have learned, have had the same experience.

The majority of accidents occur because of what the skipper does or fails to do. I have heard of many boating mishaps, but in reviewing these various misadventures, I cannot help but think about Buggsy Moran and some of the escapades in which he engaged early in his boating career.

Buggsy had been coming to the Cape for many years, staying with his family at different places in the Nauset Heights area. During those visits, he had ridden as a guest on boats of his friends, but had never owned a boat of his own or had had much experience in operating a boat. Several years ago, Buggsy retired and he and his wife, Paula, bought a house near the Mill Pond. With the encouragement of his buddies, Buggsy bought a 24-foot Agua Sport so that he, too, could cruise the waters of the Mill Pond, the Cove, and the Inlet.

He was able to obtain a mooring in the inner section of the Mill Pond, near his house, and of course, to get out to the outer waters, he had to go through the Mill Run. Years ago, there was a mill located on the Mill Run which used the tidal waters, going in and out, to turn the huge wheel for power in milling operations.

Large rocks had been placed in the water of the narrow opening between Roberts Cove and the Mill Pond and the mill itself rested on these rocks, with only a small opening through which the tidal waters rushed against the mill wheel. The mill has long since gone, but the rocks are still there, and if you do not know where the opening is, and move through with care, your propeller may feel the effects of spinning on a rock.

Buggsy knew generally about the rocks and the narrow opening, but he did not know exactly how wide the opening was or how much clearance there was above the rocks at various tides. Shortly after getting his new boat, he took it for a ride, standing proudly at the wheel, as it churned along toward the Mill Run.

The boat, however, moved too close to the side of the opening and the whirling propeller smacked a very large rock below the surface, ending up completely mangled and inoperable. Buggsy was able to hail a passing boat for a tow back to his mooring a short distance away, and eventually the propeller was replaced and the boat was back in operation. Rumor has it that Buggsy mounted the propeller on a plague which now hangs in his garage.

During this learning period, Buggsy did have other mishaps, but to his credit, he has been always cheerful and good-natured about these learning experiences. For example, one day he went to the Inlet with friends and left the boat anchored on the inside of the beach with the idea of walking to the outer side for their picnic, sunning and swimming. He took the anchor up onto the beach and carefully secured it in the sand. Off to the ocean side they all went for their fun and games.

Several hours later, they returned to the boat to head back home only to discover that the tide had gone out, leaving Buggsy's heavy boat 30 feet high and dry on the beach. Knowing and planning for what the tide is doing at all times is imperative in boating in these waters. That is one reason the local newspapers always carry the tide chart for the upcoming week.

Buggsy had forgotten that the tide was going out when he anchored, always moving fast when it does. In his defense, however, many people forget to take the tide into consideration in their boating activities, and it is not uncommon for boats to be marooned upon sand bars.

But the best story I heard about Buggsy's mishaps is one, which is very similar to he problem my Uncle Alfred had with his battery at Rock Harbor (see the "That's Not Such A Bad Fault" story, Chapter IV). Shortly after Buggsy had acquired his boat, he was having trouble starting the motor. At one time or another, everybody has a problem starting a motor; this is an endemic feature of having a motorboat. A friend suggested to Buggsy that his battery was low and should be disconnected and taken uptown to be charged. So Buggsy rowed out to his boat in his little pram to do just that.

Now you must realize that Buggsy is a big tall man, weighing around 300 pounds, and is not particularly nimble on his feet. Like most large people, however, he is affable and funloving, able to laugh at himself, a necessary characteristic for one who is learning boating "on-the-job," so to speak. He hitched his pram to his boat, clamored out of the pram into the boat, disconnected the battery, and carried it back to the pram to return to the shore.

With their rounded bottoms, prams are notoriously unstable, and after placing the battery carefully into the center of the pram, he stepped into the pram himself, forgetting, however, to disconnect the pram line from the cleat on the boat. In reaching to disconnect the line, he leaned too far,

251

causing the pram to tip inward, which in turn resulted in his losing his balance and shifting his weight. As this was happening, he grabbed up the battery, thinking that he could save it, but it only added to his lack of balance, and so over the side he went. Like my Uncle Alfred who went down with a battery in Rock Harbor many years before, Buggsy clutched the battery tightly to his chest, hoping to save it.

Buggsy reported later that initially he thought his own natural buoyancy, bountiful as it was, would be enough to counter balance the weight of the battery, but he soon learned otherwise. Like a rock, he moved straight to the bottom, about 25 feet below. As the light above grew darker the further down he went, he realized that his life was worth more than the battery, and so he let it go (as did my Uncle those many years before), and headed back up.

There he found it impossible to climb into the sunken pram and so he swam ashore pushing it along in front of him. Finally on shore, he discovered that he had lost his cellular phone and his keys during his plunge into the water. Ah yes, the joys of owning and operating a boat.

If and when this story ends up in printed form, Buggsy, I am sure, will be a skilled and experienced boatman, one who knows all the locations of the sand bars and the rocks and is always mindful of what the tide is doing. I am sure he will not have a repeat performance of the "mangled propeller", for example. But like all of us, he will be constantly confronted with a mishap of some type because there is inherent in every boat the potential for unanticipated problems and accidents.

This can sometimes be attributed to the boat itself, but more often these mishaps occur because of the inattention of lack of experience of the skipper, particularly the novice boatsman who has not yet understood fully what can happen in the operation of a boat and is not yet able to foresee all the things that may suddenly occur. Even for veterans on the water, the unexpected can suddenly create sometimes comical and other times serious mishaps. One has to be vigilant at all times, and even then you may not escape a calamity.

This story would not be complete, however, without my relating another tale about Buggsy Moran and one of his first fishing excursions on his new boat. As he became more proficient in operating his boat, Buggsy soon had the urge to fish for bass, as a number of his friends were doing. This is the story of how he caught his first bass from his boat.

Buggsy acquired all the necessary fishing gear, obtained the favored bait, collected several friends, and went out through the Inlet to the ocean waters off Nauset Beach to try his luck at trolling for bass. Unfortunately, after several hours, they had not caught any fish, and a disappointed Buggsy decided to return home.

As he proceeded along slowly toward the Inlet, another boat came toward him, and one of the men on that boat yelled over to ask if they caught any fish. When Buggsy yelled back "No", the other skipper told him to cut his motor, and the other boat moved over toward them.

When the second boat had come closer to Buggsy, one of the men yelled, "We caught too many bass, and here's one for you." With that, he hoisted a large bass up and heaved it toward Buggsy, who barely had time to get his arms up in position to catch the large fish as it descended toward him. The other boat then accelerated away, leaving a startled Buggsy holding a large bass. Buggsy literally did, indeed, catch a fish on his first fishing trip, although not in the usual conventional way.

MISHAPS ON THE COURTS

No, this is not a story about problems I encountered while trying cases in courts of law. The title, you will notice, does not read "in the courts", but rather "on the courts."

Commencing when I was a boy, and up through today, I have participated in various sports activities: baseball, basketball, as team sports, and tennis, golf and racquetball, as individual sports. I also played for three years in the fraternity touch-football league at UMass, where the games were rough and contentious. I no longer play any of those team sports, but I still do play the individual sports whenever I can.

When you play a lot of sports, you are bound to sustain an injury from time to time, and with my participation over the years, I had my share of such injuries. In looking back, however, I now realize that the bulk of my injuries were sustained either on the basketball court or a racquetball court.

Baseball, for example, has little physical contact, and with the exception of being hit by a pitched ball once in awhile, something to be expected, I had

253

no injuries during the years I played baseball. Although the intramural football was rough, again, apart from some bruises, I had no significant injuries playing during three seasons.

But basketball and racquetball were another story. In basketball, I sprained my ankle badly several times, which is not an uncommon injury. Jumping up for a rebound during a game against Provincetown, I came down with one foot hitting the side of an opponant's leg, causing the ankle to twist as the side of my foot hit the floor hard. In addition, I was smashed in the nose or side of the head several times from errant elbows of opposing players. Yes, unlike baseball, there is a lot of physical contact in basketball and injuries are more frequent.

Those unfamiliar with racquetball may wonder how it would foster injuries. But the fact is that statistics show that there are more injuries, per player, in racquetball than any other sport. You often are hit by a ball struck by your opponent, but these are usually not disabling.

But with the fast action involved and players flaying away with their rackets, whacking the ball within the confines of a small court, in close proximity to another player, the potential of a player getting hit by a racket is great. Usually injury results when a player does not realize how close another player is, and in swinging hard, hits the player either in the body, but often in the head.

This kind of thing happens more often when a player, although a fine athlete, is inexperienced in the game of racquetball. An experienced player, when he is setting up to return a shot, will recognize the closeness of another player, and instead of swinging at the ball, possibly hitting his opponent, will simply yell "hinder (meaning the hitter cannot make his shot properly), which results in the point being replayed.

I had several encounters with wildly swung rackets. The most dramatic was the time I was playing doubles at a court in Boston with several lawyers from my law firm. One of the players, a big rangy guy, was an excellent tennis player, but had played racquetball only a couple of times. Unlike tennis, which involves long arm strokes, racquetball requires short choppy wrist strokes.

We had been playing for perhaps 20 minutes when my tennis friend swung hard at the ball with his full arm stroke, and his racket came across wide on the follow through, hitting me over my left eye, above my protective glasses, neatly splitting my eyebrow. Blood began to spurt from the deep cut, all over the floor, as I attempted to staunch the flow with my hands. My friend, seeing this, feared he had taken out my eye.

The Massachusetts General Hospital was about three miles away, and with a compress held over my eyebrow to control the flow, we piled into our car, still in our playing clothes, to go to the Emergency Room at MGH. When I walked up to the admitting desk, covered with blood, the attendant looked up and casually said, "Oh another racquetball injury." It was then that I learned that most of the facial injuries, such as mine, are the result of action on racquetball courts.

Well, they ushered me into a cubicle, and a young resident closed my wound neatly and efficiently with 14 stitches. For a number of days thereafter, I had a beautiful shiner around my left eye, which required repeated explanations by me to people I encountered, often lawyers I met in court.

Perhaps six years later, while playing doubles again, another inexperienced younger player, anxious to smash the ball hard, hit me right over the bridge of my nose, resulting in a small cut, cracking the nose bone, and causing me to "see stars". The cut was minor and there is little you can do with an undisplaced nose fracture, and so I did not even go to the hospital for treatment. The nose was swollen and painful for perhaps a week, but eventually these symptoms subsided.

Having in mind the nature of the sport, the injuries described above were predictable. I did, however, sustain an injury playing basketball, which was unusual and totally unpredictable. From the age of 30 and into my forties, I played basketball each week in a pickup league at the local YMCA in Marblehead. There were usually four or five players on a side. The games could be a quite physical, and with many of the other players younger than I, I had to strain to keep up with the pace.

This one night, I was guarding the basket, with my arms up and extended, when an opposing player passed by on my right, and as he passed, his shoulder caught my extended ring finger. I heard a distinct snap, and looked at my right hand and was amazed to see the ring finger was sideways to the other fingers.

One of the players was Ed Robinson, a former basketball star at Yale, who was now a radiologist at the Salem Hospital. Ed looked at my finger and said he thought it was dislocated. He grasped the finger and pulled, and sure enough, the finger was straightened. But I then closed my fist, and pop, the finger went back to its sidewise position. Something was drastically wrong.

Off we went to the Salem Hospital, where X-rays showed that I had a complete fracture of the third bone from the end of the finger. The finger had been snapped in half, like a twig, when it hit upon and caught the shoulder of the passing player. I ended up with a cast covering half my hand and solid from the hand to beyond my wrist. I had to wear the cast for a month. During that time, I tried several cases in court, coping with the handicap of not being able to write notes with my right hand.

Fortunately, after the cast was removed, with the help of physiotherapy, and much to the delight of the orthopedic doctor who had treated me, I was able to obtain almost full function of the finger. He was worried that, with such a total fracture, I would never have full maneuverability of that finger.

This was truly a bizarre and unpredictable injury. I kept on playing basketball into my fifties, but after that, when guarding an opponent, I extended my arms defensively, but always kept my fingers half-closed to avoid any similar injury.

In my many legal battles in the courtroom, I never had any injuries, at least of the physical, visible kind, but I surely had my share of injuries on the other courts where I have competed.

SIDNEY, THE CAT

My wife Sylvia has had Siamese cats for some 30 years, years before she and I became "a number." In hitching up with her, I necessarily became the reluctant recipient of the two cats she had. Over the years, she usually had two cats at any one time, with one generation following another. Siamese cats tend to be quirky creatures, and Sylvia had appropriately given her cats strange names such as Zap, Chipper, Waza, and Zinger.

We had various dogs as pets when I was growing up, but there were never any cats in the Hopkins household in those early years. While raising a family of eight children in latter years, there were, over a period of time, perhaps three cats brought into the fold by one child or another.

Our oldest daughter Jessica, for example, had a skitterish cat during her college years, and when she was home in the summer from college, this reclusive cat never left Jessie's bedroom and could often be seen furtively peering out from a little cave she had made in the side of the mattress.

Except to wipe up the barf those cats periodically deposited, often on an expensive oriental rug, I had nothing to do with them, concentrating my attention on the dog we had. As you might imagine, these initial contacts with cats left me less than enthusiastic with them as pets and I tended simply to ignore them. Give me a dog anytime was my motto.

Of course, after Sylvia and I were married, and before that time for that matter, I had to show some interest and empathy toward the two Siamese cats she had, Waza and Zinger, and so I did make an effort to befriend them. But as noted above, they were quirky, shy and insecure and usually ran desperately under the bed whenever I approached. It was only after several years that they would even allow me to hold them.

Moreover, as with the cats that somehow had crept into the Hopkins family unit earlier, these two cats regularly barfed on the bed or on the rugs, causing permanent discolorations in the material. One time, while I was half asleep, Waza actually peed on the cover above my body. Again, although I was civil to these cats, I found them less than endearing animals.

Time went by and eventually the two cats passed away, Zinger in 1999 and Waza in April 2002. Each was buried in the enclosed garden area, which is off our master bathroom in our house in Anguilla. This had been a secure sunny area where the cats often napped, safe from the two Great Danes we had, and Sylvia felt it the appropriate place to bury them.

Although I sympathized with Sylvia as she sorrowed over the loss of her cats, I myself could not feel a great loss from their passing. Having two Great Danes who I found to be wonderful companions, I surely did not miss having a skitterish cat to complicate my life.

Sylvia spoke longingly of her cats, from time to time, but perhaps recognizing my views, said little or nothing over the next six months about getting another cat. Two days before we were scheduled to return to Anguilla on October 31 2002, Sylvia went to Boston for a hair appointment and to pick up my cousin Carol who was flying in that afternoon from Paris.

Sylvia mentioned to me about going to the North Shore to see a friend and spoke vaguely about looking at a cat at the Animal Rescue Agency in Salem. Busy with preparing for our trip to Anguilla, I paid scant attention to what she had said, never thinking that she would seriously consider taking on a cat two days before the arduous trip we were about to make.

Around 4:00 in the afternoon, I received a call from Sylvia on her cell phone. It was routine for her to call me on her return trip to let me know how she made out and when she expected to arrive home. She sounded particularly upbeat, saying everything went well and she had picked up Carol without any problem just as she arrived at Logan. They were then in Plymouth and would be home in an hour.

Then she happily went on to say, "Oh by the way, we have a new Siamese cat, male, age three years." Thinking about what her earlier cats were like and having in mind that we were to leave on a 10-hour trip less than two days away, I was absolutely dumbfounded by this announcement.

Sylvia quickly went on to describe how she came to adopt this cat from the animal shelter and explained that she and Carol had decided that we should name the cat Sidney, after my father. His name was Reuben Sidney Bernard Hopkins and a number of members of the extended Hopkins clan, including cousin, Carol, called him Sidney or Uncle Sid. This was a pretty obvious ploy they had cooked up to placate me by naming the cat after my father. They had figured that I could not refuse to take in a cat named after my father.

When they arrived home, our cat, now named Sidney, unlike his predecessors who always cringed in the corner, emerged from the cat carrier in an assured manner and immediately came over to me to rub against my leg. He was very handsome, with nice markings. I was impressed with his calm demeanor, having in mind that he had been cooped up in the carrier for three hours with strange people in an unfamiliar car for the trip to the Cape.

Sylvia then explained that she had located the cat as listed for adoption through the Internet; that she decided at least to look at the cat on her trip to the North Shore; that upon seeing his close resemblance to her earlier cats, as he sat in his cage, she burst into tears; and that, when they removed him from the cage, he went willingly into her arms, putting his paws around her neck and nuzzling her chin. She was immediately hooked. And hearing this story, and recognizing that this cat was well adjusted, responsive and affectionate, my objections began to melt away. And he was, of course, named Sidney.

Well, the rest is history, as they say. After one day at our Cape home, at 4:00 o'clock in the morning, Sidney was again placed in the cat carrier for our two-hour drive to Logan where we were to begin our eight-hour trip to Anguilla, involving three different planes. Sidney handled the long confining trip without complaint and upon arrival, he immediately settled into his area within our Anguillian home, which included the above mentioned bathroom garden, as if he had always lived there.

Sidney continues to be a warm and demonstrative cat, greeting you every time you walk into his quarters. During the night, for example, he will briefly lay across either my neck or Sylvia's neck, purring loudly and patting our faces with his paw. And in the six months he has been with us, at the time of this writing, he barfed only once, in a remote area.

We often wonder how such an affectionate, handsome cat could have become a stray, ending in an animal shelter, as he did. One thing is clear, however: Sidney did indeed change the views I have had for all those years about cats.

Sidney, the cat, in living room, Anguilla, December 2002

HIGH SCHOOL REUNIONS

Anguilla attracts people from all over the world and during our stays on the island, we meet interesting persons from various parts of the United States and Canada, from European countries, and from Third World countries. Their interests and attitudes often are similar to ours, and we have made friends with many of those we have met.

Two of these friends, from Iowa, Rick and Cindy Jennings, came over one night for wine and pizza. They have a house here on the island one-half mile from our home, and they escape the cold and snow of Iowa, where they have both lived since childhood, whenever they can, to be in the sunshine and warmth of Anguilla. Cindy retired last year from her work in occupational therapy and Rick is semi-retired from his practice as a psychologist. They are thoughtful and well versed, and we never seem to run out of things to talk about.

The Jennings have a large boat which they keep at a marina on the Mississippi River, and during the summer months, they spend their time on the boat. They live in a small town of some 6000 people, and their descriptions of the town and what it is like living there reminds me of what it was like in Orleans and other Cape towns 50 years ago.

Rick pointed out, for example, that when he needs gas for his car, he goes to the local station, pumps gas into his tank, gives the attendant in the store a wave, the attendant then makes a note of the purchase, and Rick drives away. Each month Rick goes into the store to settle what he owes on the purchases for the month. Everybody knows each other, and there is, as there should be in any community, a great deal of trust in business and social relationships.

Anyway, toward the end of our pizza evening, we somehow got on the subject of class reunions. I had had my 50th high school reunion in September 2000, and Rick and Cindy both had their 35th reunion the year before. There were approximately 180 students in Rick's senior class, and Cindy, who was from a small town, had about 30 in her class, only slightly more than the 25 students we had in my senior class in Orleans in 1950. By coincidence, both Rick and I had acted as Master of Ceremony for our respective reunions. I sort of assumed the role by default and because I have free time in my retirement and enjoy organizational work, I also did much of the planning and promotional activities for our reunion.

261

Rick pointed out that in earlier reunions he had attended, many people tried, in subtle and not so subtle ways, to impress their former classmates with how successful they had become. As I note below, I know and understand this phenomena well. A woman would refer to her daughter as "the all-star soccer player". Or another might refer to "my husband, the doctor" or note that "my son has been accepted at three Ivy League colleges". Men in the group would refer to "three houses I own" or recount how "my company had ten-million dollars in sales last year." Oh yes, we all know how that kind of thing works.

With his background in psychology, Rick recognized why these people felt it necessary to make themselves seem important, basically a sense of earlier insecurity, but in his role as MC, he tried to nullify this type of conversation in his introductory remarks. Speaking to the assembly, as they stood by their chairs before sitting down for dinner, he said, after his opening greetings, "Now I want each of you to turn to the person next to you and say 'I have accomplished a lot in life and am an important person' and the person to whom this is said shall reply 'Oh, I do recognize that'. With this dialogue out of the way, we shall all be able to talk about other, more important and relevant subjects".

This got a good laugh, and with a few exceptions I'm sure, everybody went through the charade with good humor. In a more relaxed frame of mind, they then conducted meaningful discussions, free of puffing and self-promotion.

I was, of course, very familiar with what Rick was referring to, but in my case, the type of self-promotion he described was very common at meetings of the bar association, trial lawyer conventions, and other similar events attended by members of the Bar. Most trial lawyers, always a gregarious bunch, are not known for hiding their talents and successes, and they have refined self-promotion to an art form.

But as I explained to the Jennings, the fact is that I had attended three high school reunions (25th, 40th and 50th), and I did not notice that anyone at these events was attempting to make themselves seem important. Maybe it was the small size of our class. Rick's class was larger, and perhaps the members were trying to "stand out in the crowd", something which was not necessary in our small group. Or possibly it was because one person, who was your buddy growing up, was a fisherman, while another had become a doctor. Certainly, in that situation, it is not necessary, or appropriate for the doctor to highlight his achievement. Moreover, on Cape Cod, a fisherman who works hard at this craft and leads a decent life is always respected.

I also expressed the view that the need to have yourself perceived as being successful and important seems to be more prevalent in the younger ages, when people are striving in their careers, and that this need appears to diminish as people reach their sixties. When the typical person reaches retirement age, I have found that there is a tendency for them to actually poke fun at themselves and look back, saying, "OK, I did this or that, and what's the big deal?"

Indeed, as people move into their senior years, they seem far more able to laugh at themselves, while acknowledging their idyosyncracies, shortcomings and miscues. There is no longer the compulsion to seem successful, important and always right. The one thing many of them do lament, in retrospect, is how fast the years seemed to fly by, and it's true, they surely did fly by.

Cindy said that at her recent reunion, attended by only a few classmates because of the small size of her class, the participants sat around after dinner in a group, and somehow each, in turn, began talking about a very private event, which had drastically affected his or her life. One person started this, and then the self-analysis moved around the circle, with one person, then another, offering intimate stories.

Rick, who attended Cindy's reunion, said he was amazed at what some of these folks were willing to discuss openly. Maybe the plentiful drinks and the relaxing setting worked to release the usual reservations about such things. Or maybe it's the effect of those television shows where participants are encouraged to "tell all." Certainly, nothing like that happened at any of my reunions, probably due to the fact that Cape Codders tend to be close-mouthed and more guarded.

But that is not to say that we did not enjoy our reunions. First of all, I should mention that eight of the members of our class had died, and since this left us with only 17 surviving classmates for our 50th Reunion, we invited members of the class of 1951, with whom many of us were friendly, to come to our reunion. With spouses and friends, this ended up with a total of 45 attendees for our dinner, held at the function hall, which is part of the Jailhouse Restaurant in Orleans.

We had prepared as a handout for the dinner a brochure containing about 30 old photographs, with proper captions for each. These depicted our sports teams, and the plays, parties and other events in which we participated so long ago. Although some complained that certain of their pictures were not placed in the brochure, generally, the collection and publishing of those old photos was well received and appreciated.

In addition, each member of our class received a specially selected small gift which was presented to the recipient with the reading of an appropriately humorous poem. We also had the usual contests such as who came the furthest distance; who had the most children or grandchildren; and who had been married the longest (to the same spouse, of course). With eight children and 13 grandchildren, I thought I would win (if that's the correct term) two of these categories, but as it turned out, another classmate had 17 grandchildren.

We combined our fortieth class reunions in 1990 with a reunion of the members of the baseball team which, against all odds, won the Cape Cod Championship by beating a powerful Barnstable team, scoring five runs in the bottom of the ninth inning. Members of that team were from different classes and I had not seen some of them since I graduated from high school 40 years before.

During that time, some team members had changed tremendously, while others, not at all. Although we had nametags for this event, there are always those who refuse to use them, and they often are those who have changed the most in appearances. One would come up to me and say, "Hey Steve, remember me?" As I stood there in a quandary as to who this person was, he remained in place, waiting with a smile, seeming to relish my discomfort.

Finally, he would identify himself, and I then was able to discern some resemblance to my old teammate. But you can't help wondering why it is necessary for them to go through those little guessing games. Maybe Rick could have offered some insight, but we did not cover this in the discussions we had that night.

Although the appearances of some people have changed greatly over the years, other classmates, I find, have changed hardly at all. They look almost exactly as they did 50 years ago. With this in mind, as the MC at our 50th reunion, I decided to select and announce the names of the four persons who, in my mind, had changed the least since our high school days.

In order to avoid the politics and wrangling of having several people involved in these selections, I made the choices solely on my own. I made it clear that this was not a "beauty contest" but rather simply "those who changed the least". With a brief introduction for each person, I came up with the following: third runner up, Stanley Snow; second runner up, Kate Moore; first runner up, Bruce Peters; and the winner, Norma Clark Meade. All four live in the Eastham-Orleans area. Most attendees seemed to agree with my selections.

A few people say that they find class reunions to be boring and disappointing. Others, for whatever reason, refuse to attend even though they live two miles from where the event is to take place. At our pizza get-together with the Jennings, after describing our reunions, we all agreed that it was great to be able to meet our old classmates and restore and reflect upon those earlier times. Each of us also noted that although we had not seen many of our old friends for 30 years or more, nevertheless, we were able to pick up with them immediately as if no time had passed.

During those many years of separation, we had all pursued work or career and most of us had married and had raised families. We had enjoyed successes and had faced disappointments, losses and hardships of one kind or another. Yet, with all that has happened to us through these many years, it seems as if there has been no separation of time or place, and that it was only yesterday that we had been together as teenagers, graduating from high school and looking anxiously and expectantly toward the future.

RETREIVING A FAMILY TREASURE

My Dad had been a self-employed electrician for approximately 40 years when he retired in the 1960's. IRA's did not exist in those earlier years and apart from social security, he had no source of regular income in his retirement.

Dad did, however, own a large tract of land behind our house on Hopkins Lane, which had been in the Hopkins family since the 1660's, and he laid out a road, to the north off Hopkins Lane, with a small sub-division of perhaps 10 lots, which he put on the market for sale.

In those years, the price of a lot in that type area was between $6000 and $7500 (now they would sell for more than $200,000), and by selling a lot once in a while, he developed for himself another source of supplemental income. The tract of land was large enough for about forty lots, but Dad was careful to develop lots in small increments because the Town taxed a lot at far more than they taxed undivided open land.

In 1970, or thereabouts, a young woman, who was then a guidance teacher at Cape Cod Tech, approached Dad about buying one of his lots on Captain Curtis Way, overlooking what was then called "The Goose Pond" (since renamed "Reuben's Pond"). The price of the lot was $7500, but the young woman, who was not bashful, tried to inveigle Dad to reduce the price. Dad stood firmly with the $7500 figure, and finally our intrepid teacher agreed to this amount.

After the sale, Dad, who lived nearby, sidled up to the new owner as she was making plans to build a house on the lot, and pointed out that there was a stone wall across a corner of her property in a fallen down condition and that he, Dad, would be willing to carry away the stones from the dilapidated stone wall. Our young lady, however, saw the wall, even in its fallen state, as an asset to her lot, and told Dad she wanted to retain the stones.

The stone wall in question had probably been erected by a member of our family several centuries before, and although I was not privy to the conversation Dad had relating to the wall, I realized, when I heard the story many years later, just how disappointed he must have been not to have been able to retrieve those stones in order to build a wall elsewhere.

Well, the young woman built a fine house on the lot overlooking the pond and lived there happily for several years. Having become disillusioned working in a school system and looking for something else to do, she began attending night sessions at Suffolk University Law School, along with several others from the Cape, traveling up to Boston three nights a week for her classes. Being the persistent, persevering type, she adhered to this schedule for four years until she graduated.

After passing the Bar in 1979, she moved to the North Shore to set up her law practice, buying a house in Marblehead. I was still living in Marblehead at the time, but our paths did not cross until years later. Eventually, she set up an office in Salem, specializing in criminal defense and divorce cases. She retained her house on Captain Curtis Way, however, renting it out as a source of income. If you have not guessed by now, the woman's name was Sylvia McMeen, who is now my wife.

Dad died in 1974. The years passed, and Sylvia, engrossed in her work and never having found the right guy, had never married. I, of course, married back in 1957 and over the years developed a large family. In October 1984, with most of the children grown, my wife and I, by mutual agreement, separated and began divorce proceedings. We had a verbal understanding that during the separation, we each were free to socialize as we wished, without objection or interference from the other.

In early 1985, an old friend from the Cape told me about an attractive, unattached lawyer in Salem, originally from Orleans, named Sylvia McMeen. I had a vague memory of Dad telling me about her years before. I contacted Sylvia and we agreed to meet after work for a drink at the Washington Bar in Salem. Sylvia was still living in Marblehead and I was staying in a condo in Ipswich.

The two of us hit it off immediately. First, of course, was the fact that, coincidentally, she had bought the lot her house was on in Orleans, near where I grew up, from my Father, years before. But then too, she loved Orleans and its shores as much as I. Her other interests were the same as mine. And, of course, we were both trial lawyers and could exchange stories about our travails in court. The rest is history.

We were married in August of 1990 and set up housekeeping in the Town of Manchester-By-The-Sea. In 1994, however, we left the North Shore and moved back to Sylvia's house on Captain Curtis Way. She set up a law practice in Barnstable and I continued working at my old law firm in Boston up until I retired in April 1998.

Early on in our developing relationship, Sylvia told me how much she liked my Dad and the fact that they often had drinks together after she had moved into her house. She also recounted for me the story of the stone-wall and Dad's efforts to retrieve the stones.

As it turned out, when we went back to her house in Orleans on weekends, there was a great deal of work to do on improving the yard which had become overgrown and rundown. One of the first projects I took on was the restoration of the stone-wall, which was badly fallen down. In performing this work, I pointed out to Sylvia how Dad, looking down from above, surely must be approving what I was doing.

I also kidded Sylvia about the fact that, really, I had tracked her down and hitched up to her so that this property, with the stone-wall, would someday be brought back into the family. Sylvia has no siblings and apart from her mother, few relatives you could call close.

Having now come to know my children and my grandchildren, and recognizing that her lot, with the stone wall, had been Hopkins property for several centuries, she has decided that she will arrange it so that title of the house will remain within my family. Yes, although Dad failed to obtain the stone-wall some 30 years ago, he will be pleased to learn that in years to come, it will indeed be retrieved for the benefit of the Hopkins clan.

The Hopkins stone wall (in the background)